BEYOND BASIC TURNING

D1504900

THE CREATIVE WOODTURNER

BEYOND BASIC TURNING

OFF-CENTRE, COOPERED & LAMINATED WORK

Jack Cox

LINDEN PUBLISHING CO
FRESNO, CALIFORNIA

Copyright © 1993 Jack Cox

All rights reserved. No part of this publication may be reproduced, stored in a retrieval system, or transmitted, in any form or by any means, electronic, mechanical, photocopying, recording or otherwise, without the prior permission of the copyright owner or the publishers.

Library of Congress Cataloging-in-Publication Data
Cox, Jack.
    Beyond basic turning/Jack Cox.
        p.   cm.
    Includes index.
    ISBN 0-941936-25-2:
    1. Turning. I. Title.
TT201.C68 1993
684'.083—dc20   93-27393
                                       CIP
    2 4 6 8 9 7 5 3

Published 1993 by Linden Publishing Co Inc, 3845 N. Blackstone, Fresno, CA93726
Set in 9 on 13.5 pt Bookman by Ann Buchan (Typesetters) Shepperton.

Printed in USA

CONTENTS

PROJECTS

INTRODUCTION

This book has a number of objectives, but it might be appropriate to begin by mentioning two which it *doesn't* have: firstly, it is not about 'how to turn wood'. There is already a large number of books on the market, written by well-known and respected practitioners, which deal predominantly with the presentation of tools to timber, with the objective of cutting it cleanly and efficiently. Although Chapter 10 deals with some turning techniques, it does so only to the extent which I feel is appropriate to the rather specialised subject-matter. In passing, the topic of safety is, quite deliberately, not accorded a separate chapter in its own right. To do so would be fine if the book were about woodturning techniques pure and simple; since it isn't, it would seem sensible to cover safety aspects as they occur, regardless of whether the work being performed involves turning, sawing or other activities. The book isn't about design either, at least in the sense of generating objects which are intrinsically pleasing to look at. This is a difficult enough topic to quantify in any case; what pleases one observer may well irritate another, and there are few if any 'absolutes' (although quite a number of ancient cultures managed to 'get it right' most of the time).

So what is it about? Basically, I hope, it is about ideas. Although I have been an enthusiastic woodturner for some thirty-five years, my training and professional experience are those of an engineer, and it would seem to me that there is much to be gained from a kind of 'cross-fertilisation' of the two disciplines, not only with regard to the design of ancillary jigs and fixtures, but also to that of the turned work itself. In this sense only, perhaps there is some small element of design involved.

A second objective, made possible I suppose, by my engineering background, is that of assisting readers who have little or no expertise in mathematics or geometry to be able, nevertheless, to apply them to apparently 'difficult' woodturning projects, almost without realising it. In my own personal experience, many woodworkers profess themselves to be too stupid to attempt work which even vaguely smacks of formulae or calculations. What is probably nearer the truth is that they simply lack the necessary training (and 'stupid' is a relative term anyway). I have endeavoured to present a design approach, together with a number of projects, which enables the reader to understand how the designs are derived, and hopefully to build on them further. I would suggest that, although the projects are dimensioned sufficiently fully to enable them to be copied, the dimensions (other than angles) are not really important; it is my sincere hope that the information contained herein will enable the reader to develop his or her own designs without becoming bogged-down by the mathematics. In this connection, I would suggest that Chapter 4 is read fairly early on; I can think of no better way to encourage the reader to proceed further — and it *is* a very short chapter.

A third objective is that of conservation of timber.

As a keen woodturner, I can scarcely be expected to denigrate the craft; yet there is no escaping the fact that it does tend to leave a high proportion of the original timber on the floor as shavings. Timber deserves respect from its user, regardless of the price paid for it. In this connection, I would state with some pride that, with the minor exception of a few short lengths of 'exotic', and a sheet or two of veneer, *every single piece* illustrated and described herein was made from timber offcuts which were acquired at no financial cost to me whatsoever and which, moreover, would have otherwise ended-up as 'kettle-wedges' (ie. burnt). I have of course paid a 'price' of sorts; that of rather more time spent per item than would be the case with plain turnery. The reader must expect to pay a similar price, regardless of how the stock timber is acquired; but if the work is carried out for pleasure rather than profit, what does it matter? This of course is a dead 'give-away' with regard to my hoped-for readership. I am an amateur, and this book is essentially for amateurs, particularly for those with limited facilities in terms of equipment, but with plenty of time and enthusiasm to spend on their hobby. In this connection I have avoided the use of the more exotic pieces of woodworking machinery, since descriptions based upon these are of limited usefulness to the reader who doesn't possess them. It will be found however, that a bandsaw and a disc-sander will be required in most cases. On the other hand, I sincerely hope that the more experienced and better-equipped turners (and maybe even the odd professional) will find something of interest herein, particularly if they are normally inclined to shudder and turn slightly green at the mere mention of the words 'mathematics' or 'geometry'. I derive a great deal of personal pleasure from both subjects, and use them wherever I can, regardless of the fact that I am by no means an expert in

either. One doesn't have to be an expert in a particular discipline in order to be able to enjoy it (I like woodturning too).

I have organised the book in distinct topics, each with its own chapter, and presented a number of typical projects in the second part of the book which employ the techniques outlined in the first. The approach has the advantage of limiting undue repetition but cannot, I regret, be regarded as completely successful in this respect since so many techniques are interdependent. In this respect I request the indulgence of the reader.

With regard to the vexed question of Imperial vs. Metric measure, I cannot claim to have 'got it right' (I doubt if anybody could), in the sense that the preference for imperial measure adopted herein will please everybody. Also, it may well appear that in places, I have displayed a passion for accuracy totally inappropriate to the use of wood as a working medium — a quite deliberate policy on my part for the following reasons: firstly, many of the calculations furnish an intermediate value, on the way to a final working dimension; clearly it is both unnecessary and unwise to make approximations at these points. Secondly, I contend that, particularly where joints are concerned, most woodworkers will work to a very high degree of dimensional accuracy anyway, perhaps without being entirely aware of it. For example, it is quite easy to set a pair of calipers against a steel rule, and apply the setting to turned work, either diametrally or axially, to an accuracy considerably better than plus or minus .010". Readers in any doubt are invited to make a point of conducting one or two personal experiments along these lines, particularly if micrometer or vernier facilities are available as a check, (bearing in mind that $1/64$" is almost equivalent to .015"). As a rider, it might perhaps be added that a glued joint, particularly in end grain, which started life with a gap as little as .005" in any part of it, will be perceived as a poor one by experts and laymen alike.

Finally, I have endeavoured throughout to present the material in a way which may be easily assimilated and understood (not always easy, in view of the 'nature of the beast'), and thereby to provide a 'good read'. I have tried also to produce a book which, in some respects at least, will be referred to from time to time, rather than read once and then put down and forgotten. I sincerely hope that I have managed to 'get it right' at least some of the time.

1. SEGMENTATION PRINCIPLES

The notion of segmentation is familiar enough; many books on woodturning give it a mention and most woodturners will at least try it at some time. A number of workers have delved a little deeper into the subject, and have produced quite spectacular pieces, comprising large numbers of segments, generating an effect reminiscent of highly decorated pottery. However simple or complex the piece, its construction will necessarily be bound by geometric rules and ideally by some consideration of the effect of timber movement on the finished piece over a period of time. The following notes are concerned only with basic forms of construction, together with some appreciation of the advantages and disadvantages of each.

The simplest form of segmented work is provided by segments cut from otherwise useless scraps of timber and built up in a brickwork pattern, often over four or more layers. Some care is needed here with regard to choice of timbers, since it is very tempting to utilise available offcuts in a more or less random fashion, regardless of timber type or colour. Over-indulgence in this respect can produce a result which is garish and 'cheap' in appearance, regardless of the care which has been applied to the work. On the other hand, it is possible to produce a piece from essentially bland, featureless timber which, in polished work, possesses an interest and attraction well beyond that offered by the same material used as a single piece. This particular attribute can be of advantage in terms of the utilisation of timber which 'turns well' and is relatively inexpensive, but is otherwise not particularly suited to decorative turnery. The price to be paid is, of course, that of rather more work per item.

Segments may be formed with the timber grain running in any one of three orientations with respect to the axis of the workpiece. The circumferential formation of Fig. 1(a) is perhaps the commonest, due doubtless to the ease with which segments may be extracted from odd lengths of stock. Its main disadvantage is that the mitred joints between adjacent segments are end-grain — not exactly the strongest possible glued joint. The radial formation (b) is rather less common, since it shows end-grain on both the inner and outer surfaces of a turned vessel. This particular attribute is of minor importance where the timber used is relatively hard and dense; indeed in some timbers, particularly 'exotics', it is often quite difficult to perceive grain direction. It has the advantage of presenting side-grain faces for gluing, both for mitred joints and between stacked rings of segments. It is generally less easy to extract suitable segments from offcuts without undue waste; usually the stock timber has to be prepared with a project of this nature specifically in mind. On balance, the formation is perhaps best avoided in the absence of a particularly good reason for using it. The third option might be termed the 'axial' formation. This is an inherently stable assembly with respect to timber movement as will be seen, but if the assembly involves stacked rings of segments, these will inevitably present end-grain at the glued joints, for which reason the construction must be regarded as relatively weak in this direction. The formation does, however, have one very obvious 'natural' use, that of constructing a deep vessel, such as a vase or biscuit barrel, from one single ring of segments, these being long with respect to their cross-sectional dimensions. Work of this nature is generally termed 'coopered', the segments being referred to as 'staves'. The joints are made entirely in side-grain, giving a very strong, stable formation (c).

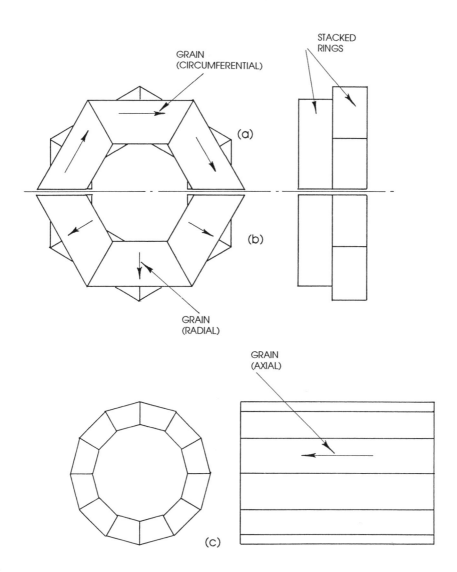

Figure 1

It is also possible to arrange a hybrid form of construction which offers a combination of side and end-grain as in Fig.2(a). It is suggested that the arrangement confers no particular advantages in terms of appearance, ease of machining or stability and is merely mentioned as a possibility. It is true that, if the grain direction is duly noted when assembling a stack of segmented rings, turning the outside of the piece will be mostly 'downhill' with consequent benefit in terms of finish, but the price to be paid is a corresponding 'uphill' problem on the inside (c). Note that the segment cutting-angle 'S' (which in this special case can scarcely be termed a 'mitre angle') is exactly that subtended by a single segment at the centre of the ring. This is *not* the same angle as the more conventional mitre angle 'B' except in the special case of six segments where 'S' and 'B' are identical anyway (it is interesting if not surprising to note that six identical segments may be assembled in either form as desired). Regardless of the number of segments, there is no direct gain or loss in terms of timber usage whichever form of construction is employed, although there may be indirect differences (due to the difference in cutting-angle) arising from the number of segments which may be extracted from a given length of stock. It is not easy to predict the relative proportions of end-grain and side-grain which will be seen in the finished piece, since this will depend on segment proportions and ultimately on the profile of the completed turning. A particular feature of the arrangement is that, dependent upon the turned profile, the joint lines can give the appearance of being angled or curved in elevation.

Figure 2

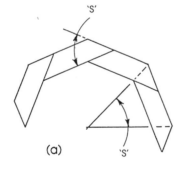

(a)

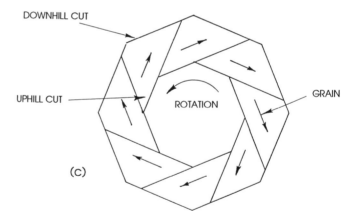

(c)

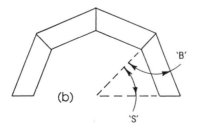

(b)

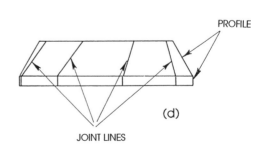

(d)

At this point it is worth examining the effect of timber movement on the various constructional forms, together with means of minimising its less-desirable consequences. Obviously, the best way of avoiding trouble is to prevent as far as possible any timber movement at the outset by stabilising it in its intended environment prior to use. This is rarely possible. The intended environment may not even be known to the maker of the piece, who often has to be content with a warning to the recipient (ie. "don't put it too near a radiator"). Moreover, even in a known environment, stabilisation can take a long time, during which the environment itself may change due to weather conditions, the presence or absence of central heating etc. In any event, it is wise to expect *some* timber movement, and to be aware of its nature and possible consequences.

Timber shrinkage or expansion occurs as a result of loss or gain of moisture. Movement is greatest across the grain, and is minimal along the grain. The latter effect has been exploited for centuries by clock-makers, who have often used wood in preference to metal for pendulum rods, due to its longitudinal stability over a wide temperature range. Cross-grain movement varies with species, and also with the position of the piece relative to the parent log; moreover, it is not even uniform within a given piece, being greatest across the growth rings. It is suggested, however, that cross-grain variations are of minor importance in terms of small items of segmented turnery, and indeed are only of relevance in the axial or coopered formation. For purposes of discussion it will be assumed, therefore, that cross-grain movement is uniform, and that the only important consideration is the difference between cross-grain and long-grain movement.

It must be appreciated that some styles of segmented work may incur stresses that will not arise at all in a 'plain-turned' piece. A simple bowl for example, turned from a single piece of timber, may move quite significantly after turning; it may become oval, or twist or cast in one direction or another. However, unless a considerable degree of movement is involved, or the drying-out process is unduly rapid or uneven, it is unlikely to split, even though it may end up as a shape other than originally intended. Segmentation, on the other hand, tends to impose somewhat unnatural stresses, due to the artificial grain orientation of the individual pieces; this propensity must be taken very seriously, since it is perfectly capable of ruining an otherwise acceptable piece of work.

The simplest and commonest illustration of the problem is that of Fig.3, which depicts one mitred corner of a rectangular construction such as a picture frame. In its original unstressed form, the joint will be a perfect 45° mitre (a). Imagine now a

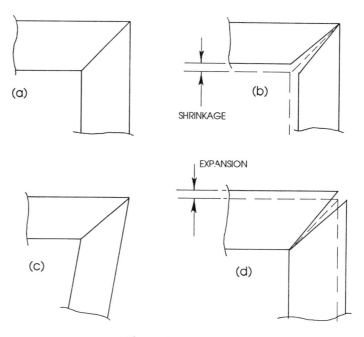

Figure 3

loss of moisture, giving rise to shrinkage: the length of the individual members will not change significantly, but their width will be reduced, giving the effect of a reduced mitre angle. In an unglued joint, given that the components remain in their original position, a triangular gap will open on the inside (b). If the joint is glued, and the two members are not otherwise constrained, the construction will close up as in (c), and the joint will remain sound. If however, the members *are* constrained to remain square, by virtue of being part of a complete four-sided frame, the joint will become stressed and may break, particularly since it is made in end-grain. A comparable effect occurs if the timber acquires moisture and increases its cross-grain dimension; in this case, a similar triangular gap will appear on the outside of the assembly (d). Since the position of each member is fixed by the presence of the others, it is clear that the relief of

stress (due to joint failure) at any one joint does absolutely nothing to reduce stress in the remainder (Fig.4(a)). It might be thought, therefore, that, given sufficient stress, *all* joints must fail. This is not the case; it is necessary only for two opposing joints to fail, thereby allowing the frame to assume the shape shown in (b), thus relieving the stress on the remaining pair of joints. Note that Fig.4 refers specifically to shrinkage; further discussion is (more or less) restricted to this form only, since it is the more likely in interior woodware.

A segmented ring of circumferential grain orientation will behave in exactly the same way. All other things (eg. joint strength) being equal, failure will occur at two diametrically-opposed points (c). In practice, differences in joint strength and perhaps shrinkage rates may cause failure to occur at pairs of joints which are not in perfect opposition, but the principle remains valid. Fig.5 offers a glimpse of

Figure 4

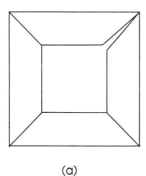

(a)

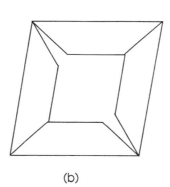

(b)

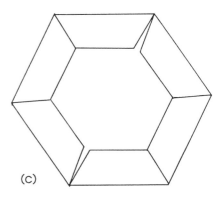

(c)

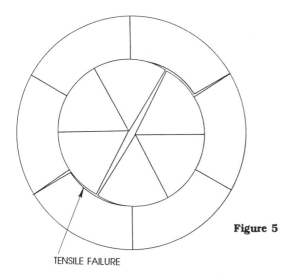

Figure 5

TENSILE FAILURE

the obvious, in that the largest gap and therefore the maximum initial stress occurs at the centre of a segmented construction. This effect remains present even for a multi-ring assembly, where the stress may actually pull the rings apart, although this latter effect is likely to occur only where the rings are fitted as 'plugs', one inside another. Fig.6 shows precisely this effect in a turned segmented bowl; the piece is about thirty years old and was made in some ignorance of the potential pitfalls outlined.

Figure 6

Given due loss of moisture, shrinkage will undoubtedly occur, and it is not possible to prevent it; it would appear possible, however, to redirect it to some extent into a form less likely to cause damage. It must be admitted that the following information is not offered as positive 'proof', since it is based upon a number of empirical tests (it is actually very difficult to *prove* anything by experiment; often the most that can be done is to reinforce a working hypothesis). If it were possible by some magical means to totally disallow the possibility of mitred joint failure and to retain the integrity of the initial planform of the workpiece, then the inevitable timber movement would be obliged to take place elsewhere. One possibility is longitudinal compression at the outer edges (timber *is* compressible in this way). It would appear more likely, however, that the movement is redirected such that it takes place predominantly in the depth (ie. elevation profile) rather than the width, and may therefore go totally unnoticed. (Wood is known to possess a degree of elasticity; typical values of Young's modulus may be found in reference books). Be that as it may, it is undoubtedly possible to put the hypothesis to use by embodying suitable joint-protection into many designs.

In the case of a bowl or vase with circumferential grain orientation, the outer rings will rarely present a problem; in the first place the actual movement is unlikely to be sufficiently large to stress the joints unduly; in the second place, it is normal to add depth at the periphery of the vessel by building up layers of segmented rings with the joints staggered in adjacent layers. The support offered by side-grain gluing, plus the shear-strength of the adhesive (and the timber) will resist any tendency for mitred joints to pull apart. The inner rings are likely to present the biggest problem, partly because the stresses are greatest in this area, but

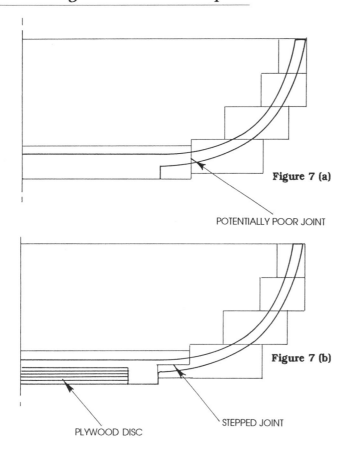

Figure 7 (a)

POTENTIALLY POOR JOINT

Figure 7 (b)

PLYWOOD DISC

STEPPED JOINT

also because, in many cases, there is a strong temptation to fit adjacent rings one inside another (Fig.7(a)), rather than employ a stacked construction. It is strongly advised that this practice be avoided wherever possible, partly because the resultant tensile joint is relatively weak, but also because it is often quite difficult to obtain the class of fit that will do justice to the adhesive and obtain the strongest possible joint in the circumstances. It is preferable to avoid this type of joint altogether or, where this is not possible, to employ a stepped construction to give a predominantly shear-stressed joint (b). Matters may be further improved by using a hidden disc of birch ply at the centre. In passing it may be noted that in the case of timber *expansion* the effects are reversed, with the greatest stresses occurring at the periphery. Unobtrusive protection is rather less easy in this case; this applies also to the radial formation of Fig.1(b) under shrinkage conditions.

Fig.8 shows the general effects of timber shrinkage on fully-triangular 'one-sixth' and 'one-twelfth' segments, where the dimension 'w_1' represents the

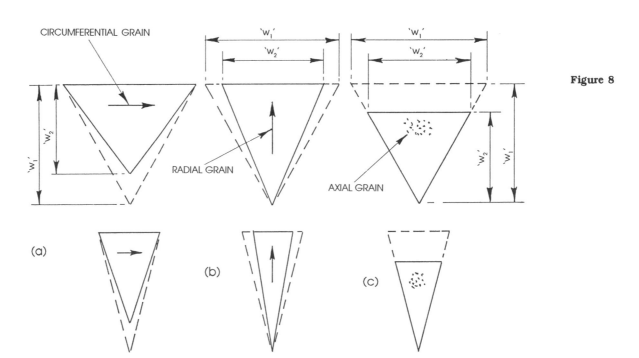

CIRCUMFERENTIAL GRAIN

RADIAL GRAIN

AXIAL GRAIN

Figure 8

(a)   (b)   (c)

original size and 'w$_2$' that after shrinkage. Comparison of the two forms so far discussed shows that there is little to choose between them, although it is clear that the greater the number of segments, the smaller the gap between any adjacent pair. The overall effect will be much the same of course, but the stress on any one joint will be reduced, thereby allowing *all* joints to contribute more to the 're-direction of movement' mentioned earlier. The axial or coopered formation shows a distinct improvement however. In fact, given uniform cross-grain shrinkage with respect to direction, no stress whatsoever is placed upon timber or joints, since the timber merely changes its overall size, its shape remaining unaltered. In this case, no form of joint protection is necessary. There is, however, one indirect problem: coopered pieces, such as biscuit barrels and the like, invariably have lids. If a lid is constructed in one of the other segmented forms or if, to simulate a barrel-like appearance, it is 'planked', then it is possible to be a little too clever

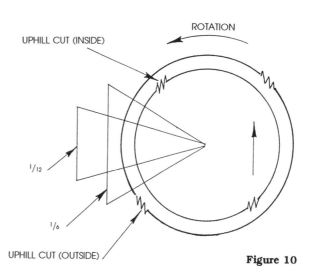

Figure 10

Figure 9

by making the fit unduly snug to begin with, in which case it will be almost impossible to remove the lid after a while. Fig.9 shows the effect and its cause. Close examination reveals that the barrel has remained circular and the lid has become oval. It is also clear that, since the lid is oval, and the barrel is an interference fit in two places, *both* have shrunk somewhat since they were made. For the same reason, the base also should be made a fairly easy fit, and attached with an adhesive which allows a little 'creep', such as PVA.

The turning of a plain unsegmented bowl mounted such that the grain is at right angles to the turning axis invariably gives rise to a certain roughness at two specific locations, regardless of the tools used or the skill of the turner (Fig.10). The effect occurs in the general cross-grain area, and most particularly at the point where this area begins to change to 'uphill' side-grain; note that it does not occur in the corresponding area on the 'downhill' side of the cut, since the cutting action here is rather like that of sharpening a pencil or planing 'with the grain'. The roughness is due to the lack of mutual support offered by the wood fibres. Readers who have not experienced turning a segmented blank of circumferential grain orientation will undoubtedly be pleasantly surprised by the relative absence of such roughness, since even for a 'one-sixth' segment, the 'uphill area' is largely eliminated. Matters improve still further as the number of segments is increased. Figs.11 and 12 provide some illustration of the effect that circumferential segmentation can have on the turning process. In both cases it can be seen that the shavings tend to fall from the work and lie on the

Figure 11

Figure 12

toolrest, rather than fly off at high speed. This is indicative of the low energy with which they leave the parent stock, which in turn demonstrates the ease with which they are being cut. The effect is generally independent of heaviness of cut, but does actually depend somewhat on lathe speed and timber type. The same considerations apply to finish, which normally causes end-grain timber to appear darker than neighbouring side-grain timber; moreover, finishing materials tend to get 'mopped-up' more on end-grain (although both effects are considerably less marked with hard, dense timbers). Radial-formation segmentation will of course present continuous end-grain to the turner. Coopered formation will present no more or fewer problems than plain 'axial-grain' turning of any kind.

Any group of segments which have been machined to fit together 'normally' (ie. with their mitred joints lying on radial lines passing through the centre of the assembly), will also fit together perfectly if they are twisted slightly in plan view such that their edges are staggered, and the joint lines no longer radial (Fig.13(a)). On the face of it, the arrangement has little to recommend it since it

creates a hole in the centre with virtually no corresponding advantage in terms of increase of outer diameter, and therefore wastes more timber than the conventional assembly. The formation is also rather more difficult to assemble. On the other hand, it is possible to make a positive feature of the mitred joints by using strips of contrasting veneer between them for example. One may also utilise a timber with a distinctive striped pattern to produce a kind of 'Catherine-wheel' pattern. Both effects work best where plenty of surface area exists to display them, such as platters or shallow bowls. The possibilities inherent in the regular serrated periphery of this type of assembly are worth a look; attractive vessels may be made by leaving this alone (or part-turning it). An attractive extension of the idea is that of making the segment joint-lines curved rather than straight. This technique offers a number of decorative possibilities and, as will be seen, also contains a fair number of surprises. It will be developed more fully in Chapter 2, along with a form of 'stave-segmentation' which is particularly suited to 'between-centres' turning and, in terms of grain orientation, corresponds closely to coopered work.

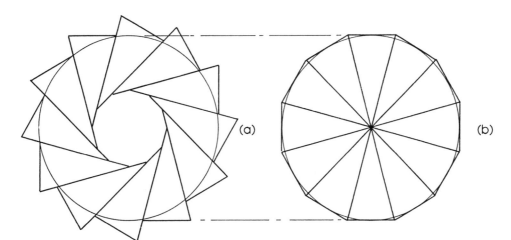

(a)　　　(b)

Figure 13

2. SEGMENTATION: *Design and Marking Out*

It is a mistake to rush things when dealing with segmented work. The fact that it is a very facile means of dealing with offcuts carries its own pitfalls. It has been seen that certain forms of construction can, in the absence of appropriate planning, bear a risk of joint failure due to timber movement. An unduly hasty approach can lead to other disappointments. It is quite easy, for example, to make the mistake of assembling a stack of segmented rings which, as seen in the solid, appears substantial enough to allow plenty of latitude when turning, only to find out the hard way (ie. on the lathe), that the available bowl profile range is very restricted. Problems of this nature can be easily avoided by a few profile sketches, together with an easy-to-use method of determining segment dimensions.

At this point it may be appropriate to mention that, although dimensions are preferentially given in inches, many of the fractions will be presented as decimals (because this is the normal manner of performing calculations); the point is discussed further in Chapter 4. These may easily be related to sixteenths etc., by reference to the Conversion Table on p. 251. To assist readers with a preference for metric dimensions, major dimensions on projects are given in metric measure in brackets immediately following their Imperial equivalents.

When contemplating the making of a segmented piece, it is helpful to have some means of playing 'what-if' games prior to cutting, or even marking out the timber, particularly if the latter is in the form of random offcuts. Indeed the nature of the project itself may well be decided by the determination to use up otherwise scrap stock. It is important, therefore, to know just how much useful turning-timber is available from a given segment. To give a simple example, the one-sixth segment of Fig.14 will yield useful timber between the two arcs, the shaded area representing waste. Equally importantly, the vertical profile must be contained by the rectangle shown in the elevation. Matters are considerably improved as the number of segments is increased, as shown in (b), which repre-

Figure 14

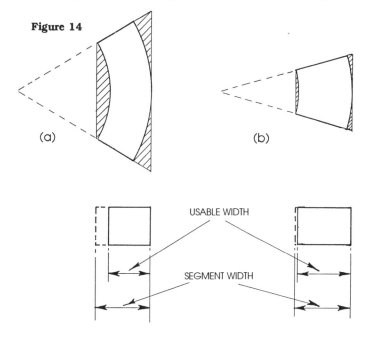

(a)

(b)

USABLE WIDTH

SEGMENT WIDTH

sents a one-twelfth segment of identical outside diameter extracted from timber of the same width and thickness.

The safest way to plan a project is to decide upon the required inner and outer profiles and draw an elevation cross-section which specifies both. This is used to determine the actual turned widths of each of the stacked rings (including a little waste allowance) as shown in Fig.15(b). One must then decide upon the number of segments per ring and then, *in the absence of other means*, draw a part-plan to determine by measurement the actual usable size of the segments required for each ring. Fig.15(a) shows the general idea for a single ring, based upon six segments. At this point, it is as well to examine the timber stock available, to see if it is adequate for the purpose (a method of doing so is given later); if it is not, then the process needs to be repeated with appropriate modifications to the profile.

No pre-planning process can avoid the drawing of the elevation-profile, and subsequent determination of the required ring-widths, but it is by no means necessary to draw a plan to obtain the associated full-segment dimensions, since other means are readily available, and are far less time-consuming. Given that the required outer diameter and width of each ring have been determined from the profile, the remaining dimensions may be obtained from Nomograms 1 and 2 as (p. 56) follows: to obtain segment length 'l' from Nomogram 1, it is merely necessary to lay a straightedge between the known values of 'N' and 'o' on the outer scales to read off the value of 'l' directly on the centre scale. (Non-mathematical types please note — it really is that simple!). The right-hand scale also gives the required mitre angle 'B' directly opposite the corresponding value of 'N'. This should be used only as a check however. It is far better, certainly where

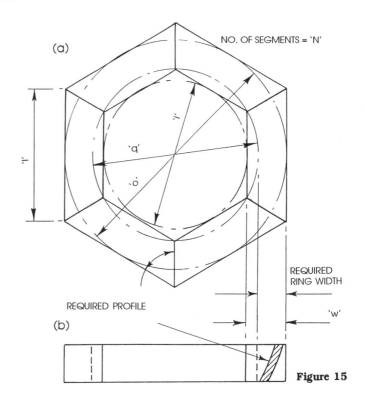

Figure 15

the angles are not 'round figures', to use the simple formulae included on the Nomogram to obtain the value of 'B' and, where necessary, the centre angle 'S'. True segment width 'w' may be obtained from Nomogram 2, although the method here requires a little additional simple arithmetic. It will be seen from Fig.15 that the ring has a required inner diameter 'q', which may be readily determined from the profile. The 'true inner diameter' of a made-up assembly of segments is given by 'i'. Nomogram 2 gives the value of 'i' on the centre scale from a straightedge placed across the known values of 'q' and 'N' on the outer scales. To obtain the width 'w' of the segment, it is merely necessary to subtract the value of 'i' from the value of 'o' and divide the result by two. The operation is quite easy, and may be accomplished very quickly, as the following example will show.

From Fig.15, assume that the required outer diameter 'o' is 10" and the number of segments is six. On Nomogram 1, a straightedge between 10" on the 'o' scale and '6' on the 'N' scale will give the value of 'l' on the centre scale as 5.8". Note in passing, that a straightedge between '100' on the 'o' scale and '6' on the 'N' scale will yield '58' on the 'l' scale (ie. a scale-factor of ten); indeed in this particular case, it is the preferable course of action, since it extracts the best accuracy from the Nomogram. As mentioned in Chapter 4, linear dimensions may be scaled up or down in this way, as convenient. The mitre angle 'B' may also be checked on the right-hand scale at 60°.

Assume now that the required inner diameter 'q' is measured directly from the elevation of Fig.15 at 9". On Nomogram 2, a straightedge between '90' on the left-hand 'q' scale and '6' on the right-hand 'N' scale will give a value of '78' (ie. 7.8") on the centre 'i' scale. Subtracting 7.8" from 10" gives 2.2". Dividing the result by two gives the segment width 'w' as

1.1". With a little practice, Nomogram results may be obtained far more rapidly than by drawing a part-plan, even for the simple case involving six segments. Nomograms are even more useful with awkward segment numbers since they will cope with these just as easily; by contrast, it can be quite difficult to draw accurate plan views involving odd numbers of segments. The methods so far outlined will now be applied to the layout of a shallow bowl (suitable as a first exercise) of about 8" diameter and 1½" depth (200x38mm), comprising three stacked layers each of six segments, as shown in Fig.16. The elevation may be set out by drawing four horizontal lines spaced ½" apart, to represent the three layers. A convenient vertical centre line is drawn and the required inner and outer profiles determined for one-half of the bowl by freehand drawing on one side or the other of the centre line. Sometimes it helps to visualise the profile if both halves are drawn, a task easily accomplished with the aid of squared paper. Vertical lines are now

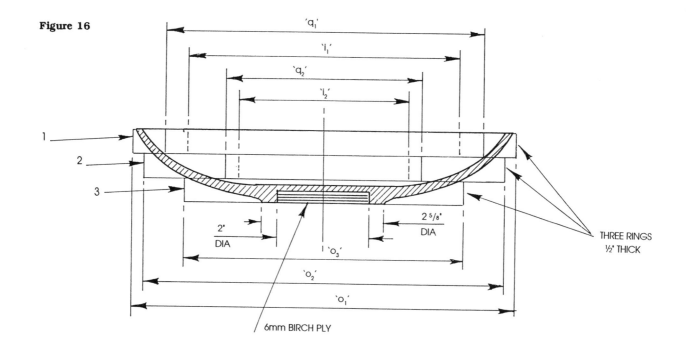

Figure 16

drawn on each layer, representing the ring-widths necessary to encompass the profile. From this information, the required inner and outer diameters for each ring may be measured. It then remains only to use Nomograms 1 and 2 as previously described to determine the segment lengths and true widths, the latter being shown as dashed lines on Fig. 16. To assist in checking the results, the values which should be obtained are given in Table 1, these particular figures being given as decimals, since one or two of them do not resolve into practical fractions. Note that the entire process may be carried out without drawing a plan view.

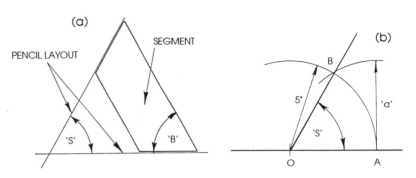

Figure 18

TABLE 1   (Inches)

RING no.	'o'	'q'	'l'	'l'	'w'
1	8.25	6.75	4.75	5.84	1.20
2	7.75	4.25	4.47	3.69	2.03
3	6.00	–	3.47	–	3.00

Marking out of individual segments will generally be carried out as shown in Fig. 17(a), with segments reversed and overlapped to minimise timber wastage. This requires dimension 'l' to be marked alternately on both edges of the timber. Additionally,

some machining processes are made easier by flipping the stock from one face to the other; thus for accuracy's sake both faces should be parallel and the timber the correct width. Uniformity of stock thickness from one piece to another is of less importance, since this need present only a minor inconvenience both during segment machining and subsequent assembly of individual rings. At this point it may be noted that it is common practice for the 'indirect' mitre angle 'B' to be used for marking out, by setting a combination-square or sliding-bevel. If direct-machining methods are used (ie. with no marking out), this angle would also be that to which the machine is set. The angle which really matters, however, is that subtended at the centre of the ring of segments (shown as 'S' in Fig. 18) since it is this angle which actually determines the fit of

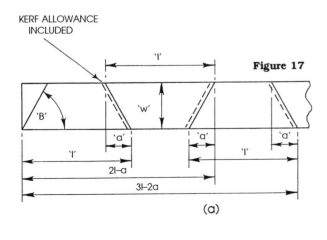

Figure 17

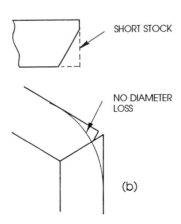

the segments. It is helpful, particularly where a large number of segments per ring are used, to construct a simple pencil layout as drawn in Fig. 18, against which the accuracy of this angle on individual segments may be checked. Fig. 19 illustrates the practical application of the layout.

The angle may be obtained for all constructions from 'one-third' to 'one-sixteenth' segments from Fig. 18(b) and Table 2 as follows: a straight baseline is drawn, and a pair of compasses set to exactly 5" is centred at 'O' to draw an arc cutting the baseline at 'A'. The compasses are now re-set to the dimension indicated in Table 2 against the required value of 'N', and a second arc, centred on 'A' drawn to intersect the first arc at 'B'. A straight line joining 'O' and 'B' will be at the required angle to the baseline. The method is inherently capable of a

'w' = 5

'N'	'a'
3	8.66
4	7.07
5	5.88
6	5.00
7	4.34
8	3.83
9	3.42
10	3.09
11	2.82
12	2.59
13	2.39
14	2.23
15	2.08
16	1.95

TABLE 2

$$a = \sqrt{50 - 50.\cos\left(\frac{360}{N}\right)}$$

Figure 19

high order of accuracy since it utilises linear dimensions to create angles, and it is usually very much easier in a small workshop to set out linear distances accurately, rather than angles. The second part of the 'what-if?' process is that of estimating whether the available stock is sufficient to meet the proposed requirement (and if not, whether it is possible to modify the requirement to suit stock availability). In view of the way in which segments may be overlapped to maximise stock usage, it is rarely easy to determine by inspection how many segments may be extracted from a given length of stock. It is of course possible to bring the timber to the necessary width and thickness and then mark out directly. The problem with this approach is that, if the available timber is insufficient, some modification of the original design may be called for; this in turn might require different timber dimensions — but the timber has already been marked out (and possibly cut!). The converse may be true, in that the first attempt is seen to waste some of the available stock, which may in fact be sufficient to support a larger turned piece; again if the timber is cut, it may be too late. It is precisely in a situation of this kind where a little arithmetic is of tremendous benefit, despite its lack of appeal to many readers. In any event, the following method is offered, since it involves only measurement of the stock timber, simply to determine what sizes may be extracted from it, with no cutting (or even marking out), prior to the final decision.

From Fig.17(a) it may be seen that the minimum stock length for one segment is the segment length itself 'l' (which, for estimation purposes, can include a saw-kerf allowance); two segments will require twice this length, minus the distance 'a'; three segments will require three times 'l' minus twice 'a', and so on. The dimension 'a' is itself determined by the mitre angle 'B' and the required stock width 'w'. The value of 'a' is not required to a high degree of precision and may be obtained by simple measurement on a sheet of squared paper, given that some means of drawing the necessary angle is available. It may, however, be determined far more easily by using Nomogram 4; one of the advantages of the set of Nomograms provided is that they solve basic trigonometrical equations, which themselves have a wide range of applications. It is therefore often possible to use the Nomograms for purposes other than those for which they were originally designed. Such an example is now given: referring to Nomogram 4, a straightedge laid between the known value of 'w' on the left-hand (h) scale, and the known value 'B' on the centre (A) scale, will give the corresponding value of 'a' on the right-hand (k) scale. Diagram N.4(c) accompanying the Nomogram explains the process; it can be seen that the 'h','A' and 'k' scales are temporarily re-assigned as 'w','B' and 'a' scales respectively, for the purposes of this calculation only. Given the necessary value of 'a', the remain-

ing calculations are a matter of simple arithmetic which may be performed as many times as necessary in the comfort of an armchair. It is worth mentioning that procedures of this kind, performed at leisure, can go a long way towards avoiding the kind of mistakes often made in the workshop as a result of undue haste. A little thought can spare a lot of wood! One further small saving is possible (when the occasion presents itself): from Fig.17(b) it is evident that some shortfall in available stock length can actually be accommodated with a little forethought. Obviously, one must be careful not to overdo things, and marking out and machining may become a little more difficult, but it is a perfectly viable technique.

Similar considerations apply to the preparation of staves for plain, parallel-sided coopered work (Fig.20). If the finished piece is intended to be

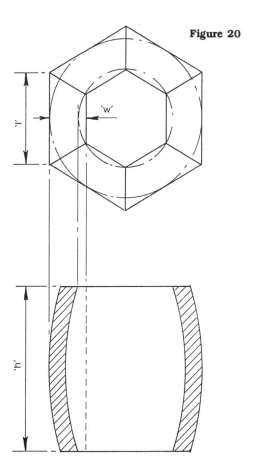

Figure 20

significantly tapered in profile, however, there is much to be gained by tapering the basic assembly to begin with. Fig.21 shows that the staves in a tapered assembly will be wider at one end than the other, by virtue of the difference in the outer diameters 'o_1' and 'o_2'. The stave widths (equivalent to segment lengths in a stacked-ring assembly) are shown as 'l_1' and 'l_2' respectively. These may be obtained from Nomogram 1 as previously described, after deciding upon the required values of 'o_1' and 'o_2'. It is also clear from (b) that the true stave length 'v' is not the same as the overall height of the piece 'h'. Given that the elevation drawing has been

carefully constructed, it is possible to obtain 'v' by direct measurement. It is equally possible (and more convenient on occasion) to obtain 'v' from Nomogram 3, given that 'o_1', 'o_2' and 'h' are known. From Fig.21(b) it can be seen that the difference in the two outer diameters can be split into two equal 'overhang' dimensions, shown as 'k'. The value of 'k' may be obtained by subtracting 'o_2' from 'o_1' and dividing the result by two. Armed with this information it is necessary only to lay a straightedge across the values of 'h' and 'k' on the outer scales of Nomogram 3 and read the resultant 'v' on the centre scale. One must be careful to apply the true

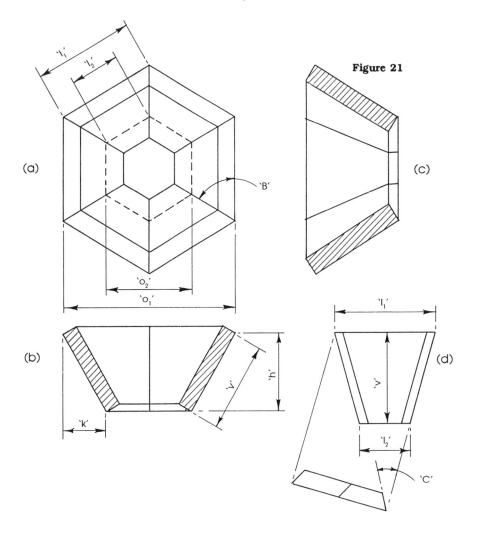

Figure 21

value of 'h' as shown; the presence of the inevitable waste at each end can be a little confusing in this respect. The planform of the stave may now be sketched as in (d). Note that Fig.21 is intended to demonstrate only a limited number of design features, and the stave thickness, although shown arbitrarily, is not actually under consideration for the moment.

The true mitre angle 'C' between staves is a little more difficult to obtain. It might be thought that this is simply the normal plan-view angle 'B' as determined by the number of staves in the assembly, but it most certainly is not! The new mitre angle will be rather larger than 'B', to an extent determined by the slope angle of the sides. This is not exactly the easiest of concepts to visualise, but a graphical example is given in Fig.22. Imagine first, a plain box, square in plan and rectangular in elevation. The mitre angle for such a construction would obviously be 45°. Imagine now the same box with all four sides sloped in elevation to an angle 'A' (in this case also made 45° for convenience) as shown in Fig.22 (a) and (b). The new mitre angle would be best observed by holding the box and sighting along one of the joint lines. The remainder of Fig.22 does precisely this by geometric construction, culminating in view (d) which shows the new mitre angle 'C' as being considerably larger than 45°. The angle is in fact 60° for this particular object, and could be so measured, given that the entire drawing is made with sufficient accuracy. As might be imagined, drawings of this kind are not particularly easy to execute with accuracy. In passing, it is of interest (although arguably not particularly useful) to note that the slope angle 'D' at the corners as shown by view (c) is considerably less than the side-slope angle 'A'. The value of angle 'C' may be calculated with the aid of Nomograms 5 and 6, (with no necessity for geometric construc-

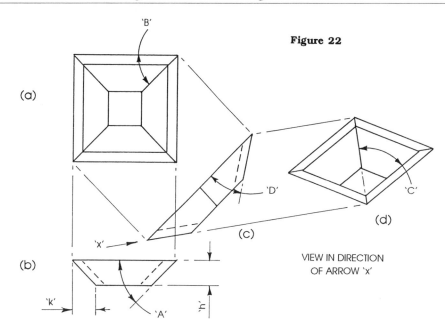

Figure 22

VIEW IN DIRECTION OF ARROW 'x'

tions of any kind), once the values of angles 'A' and 'B' have been chosen. It is first necessary to obtain the value of angle 'A' (where this has not actually formed part of the initial construction). This can be derived from the known values of height 'h' and overhang 'k' in conjunction with Nomogram 4. It is assumed for the moment that the elevation (b) has been arbitrarily drawn to the required shape, with sufficient accuracy to enable measurements to be taken from it. It is also assumed that the value of 'A' is not known, but needs to be determined from linear measurement on the elevation. One may then proceed as follows: the value of 'h' is chosen (as an example) at 2". By measurement, the value of overhang 'k' would be 2" also. Using the convenient value '20' on the outer scales of Nomogram 4 will give the value of 'A' directly as 45° on the centre scale. In order to obtain 'C' one must first find the value of the corner slope angle 'D'. This angle is not of direct interest but the nature of the formulae involved makes it a necessary intermediate Nomogram step. The value of 'D' is obtained from Nomogram 5 by laying a straightedge across the known 45° value of 'A' and the number of segments 'N' (in this case, four) on the outer scales, and reading off 'D' as 35.3° from the centre scale. The value of 'D' thus obtained is now transferred to Nomogram 6 and used in conjunction with the same value of 'N' to give the true value of 'C' as 60° on the centre scale.

It has been previously noted that the Nomograms solve general trigonometrical formulae, and they may therefore be pressed into service for purposes other than their basic ones. It is often quite difficult to plane, saw or sand a mitre angle to the degree of accuracy demanded, generally due to the difficulty in setting-up machine tables or fences. Much depends upon the machine of course, but in many cases the angular divisions available are of limited definition or possibly non-existent. A setting-up template may be constructed from card with the aid of Nomogram 4 and its associated Fig.N4(b), by selecting a convenient value of 'h' on the left-hand scale and using this in conjunction with the required setting angle on the centre scale to derive a value of 'k' on the right-hand scale. The template is now constructed by setting out the values of 'h' and 'k' on a piece of card as shown in Fig.23 and cutting along the diagonal line thus derived.

Incidentially, the cut is best made with a sharp knife and steel straightedge rather than scissors, for best accuracy. It may also be noted in passing that the construction of Fig.18 will serve exactly the same purpose where convenient, and may be used in conjunction with Nomogram 11. Note that the Nomogram also assumes an initial compass setting of 5", and also that it is of the 'direct-reading' type, and does not require a straightedge. A template of this type, although potentially highly accurate, requires care in use. It must be placed such that it is at right angles to the table in plan, and simultaneously at right angles to the cutting-plane of the sanding disc (or saw) in elevation, as shown in Fig.24(a). Any errors in this respect will give a misleading result, as may be shown by the simple expedient of rotating the base of the template slightly on the table and observing the angular gap which appears in the cutting plane (b). Further, the angle may be apparently corrected by rotating the template slightly in the cutting-plane also (c). Thus it can be seen that errors in presentation of the template will produce a result which is quite meaningless; it follows that machine-table setting errors can arise as a result. One faces exactly the same problem when using a sliding-bevel to check a mitre angle. The stock *must* be held at right angles to the edge of the work, as shown in Fig.25.

It is appreciated that the use of the Nomograms as described may appear somewhat complicated to readers unused to this type of work. The design of Fig.26 is therefore offered as a simple example of their use. The drawing shows a six-stave curved pot, rather wider towards the top than at the bottom. As can be seen from the elevation, a plain parallel-sided coopered construction would require timber of appreciable thickness 'w$_2$', leading to severe difficulties in machining the staves, and so much wastage that one might as well turn the piece

Figure 23

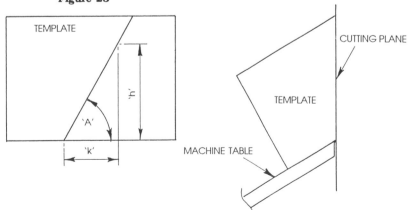

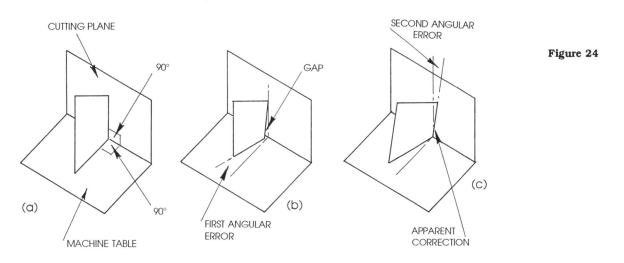

CUTTING PLANE
90°
90°
(a)
MACHINE TABLE

GAP
FIRST ANGULAR ERROR
(b)

SECOND ANGULAR ERROR
APPARENT CORRECTION
(c)

Figure 24

from the solid and be done with it. On the other hand, a taper applied to the initial construction will allow an appreciable thickness reduction to 'w_1.' Some care is necessary when determining the value of 'q' for a tapered construction. For values of 'A' greater than about 60° it is safe enough to measure 'q_1' directly as shown, particularly if a fairly generous waste allowance is given. For smaller values of 'A', the error may become unacceptable. In this case it is safer to determine the value of 'q_1' either as shown in (b) or more easily perhaps, by measuring the true *required* thickness directly from the elevation, multiplying by two, and subtracting the result from 'o_1'. The required stave thickness as estimated on the elevation sketch will almost certainly be determined by the required inner profile at the bottom, even though the bottom is made 'open' and finished off with a plain plug afterwards. The requirement will almost certainly give plenty of latitude at the top of the pot which may as a result be incurved if desired (pots often look better this way).

The desired value of 'o_1' is 6" and the number of segments 'N' is 6. From Nomogram 1, the length 'l_1'

of the top end of the stave is given as just under 3.5". The desired value of 'o_2' is 3" giving a value of 'l_2' from Nomogram 1 of just under 1.75". The required inner diameter at the top is determined by measurement as previously described, at 4.5". From this value, the true inner diameter may be obtained from Nomogram 2 at 3.9". Subtracting this value from 6" and dividing the result by two gives a value of 'w' (in

Figure 25

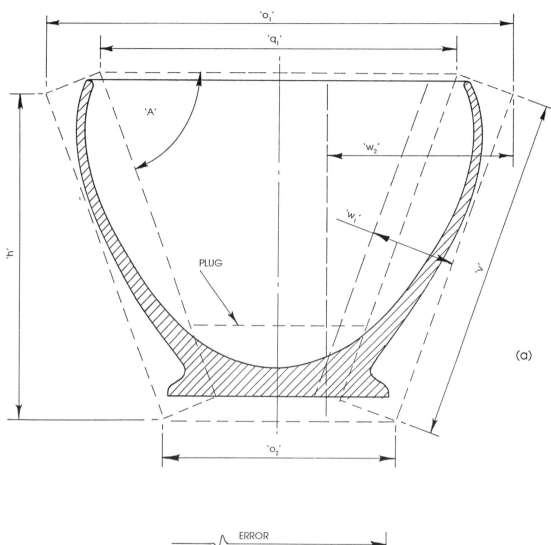

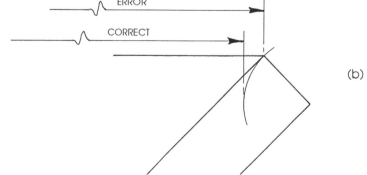

Figure 26

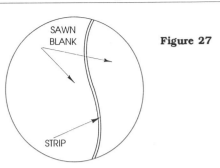

Figure 27

thio case, the stave thickness) of 1.05". It is very important that the derivation of 'i' is made with reference to the *larger* value of 'q' (ie. 'q_1'), since this will give a larger (and correct) value of stave thickness. It is now necessary to derive the true stave length 'v'. The values of 'o_1' and 'o_2' are known at 6" and 3" respectively. By subtraction and dividing the result by two, the value of overhang 'k' is found to be l.5". From this result and the desired value of 'h' of 4", Nomogram 3 gives the true stave length 'v' as 4.25". Similarly from Nomogram 4, using the same values of 'h' and 'k' the slope angle 'A' is given as 69.5°. Given the value of 'A', it is now possible to use Nomogram 5 to derive the intermediate angle 'D', at 66.7° and transferring this value to Nomogram 6 gives the true mitre angle 'C' at just a little over 62° (actually 62.07° by calculation). As a small practical consideration, the bottom plug is tapered in the design shown. It is necessary in this particular case in order to maintain the internal profile but, for reasons given in Chapter 8, a parallel-sided plug is preferable as a general rule. Note also that, given the timber grain is axial in both body and plug, the construction may be deemed safe in terms of timber movement (see Chapter 1).

A particularly fascinating area for exploration is that arising from making the segments curved rather than straight. This approach is not to be confused with the idea of sawing a curved line through a blank board and gluing the pieces back together with a strip of contrasting veneer between them (Fig.27). Attractive though the technique is if used with restraint, the only difficulties posed are the purely manual ones of sawing and re-assembly. Constructing a perfectly fitting ring from a collection of identical curved-joint segments is an altogether different proposition. To begin with, one can forget the idea of 'free-form' curves for the joints since re-assembly requires a shift in the

relative angle between the pieces, and this cannot be accommodated with anything other than a circular arc. It is also necessary to appreciate the fact that there is an implied angular relationship between two adjacent segments. In its simplest form, this will comprise the normal angles 'S' and 'B'. In addition, the upper and lower limits of the curve must coincide with those of the equivalent straight-line joint (Fig.28). This arrangement also permits the most convenient usage of stock timber, since all segments may be cut at a single setting of a simple cutting-jig (to be described later), with minimal wastage. In passing it may be noted that, on subsequent assembly, the joint is not obliged to be radial but, for ease of calculation and subsequent machining, it is laid out as though it were. The foregoing statement demands a little further explanation: Fig 28(a) shows a six-segment construction with radial curved joints, and an equivalent centre angle 'S' of 60°. The segments are cut as in Fig.29, a method which, incidentally, works for any desired mitre angle. Fig.28(b) shows a fully closed five-segment assembly using *exactly* the same seg-

Figure 28

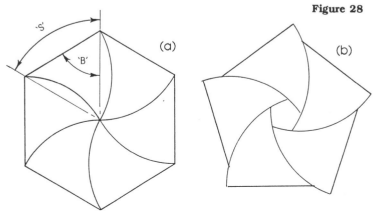

(a)   (b)

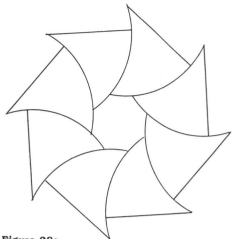

Figure 28c

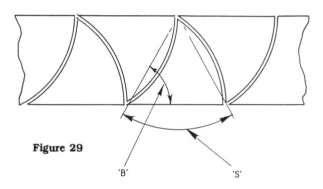

Figure 29

'B'   'S'

ments non-radially to begin with. By way of explanation, consider the assembly of Fig.30(a). This particular design has all the outer corners meeting perfectly — ie. with no steps between them. In order to meet this requirement *and* that of non-radial alignment, it is necessary for the equivalent straight-line mitre angles 'B$_1$' and 'B$_2$' on both sides of any single segment to be unequal. This poses severe setting-up difficulties when actually cutting the segments, and also leads to a great deal of wastage (shown shaded in (b)), no matter how cunningly the segments are laid out on the parent stock. Accordingly, the method has little to commend it.

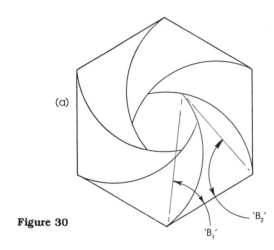

Figure 30

(a)

'B$_2$'

'B$_1$'

(b)   WASTE

'B$_1$'   'B$_2$'

ments as in (a); this is achieved by re-alignment of segments into a non-radial format. An eight-segment assembly of slightly different form, again using the same segments, is shown in (c). Note that both non-radial assemblies have, by definition, a hole in the centre. Thus, it is possible to set up non-radial arrangements with segments which have been cut radially (ie. in the simplest possible way). There is of course some wastage of timber if the outer serrations are subsequently turned away, but this is only of importance when the displacement between adjacent segments is itself large. In any case it is insignificant compared with the wastage incurred in attempting to cut the seg-

Although not immediately obvious by inspection, the angle 'S' subtended at the centre of a given segment remains constant regardless of where it is measured (Fig.31(a)), given that both curved flanks are of equal length (as they will be if cut radially). Matters change dramatically however when one segment is re-aligned relative to its neighbour as shown in (b). The effect of such a shift is to alter the angular displacement between segments. This is a most important concept, which leads to the ability to form a perfectly closed ring with either a lesser or a greater number of *identical* segments than required for a plain radial arrangement, as demonstrated by Fig.28.

It can be seen from Fig.31 that there are two possible methods of segment re-alignment. Anti-clockwise rotation of the left-hand segment relative to its neighbour leads to an increase in the total effective angle between them as in (b), and thereby leads to a reduction in the number of segments required for a fully closed ring. Clockwise rotation as shown in (c) gives a decrease in angle and an increased number of segments per ring. This latter arrangement needs to be handled with care, since it is possible to decrease the angle to such an extent that the ring will never close, however many segments are used. An effective way of studying segment behaviour, and indeed of planning a curved-segment project of any kind, is to cut a number of segments from card and arrange them in various combinations. It will most certainly be found initially that perfect closure of a ring (other than the plain radial arrangement) is quite difficult to achieve. This is because (given a requirement for equal displacement between segments) every segment in the construction must be very precisely aligned relative to its neighbour; thus any minor adjustment required for perfect closure must be made to *all* segments. It will be found, however,

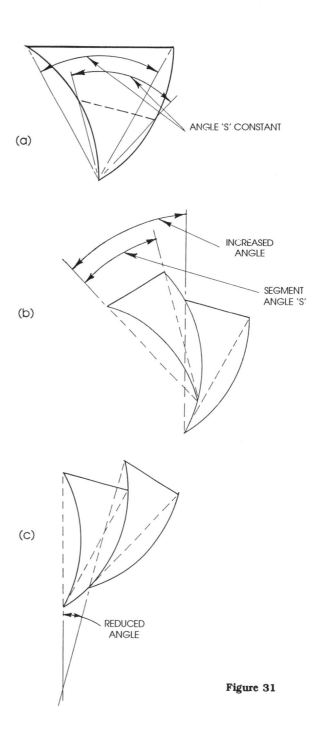

(a) ANGLE 'S' CONSTANT

(b) INCREASED ANGLE — SEGMENT ANGLE 'S'

(c) REDUCED ANGLE

Figure 31

that a deliberate mismatch in one segment pair *can* be accommodated by adjustment of the remainder, given sufficient time and patience. Such activities could well give the impression that the whole business is a matter of guesswork. This is by no means the case; any desired arrangement, comprising any combination of centre angle and radius of curvature may be predetermined very easily, with no mathematical or geometrical expertise on the part of the designer. Given observance of the few simple steps to be outlined, there is no need even to draw the proposed arrangement (which is perhaps as well, since such constructions are far more difficult to draw than to make). There is, unfortunately, one area where calculations do become sufficiently cumbersome to be inappropriate for practical use, and that is in the determination of the maximum turned diameter available from a given non-radial arrangement. This is, however, a relatively simple matter to resolve with the aid of segments cut from card.

To take a very simple example, a five-segment construction derived from 'one-sixth' segments will be described. The equivalent 'straight-line' centre angle 'S' for a one-sixth segment is easily found from the formula given with Nomogram 1 to be 60°, as shown in Fig.32(a). The value of 'S' for a five-segment construction is similarly determined at 72°. Thus the angular increase 'P' to be made by re-alignment is the difference between these two values, i.e. 12°. Anti-clockwise rotation of the left-hand segment is obviously made by sliding the curved flank against its neighbour; the rotation must therefore take place around the centre 'O' of the arc forming the 'joint line'. This in turn gives a displacement distance 'y' at each end of the joint line, a distance which is easily (and quite correctly) measured with a rule as a 'straight-line' measurement. In practical terms (i.e. with segments cut

(a)

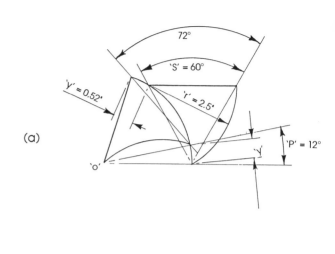

(b)

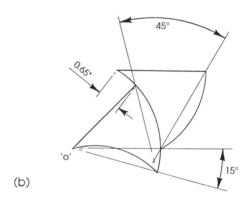

(c)

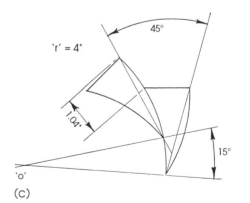

Figure 32

from timber) the centre point may well be somewhat badly defined; it is better therefore to use the outer edges to make the measurement. In order to correctly align a pair of segments, therefore, it is necessary only to mark the distance 'y' on one of them and use the mark as a point of alignment with the other (again, an exercise which may be tried out with card segments). It is of course necessary to determine the value of 'y'. This is effected with the aid of Nomogram 7 as follows, using the numerical values given in Fig.32(a) as an example: it has been shown that the required value of 'P' is 12°. The value of 'r' is a matter of choice and is given for convenience as 2.5" in this case. To use Nomogram 7 in this particular application it is necessary to halve the value of 'P' (the value of 'r' may be used as it stands), giving 'working values' to be applied to the Nomogram of 6° and 2.5" respectively. These values are used with a straightedge on the outer scales of Nomogram 7 to give the value of 'y' directly as 0.52" (actually, the value '25' is used on the 'r' scale to yield '5.2' on the 'y' scale (ie. a scaling factor of ten). Note that the overall dimensions of the segment are not relevant to the calculation; in other words the segment may be made any desired size for any fixed value of 'r', without affecting re-alignment behaviour.

An increase in the number of segments may be similarly accommodated. Fig.32(b) shows a pair of one-sixth segments arranged to give a closed ring of eight, the centre angle for which may be determined as 45°. Thus in this case a clockwise rotation of the left-hand segment is required to reduce the 60° angle to 45°, i.e. a rotation of 15°. Using the same value of 'r' as previously, the Nomogram 'working-values' are 7.5° and 2.5" respectively, giving 'y' as 0.65". The foregoing two examples correspond with the complete assemblies shown in Figs.28 (b) and (c). The third example uses one-

twelfth segments (an equivalent centre angle of 30°) to form a closed ring of eight. This requires an *increase* in angle from 30° to 45°, giving 'P' as 15°. The value of 'r' is arbitrarily increased in this case to 4". Nomogram 'working values' are therefore 7.5° and 4" respectively, giving 'y' as 1.04".

A further example is offered (Fig.33) in order to illustrate the versatility of curved-segment assemblies. In this particular case a twelve-segment construction is made, using two different sets of six segments, the difference being the value of the centre angle 'S'. Arrangements of this nature work extremely well if the two sets are made in contrasting timbers, or if the segments are separated by contrasting veneer slips. If they are given centre angles of 35° and 15° respectively, this gives a total angle of 50° for a pair. Six such pairs will give a combined centre angle of 300°. Since a full circle encompasses 360°, this leaves 60° to be shared as

Figure 33

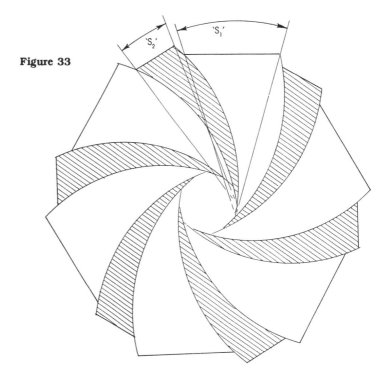

'offset' between twelve segments, ie. 5° each. For an arbitrary radius of curvature of 3" the offset value 'y' is found to be 0.26". In practice it will be found a trifle difficult to mark these offset values on all segments with complete accuracy; there is bound to be a little minor shuffling of segments to achieve perfect closure.

It is one thing to cut segments from card, and quite another to cut them from timber. Obviously the cutting of matching curves demands a bandsaw or power fretsaw; this topic is discussed fully in Chapter 5, including the construction and use of the necessary pivoted jig which enables circular arcs to be cut accurately. Such devices are commonplace, but an extra requirement in this case is a means of predetermining the position of the fence

relative to the pivot such that the start and finish of the desired arc occcur at the corresponding points of the equivalent straight mitre line. Figs.34 (a) and (b) show that the fence may need to be above or below the pivot point by a distance 't', dependent upon the required values of 'B', 'w' and 'r'. The value and position of 't' may be determined by the simple geometric construction shown in (c). Two parallel lines are drawn, separated by the known timber width 'w'. A straight line is drawn across the two parallel lines at the desired angle 'B'. A pair of compasses, set to the required value of 'r' is then centred upon points 'E' and 'F' in turn, to strike a pair of arcs intersecting at 'G', which is actually the centre of rotation. Thus it becomes immediately obvious whether the 'fence-line' is above or below

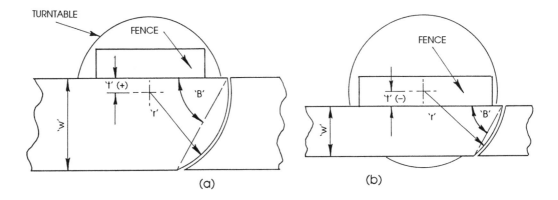

(a)   (b)

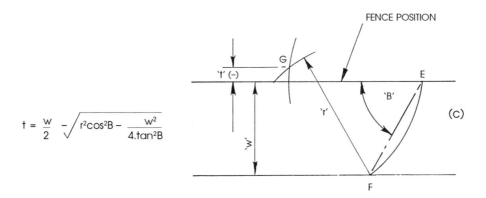

$$t = \frac{w}{2} - \sqrt{r^2\cos^2 B - \frac{w^2}{4.\tan^2 B}}$$

(c)

Figure 34

the pivot point, and the distance 't' may be measured directly. Alternatively, 'mathematical types' may care to use the formula shown on Fig.34. In this case, a positive result indicates that the fence is placed above the pivot point, and a negative result the converse. Unfortunately this particular formula does not lend itself to easy use of

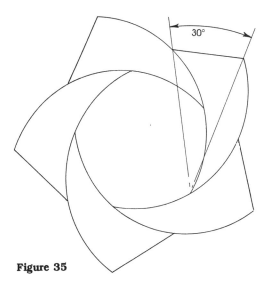

Figure 35

Nomograms. To close the discussion on curved assemblies, Fig.35 shows a somewhat exaggerated example using only five 'one-twelfth' segments. Clearly, as a fully-turned piece, this would give rise to unacceptable timber wastage and would be scarcely worth the bother of making. If the piece were made from fairly thick stock and the serrated outer profile left alone, the inside could be lightly turned and fitted with a suitable centre, thereby creating an attractive vessel.

One final form of segmentation may be discussed with advantage, that of using long triangular strips to successively build up a multi-segment cross-

sectional arrangement as shown in Fig.36. This particular construction is best suited to the essentially 'square' formation shown since more complex assemblies lead to severe practical difficulties in machining and assembling the parts. The turning process gives rise to a characteristic pattern of elliptical and 'mushroom' shapes, although these can be made to appear more complex by the incorporation of plenty of beads and coves in the workpiece; indeed this particular form of construction is best suited to ornate turnery. The assembly also needs to be built up from two different timber types in alternating 'squares'. It is suggested, however, that the contrast between timber types is not too great, since this can give a somewhat garish and 'overdone' appearance.

As can be seen, the assembly is built upon a small core of square cross-section from successive sets of four isosceles triangles with an apex angle of 90° and base angle of 45°, to form further squares, with an angular offset of 45° between successive squares. The side length of each square is $\sqrt{2}$ times its immediate predecessor (roughly 1.41 times). From this it follows that the multiplying factor between semi-adjacent squares is 2. Thus, apart from an initial calculation involving $\sqrt{2}$, the determination of the remaining sizes merely involves a 'times-two' factor. Fig.36(a) shows the relationship, based on a central square of side length 's'.

It is convenient to cut the triangular sections from square-section stock, the side lengths in this case being half those shown in Fig.36(a). For example, it may be seen from (b) that (neglecting saw-kerf allowance), the size of the stock square for the third layer is the same as that for the centre square. Fig.36(c) demonstrates the loss in side length arising from saw-kerf and clean-up allowances. As previously noted, these are perhaps best dealt with on a trial-and-error basis.

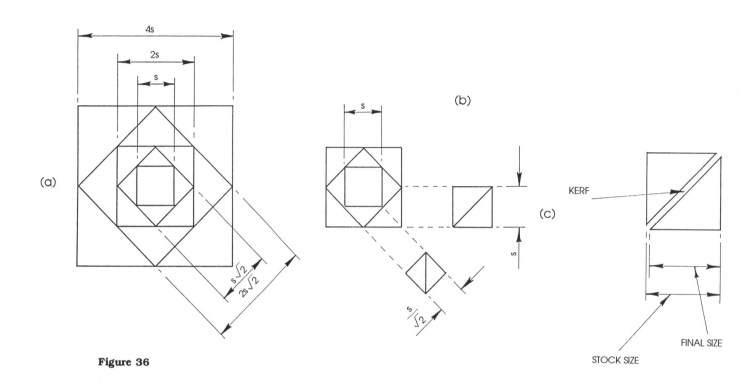

Figure 36

It is possible to employ further segmentation techniques, either for basic constructional purposes or as a form of 'inlay work' (for want of a better term). The combination of segmentation and turnery does, in many cases, create the impression that straight joint lines are actually curved, a technique which may be effectively exploited with strips of veneer glued between segments. Some of these ideas will be illustrated in a number of projects to be described but, as a conclusion to this chapter, Figs. 37 and 38 show the segmented platter and tapered-stave vessel described and fully-dimensioned earlier, since they provide an introduction (and relatively easy exercises) with respect to the segmentation and assembly techniques discussed in this and subsequent chapters.

Figure 37

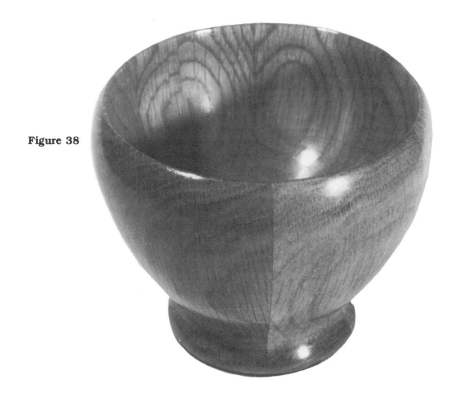

Figure 38

3. OFF-CENTRE TURNERY: Design Considerations

One of the pleasures of turnery is that of watching the shape of the workpiece gradually evolving under the action of the tool. In this sense, the fact that the workpiece is actually revolving might almost be regarded as irrelevant, since it will show the same profile whether the lathe is running or not. The situation is slightly different if part of the work involves, for example, a 'square-to-round' transition, as often required in between-centres work for table legs and similar items, or the rather technically-demanding faceplate turning of vessels which retain a non-circular cross section over part of their profile. In the first place it is much more difficult to see what is actually going on during the turning, since the non-circular portion of the work can only be observed as a kind of 'ghost-image' which gives no real idea of its true shape. Many an accident has occurred to the workpiece, the worker or both, as a result. On the other hand, since the work revolves on one single axis of rotation from start to finish, the final result is usually predictable even before the first cut is taken, and any attendant difficulties are normally those of tool-handling imposed by the intermittent cutting action. Any form of turning which involves changing the axis of rotation during the course of the project usually requires a little more planning if unpleasant surprises are to be avoided. The intermittent cutting demands on the manual skills of the turner are much the same, although the ghost-image may be rather more difficult to see in some cases. The biggest problem, however, lies in the prediction of the result.

Perhaps the simplest possible case is that of turning a workpiece between-centres, of approximately oval cross section. This is achieved by marking *two* axes of rotation at each end of the workpiece, and using each in turn. It is a common-enough practice, the desired result often being arrived at by trial-and-error. This may well be acceptable if the final required cross section is a fairly close approximation to a circle (achieved by a close spacing of the centres, as in Fig.39(b)). On the other hand, where the 'aspect-ratio' (ie. the ratio between width and thickness of the cross section) is fairly large, some form of preliminary drawing at least, is indicated. It can be seen from Fig.39(a) that, as the distance between centres is increased, the aspect ratio is increased also. Further, the cross-sectional profile becomes noticeably less continuous, in the sense that it exhibits distinct points at both ends; these may of course be rounded by subsequent hand sanding if desired. Any project of this nature would normally pre-require some idea of the final cross-sectional width and thickness of the completed oval. Indeed, in order to avoid undue wastage of timber it is sensible to utilise stock material which is reasonably close to the required final dimensions, particularly if a number of identical pieces such as table legs or balusters are to be made. Whilst it is quite possible to determine all necessary parameters mathematically, the result-

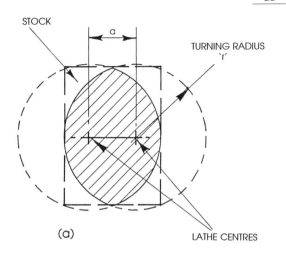

STOCK

TURNING RADIUS
'r'

LATHE CENTRES

(a)

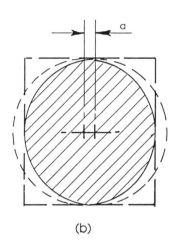

(b)

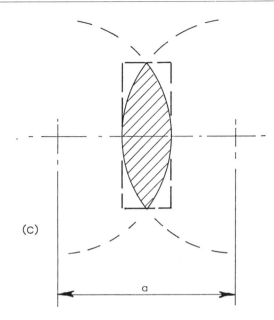

(c)

Figure 39

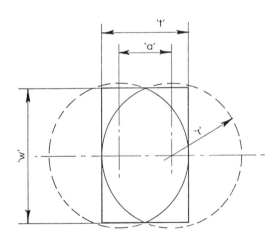

$$t = 2r - a$$

$$w = \sqrt{4r^2 - a^2}$$

$$a = \frac{2r(n^2 - 1)}{n^2 + 1} \quad \text{where } n = \frac{w}{t}$$

Figure 40

Figure 41

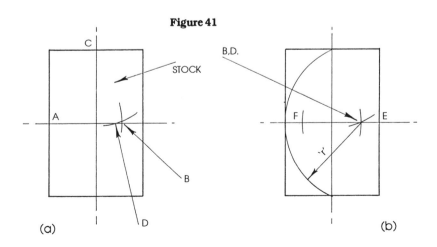

STOCK

(a)

(b)

ant formulae are perhaps a little difficult to handle by non-mathematical readers, even with the aid of Nomograms. For completeness' sake, however, the relevant formulae are given in conjunction with an explanatory diagram in Fig.40, for the benefit of readers in a position to use them. The alternative geometrical approach is given in Fig.41. Whilst this is quite simple, requiring only a rule, pencil and compasses, it does involve trial-and-error with, unfortunately, a high percentage of the latter, in that several attempts will generally be required to achieve acceptable accuracy.

It is first necessary to draw a rectangle embracing the required cross-sectional profile, plus horizontal and vertical centre lines. The compasses are now set to an arbitrary dimension and, with the point centred at 'A', an arc is struck to cross the horizontal centre line at'B'. The compasses are now centred at 'C' and a further arc struck to cross the centre line at 'D'. The compasses are re-set to a further trial dimension, and the process repeated, the ultimate objective being to make the arcs intersect at the same point *on the centre line,* thus making 'B','D' and the centre line coincident. It will now be found that this point will give one of the required pair of lathe centres with the compasses automatically set at the required radius 'r'. The second centre is easily found by placing the point of the compasses on the other flank at point 'E' and striking an arc to intersect the centre line at 'F'.

It is of course, one thing to determine the radius of curvature, and quite another to actually turn to that radius on the lathe, since the use of calipers is quite out of the question, regardless of whether the workpiece is revolving or not. In order to accomplish this particular task it is necessary to draw a bold, easily visible centre line along the full length of the workpiece on *both* 'short faces' as in Fig.42. When the work is revolving in the lathe, these lines will be visible, as will the progress of the cut (although they will be ghost-images). All that is necessary is to turn up to these lines; the profile will then be generated correctly. Any uncertainty may be dispelled by stopping the lathe occasionally. With this type of turnery there exists a kind of 'theoretical maximum' aspect-ratio, which occurs when the centres are placed exactly on the extreme flanks of the rectangular stock. This cannot be accomplished in practice without some special mounting provision of course, but for interest, this maximum gives an aspect-ratio of just over 1.7, (strictly $\sqrt{3}$). Beyond this point, the centres lie outside the blank (Fig.39(c)), which not only requires some thought with regard to mounting arrangements but also opens up a very interesting range of possibilities.

Clearly, one way of turning a piece of this kind would be to mount the blank on the periphery of a pair of disc mandrels which themselves are held between centres. It would be necessary to devise some means of re-positioning the blank (ie. by locating-pegs) after turning the first face in order to deal with the second. It would also be necessary at a minimum, to position a similar blank on the opposite side of the discs in order to stabilise and balance the assembly. Even better is to mount several blanks to form a cage and turn the lot simultaneously; this not only improves the overall

Figure 42

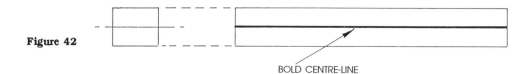

BOLD CENTRE-LINE

balance of the assembly but makes the actual turning very much easier (and safer) by reducing the gap between workpieces, and, therefore, the intermittency of the cutting action. Fig.43 shows the general arrangement. The idea can be extended to encompass cross-sectional profiles involving three or more facets. It is, however, necessary to devise rather more complex arrangements of dowels and holes to rotate and locate the workpieces on the mandrels. Fig.44 shows one such arrangement, based upon the equilateral triangle. It can be seen that this particular shape is ideally suited to a 'six-station' mandrel, given that the blanks are sawn to a triangular cross section to begin with.

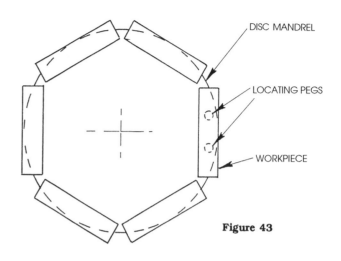

Figure 43

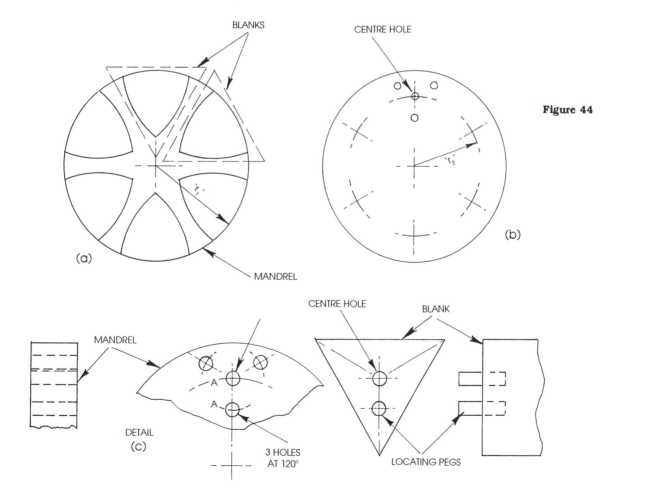

Figure 44

The blanks must each be fitted at one end with a pair of locating pegs which enable them to be re-positioned on the mandrel for turning each face in succession. One pin must be at the centre of the triangle; the other is located at a convenient distance from it. The other end of each blank needs to be fitted only with a single centre pin, to be used with a similar but rather simpler mandrel running on the tailstock live centre. The mandrel must be carefully marked out and drilled with six 'work-stations' as shown in Fig.44 (b) and (c). The centre hole of each work-station must be placed on a common 'pitch-circle radius' such that the blank, when mounted, may be turned to the required outer radius ('r_1' in Fig.44(a)). This is much easier than it might appear, once the required outer radius is known.

It is necessary to digress slightly at this point, in order to determine the curved equilateral cross section, as shown in Fig.45(a). Profiles of this

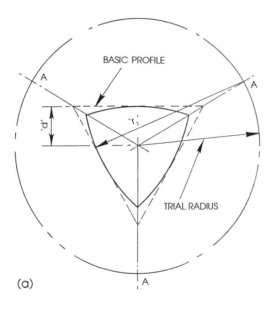

(a)

Figure 45

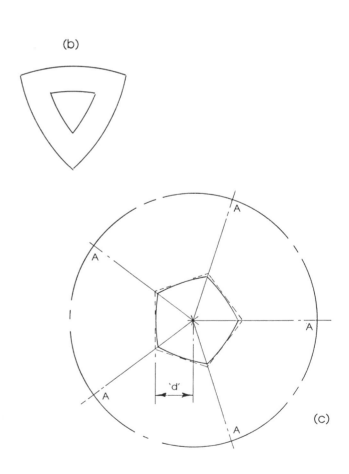

nature are best planned with the aid of geometry, since the appearance of a finished turned piece will depend a great deal upon the relationship between the width of the facets and their radius of curvature. The construction itself is quite simple, but requires some trial-and-error in order to arrive at an attractive shape (an assessment which is entirely at the discretion of the turner). Firstly, a plain equilateral triangle, shown by the dashed lines in (a), is drawn which would, at a guess, embrace the finished profile. The corner-angles are now bisected with three lines (shown chain-dotted); these should meet at the centre, and should be extended for a fair distance. A pair of compasses is now set to a convenient trial radius and a circle drawn cutting the three radial lines at points 'A', these being the trial centre points for the curved profile. The compasses are now centred on any one of these three points and adjusted so that they draw an arc which just touches the opposite face of the triangle. The profile is completed by drawing two further arcs on the remaining centres. The whole procedure is repeated as many times as desired until a pleasing result is obtained. It must be noted that the radius 'r_1' thus obtained is actually that which will be turned on the lathe, which must consequently be capable of handling a workpiece of effective diameter of rather more than twice the value of 'r_1', since the points of the fully mounted set of blanks will increase the effective diameter somewhat; this can be seen from Fig.44(a).

To return to the business of laying out the mandrel: the radius 'r_1' has been found, and a circle of this radius is now drawn on a sheet of paper. The distance 'd' shown in Fig.45(a) is carefully measured and used to establish the radius at which the centres of the blanks are mounted, shown as 'r_2' in Fig.44(b). The circular construction is divided into six equal sectors, their intersection with the smaller circle giving the centre points of the work-stations. The work-stations themselves may then be set out in accordance with the detail (c) in Fig.44, although it would be rather pointless to do this on paper. The task is better carried out directly on the mandrel, since all required dimensions are known. (More details of marking out and making mandrels are given with a number of projects which require them). Note that the basic triangular profile has only been used thus far to establish the maximum turning dimensions. When actually sawing the blanks, they should be made slightly larger, to accommodate a little 'turning-allowance', as shown in Fig.44(a). It is not suggested for a moment that pieces of this kind are turned as plain parallel-sided sticks; their usefulness and appeal would be severely diminished if this were so. Accordingly, some variation in side profile is to be catered for. Methods of dealing with some of the problems encountered are given later but for the moment, it is merely pointed out that the mandrel must obviously accommodate the *largest* cross section, and layout must be based upon this. It should also be appreciated that variations in turned 'diameter' will give rise to some modification of the cross-sectional profile. By way of example, Fig.45(b) shows two such profiles: these would be arrived at by the normal off-centre turning process on the same piece; they demonstrate that the smaller the cross section, the 'flatter' it appears, although the radius of curvature is in fact smaller, an optical illusion caused by the significant reduction in facet width. The method of layout may be extended to four or more sides. Fig.45(c) shows a five-sided layout. Whilst this is by no means impossible to manage, it is necessary to point out that the practical difficulties associated with turning a significant number of matching facets represent a fairly stiff examination of the skill of the turner.

Slightly more ambitious is the turning of profiles which have unequal facets as shown in Fig.46. The basic shape (which is again one of personal preference) is laid out in accordance with the procedure shown in Fig.46(a). A horizontal centre line is drawn, together with a vertical line which intersects it at some convenient point. Two arbitrarily chosen equal distances are marked on the vertical line on either side of the centre line, to give the two points 'A'. From these points, two arcs are drawn at a convenient radius r_1. The compasses are now centred at the intersection 'B' of the two original lines, and a further arc struck at radius r_2, cutting the centre line at point 'C' (the radius r_2 may or may not be equal to r_1 as desired). With the compasses set at r_2 and centred on 'C' the final arc is struck to complete the profile. Again, the entire process may be repeated as often as necessary until a satisfactory result is achieved. The positions of a pair of location holes ('D' and 'E') are now marked at suitable positions. The distance between 'D' and 'E' should be a convenient round-figure, since it will be used to determine the centres of the two locating pegs on the blanks, in addition to striking arcs on the mandrel. The distance from point 'B' to hole-centre 'E' should be treated similarly, since it will be found of importance when designing the mandrel to hold the blanks for turning the short final flank of the pieces (ie.r_2). It remains to transfer the hole positions on to a mandrel suitable for turning the pair of long flanks. This is done quite easily by measuring the distances 'AE' and 'AD' (ie. from either of the points 'A' to the centres of the two locating holes) shown on Fig.46(b) as r_3 and r_4 respectively. A pair of concentric circles are now drawn on the mandrel to these radii, and divided into six equal sectors (Fig.46(c)). Finally, with the compasses set to the chosen distance r_5 (between the pair of location

holes) and centred at the intersections 'F' on the smaller circle, six arcs are struck on the outer circle, thereby locating the six pairs of holes as required. Note that the outer radius of the disc-mandrel is made equal to the turning-radius r_1. This enables the mandrel itself to become a convenient reference point when turning the blanks. It is always a great help to make such arrangements wherever possible, and thus applies equally to the tailstock mandrel which, as a result, may be of a different overall diameter from that of the headstock mandrel. In this way, some means of gauging the finished dimensions of the blanks is actually furnished by the mandrels themselves (at the two ends at least). In common with the equilateral arrangement previously described, it is necesary to have only one hole per work station on the tailstock mandrel (conveniently, that marked 'E' on Fig.46).

As drawn, the arrangement depicted in Fig.46(d) would appear to cater for only one of the pair of long flanks on each blank. However if, after turning the first flank, the blanks are removed and the mandrel reversed on the headstock, the blanks may now be replaced and the second flank turned as a mirror-image of the first, as shown by the dashed lines on blank 'A' in Fig.46(d). It is of course necessary to arrange that the mandrel may be reversed in this way, *and* retain its concentricity. This is quite easily managed, and will be described later. The turning of the remaining (short) flank is easily accomplished with the aid of a mandrel which places the locating pegs in a radial arrangement. As an example, the mandrel shown in Fig.44 could be utilised, with only those holes marked 'A' in detail (c) being used. Due attention must of course, be paid to the desired radius of curvature and the position of this flank with respect to the locating holes. The 'cutlery-handle' project features a fully-dimensioned set of blanks and mandrels based upon the design methods outlined here.

Finally, it is worth noting that each of the finished 'blanks' may be further modified by partial turning as individual items, either between-centres or faceplate mounted, as appropriate. This technique is featured in a number of projects. In the meantime, Figs.47-50 give some indication of the effects which may be obtained.

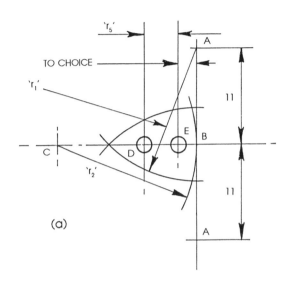

(a)

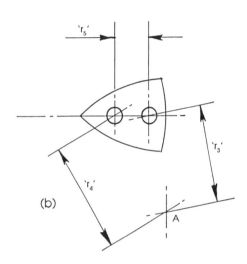

(b)

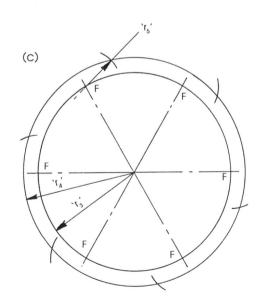

(c)

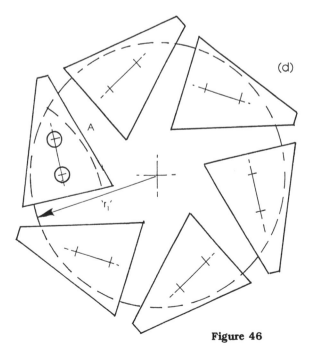

(d)

Figure 46

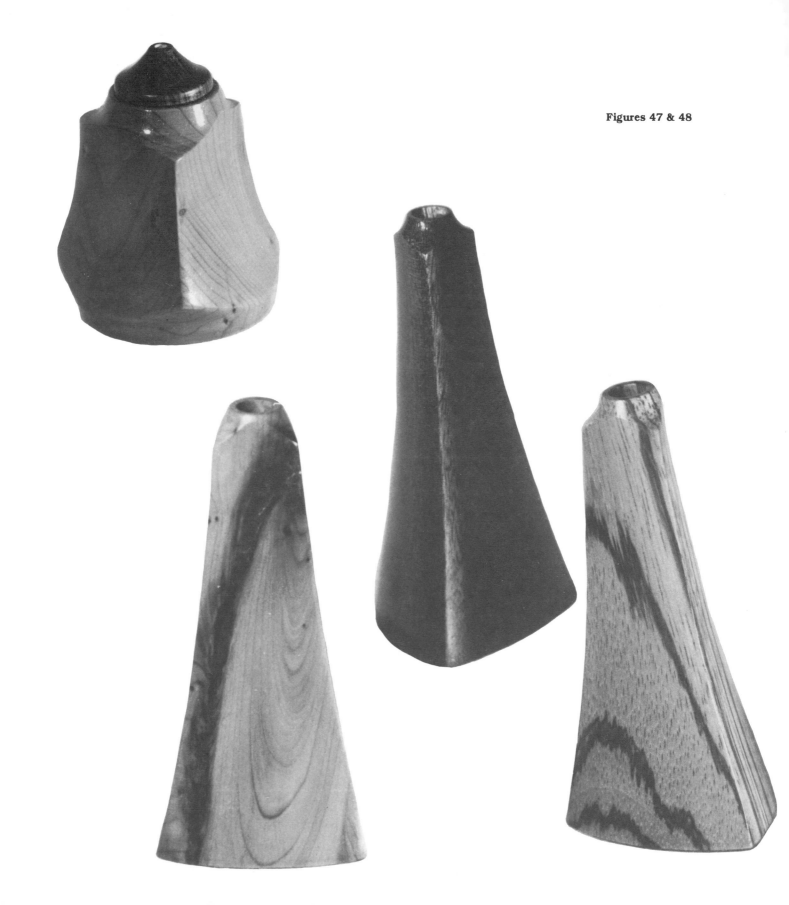

4. THE NOMOGRAM

Many woodworking projects may be successfully undertaken by the application of craft skills pure and simple, these being essentially an understanding of wood and its behaviour, plus the necessary skill with hand tools and, where appropriate, machinery. Others will require something more. For example, the woodcarver or marquetarian specialising in rendering real-life objects in their chosen media clearly require artistic ability, in addition to skill with tools. Similarly, many forms of woodwork, particularly those involving complex joints or compound angles of one kind or another, will require the application of geometry and mathematics if mistakes and disappointment are to be avoided. It might be argued that the turner has little or no need of such things. It is certainly true that the turning of a bowl or a table leg from a single piece of timber, however ornate the design, will not

Figure 51

place particularly severe demands upon the mathematical or geometrical skills of the turner. On the other hand, the design of a segmented piece can scarcely be carried out without some ability in these disciplines. Moreover, some forms of 'off-centre' turnery will demand some prior knowledge on the part of the turner, of just how things are going to turn out (in both senses of the phrase).

It is appreciated that the application of mathematics does presuppose appropriate training (coupled perhaps with a liking for the subject), and that many people, whatever their other skills, do not possess these attributes, and are consequently rather frightened off any projects which appear to require them. This is a pity; such a self-imposed limitation is entirely unnecessary, since a means exists whereby many of the problems encountered may be easily solved by those with no mathematical or geometric knowledge whatsoever. Indeed it may be regarded as the mathematical equivalent of 'painting-by-numbers'. The method involves the use of a graphical device known as a 'Nomogram', comprising a set of (usually) three scales drawn on a sheet of paper, each scale representing a particular range of dimensions or angles. All the user has to do, is to lay a straightedge across the scales in accordance with one or two simple instructions, and to read off the required answers directly (Fig.51). It is the task of the Nomogram designer to ensure that the Nomogram performs the required function to an acceptable degree of accuracy.

Nomograms do in fact solve mathematical equations, but the important point is that it is not in the least necessary for the user to understand the equations themselves. Thus, although mathematical devices such as 'tangent', 'square-root' or whatever, may actually be used in a Nomogram, it is by no means necessary for the user to understand them, or even to be aware that such things exist. The relevant equations are actually given on the Nomograms; these are, however, only for the benefit of the reader who prefers to use them directly.

In order to demonstrate the Nomogram principle, one may take as an elementary example, the simple addition of two small numbers, say, '5' and '2'. One would scarcely bother to design a Nomogram for simple addition and subtraction of numbers, but the very simplicity of the task provides an ideal means of illustrating the idea. Fig.52 shows a Nomogram which solves the problem as follows: laying a straightedge across the 'a' and 'b' scales such that it intersects the 'a' scale at the value '5' and the 'b' scale at the value '2' gives the required value of '7' on the 'c' scale, as indicated by the line drawn across these values. As may be seen by a few simple experiments, the selection of any pair of values on the 'a' and 'b' scales will yield their sum on the 'c' scale. Thus the Nomogram solves the simple equation: [c = a + b]. By mental arithmetic, if 5 + 2 = 7, then it follows that 7 - 5 = 2, and 7 - 2 = 5. The Nomogram can be made to solve these two equations also, by using it 'in reverse'. To take the same example, to subtract 'a' from 'c', a straightedge between '7' on the 'c' scale and '5' on the 'a' scale would give '2' on the 'b' scale. Similarly the 'b' and 'c' scales may be used to furnish a result on the 'a' scale. This method of use does have one minor disadvantage: any error of alignment made when setting the straightedge between two adjacent scales will tend to be magnified on the remaining

scale. The effect can be particularly severe if the pair of scales used to position the straightedge are fairly close to one another (as many of them are). The method is thus not really the best way of using a Nomogram. In general, Nomograms are designed to give the best (ie. the most accurate) solution to a particular equation over the range of values most likely to be encountered; this will normally mean that the 'known' values are on the outer scales and the 'unknown' (ie. the required) value is found on the centre scale. Any other method of use will occur only where a Nomogram designed for one particular application may be pressed into service for another. Two rather more useful examples will now be given:

Nomogram 9 demonstrates multiplication and division of numbers. It is perhaps as well to note at the outset that this particular Nomogram actually has five scales, although only three are used at any one time. The left-hand 'b' scale is a single common scale, used for both multiplication and division. The right-hand and centre scale-sets each comprise a pair of scales. The right-hand scale of each

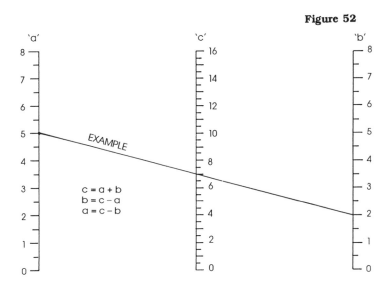

Figure 52

$$c = a + b$$
$$b = c - a$$
$$a = c - b$$

set ('c' and 'a') are used for multiplication; the left-hand pair ('e' and 'd') are used for division. The method of use is as follows: to multiply '8' by '3' for instance, the straightedge is laid between '8' on the 'b' scale and '3' on the 'c' scale, to give the result '24' on the 'a' scale as shown by the 'Example 1' line. The division of the same pair of numbers is accomplished by placing the straightedge across the 'b' and 'e' scales, to give a result just a little less than '2.7' on the 'd' scale as shown by the 'Example 2' line. The general nature of the Nomogram also makes it possible (although unnecessary in this case) to use it 'in reverse' as previously described. The supplementary formulae on the Nomogram indicate the functions which may be performed thereby. The reader is invited to experiment with these in order to gain familiarity with Nomogram use. In passing it may be noted that this particular Nomogram, although perfectly operational, performs nothing other than multiplication and division of numbers, ie. it does not solve any 'difficult' mathematical equations. For this reason it is to be regarded as a simple demonstration, rather than a tool for handling specific woodworking problems.

Nomogram 4 demonstrates a simple trigonometrical application which regularly crops up in woodworking activities (whether one is aware of it or not), and which involves one of the properties of the right-angled triangle. This particular Nomogram, (which will be encountered again in Chapter 2 in the role for which it was designed) determines the value of angle 'A' when the base distance 'k' and the height 'h' are known. (Fig.N4.(b)). For example, if the base distance 'k' is known at 10 metres, and the height 'h' is known at 50 metres, the straightedge may be laid across the Nomogram to intersect these values on the 'k' and 'h' scales and the required angle read off directly on the 'A' scale at 78.7°. Again, the Nomogram may be used

'in reverse' in order to determine, for example, 'h', when 'k' and 'A' are known (given due care with the straightedge). It is worth noting at this point that the example given relates to 'metres' but the 'k' and 'h' scales do not actually indicate this or any other type of unit. In fact, the choice of unit is entirely up to the user, and it makes no difference to the behaviour of the Nomogram, provided that the same units are used for both scales in any single calculation. It is also possible to alter the 'dimension' scales of the Nomogram in order to better suit the dimensions of the task in hand. For example, it is perfectly in order to mentally multiply all the dimension marks on the 'k' and 'h' scales by five, thereby giving both scales a maximum scale range of 500 units. It is, in fact, much the same as applying scale-factors to the dimensions of the piece under construction, just as one might do on a drawing. Note, however, that whatever scale changes are made to the line-dimensions, *all angles remain unchanged*. It is most important to realise that it is not possible to apply scaling factors to the 'angle' scales on *any* Nomogram. It may help to appreciate the point by considering any drawing involving both linear dimensions and angles. It would be quite in order to make a drawing larger or smaller as desired, by applying a scale factor to the linear dimensions. If however, the angles are changed in any way, the drawing would cease to make sense. Nomograms behave in exactly the same way.

Finally, the reader will doubtless have noticed that most of the scales on the Nomograms are 'non-linear', with the divisions being somewhat more cramped at some parts of the scale than at others. This is unavoidable, due to the nature of the mathematical operations being performed. It is always possible to design an acceptably-accurate Nomogram, covering a limited range, to suit a particular application, but 'limited range' also implies limited usefulness. All the Nomograms are designed specifically for woodturners and, it is hoped, will embrace most popular applications.

The use of each Nomogram is described in detail in the chapter or project which makes use of it and a brief summary is included at the end of this chapter, indicating where the Nomograms are used, or giving specific applications, as appropriate. Their usefulness may be readily extended by choice of metric or Imperial dimensions as appropriate to the physical size of the work in hand, and also by applying scaling factors either to the Nomograms or the project drawings, as previously described. Changes of this nature can be particularly useful in avoiding the more cramped portions of the scales, and thereby enhancing accuracy. This is a major reason for the choice of 'one-tenth' subdivisions. The absence of 'eighths' and 'sixteenths' etc. will perhaps be deplored by readers accustomed to working in these units, but they are a necessary omission, made in the interests of the acquisition of a greater working range. A further reason is simply that the use of any Nomogram implies a calculation, the result of which will rarely be obliging enough to emerge as a convenient fraction. In other words, the use of a calculator of any kind implies a decimalised result, since this is the way that most of them present their results.

LIST OF NOMOGRAMS

NOMOGRAM 1.   Trigonometrical. (see Chapter 2)

NOMOGRAM 2.   Trigonometrical. (see Chapter 2)

NOMOGRAM 3.   Trigonometrical. (see Chapter 2)

NOMOGRAM 4.   Trigonometrical. (see Chapter 2)

NOMOGRAM 5.   Trigonometrical. (see Chapter 2)

NOMOGRAM 6.   Trigonometrical. (see Chapter 2)

NOMOGRAM 7.   Trigonometrical. (see Chapter 2)

NOMOGRAM 8.   Trigonometrical. Similar to Nomogram 7, but with different scaling factors. Useful for solving problems requiring a regular polygon inscribed in a circle.(See Fig.N8.(a).

NOMOGRAM 9.   Multiplication and division. May be used for this purpose, but essentially for demonstration.

NOMOGRAM 10.   Trigonometrical. Allows design of turned ball or ellipsoid by steps. Designed specifically for use with 'ellipsoid' range of projects.

NOMOGRAM 11.   Trigonometrical. Template layout. (See Chapter 2.) Direct-reading Nomogram.

NOMOGRAM 12.   Trigonometrical. Multiplies or divides by a fixed factor of $\sqrt{2}$. Direct-reading Nomogram.

NOMOGRAM 13.   Trigonometrical. Multiplies or divides by a fixed factor of $\sqrt{3}$. Direct-reading Nomogram.

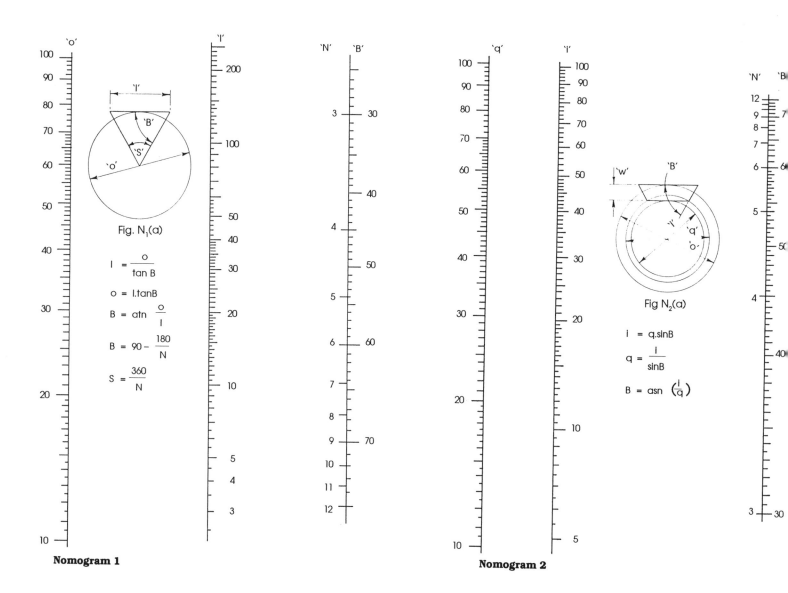

Fig. N₁(a)

$$l = \frac{o}{\tan B}$$

$$o = l.\tan B$$

$$B = \text{atn } \frac{o}{l}$$

$$B = 90 - \frac{180}{N}$$

$$S = \frac{360}{N}$$

Nomogram 1

Fig N₂(a)

$$i = q.\sin B$$

$$q = \frac{i}{\sin B}$$

$$B = \text{asn}\left(\frac{i}{q}\right)$$

Nomogram 2

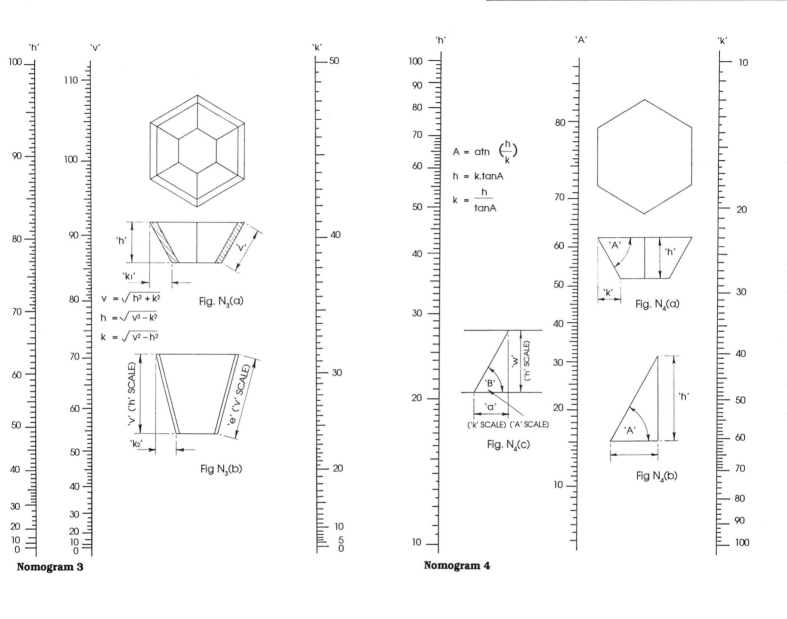

'h'   'v'   'k'

A = atn $\left(\dfrac{h}{k}\right)$

h = k.tanA

k = $\dfrac{h}{tanA}$

'h'   'A'   'k'

v = $\sqrt{h^2 + k^2}$ Fig. N₃(a)

h = $\sqrt{v^2 - k^2}$

k = $\sqrt{v^2 - h^2}$

Fig N₃(b)

Fig. N₄(a)

Fig. N₄(c)

Fig N₄(b)

Nomogram 3   **Nomogram 4**

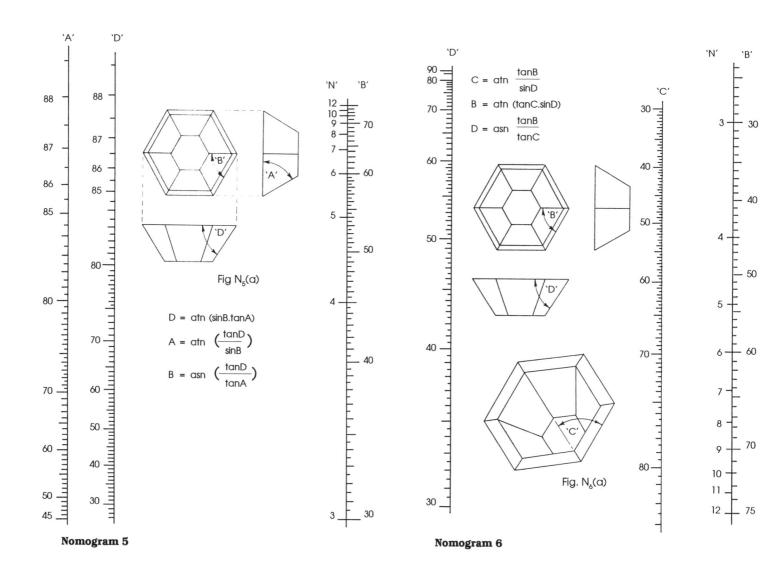

Fig N₅(a)

$$D = atn\ (sinB.tanA)$$

$$A = atn\ \left(\frac{tanD}{sinB}\right)$$

$$B = asn\ \left(\frac{tanD}{tanA}\right)$$

Nomogram 5

$$C = atn\ \frac{tanB}{sinD}$$

$$B = atn\ (tanC.sinD)$$

$$D = asn\ \frac{tanB}{tanC}$$

Fig. N₆(a)

Nomogram 6

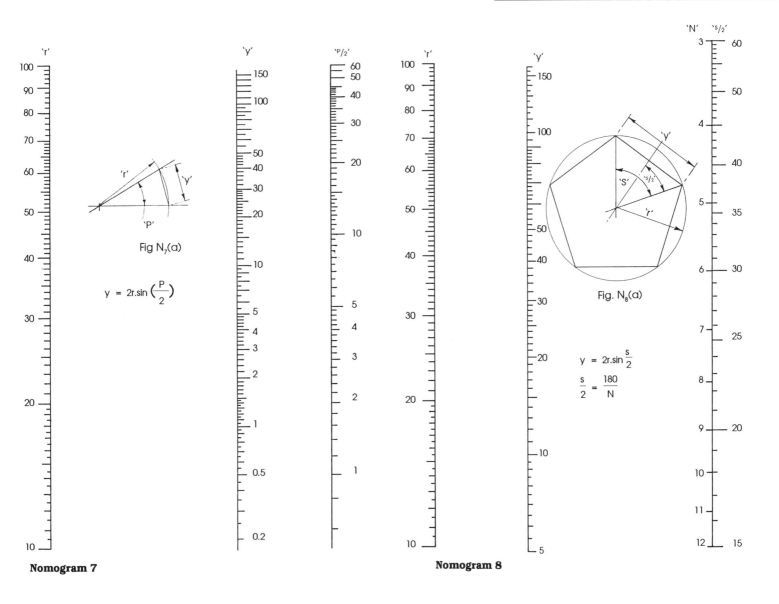

Fig N₇(a)

$$y = 2r.\sin\left(\frac{P}{2}\right)$$

Fig. N₈(a)

$$y = 2r.\sin\frac{s}{2}$$

$$\frac{s}{2} = \frac{180}{N}$$

Nomogram 7

Nomogram 8

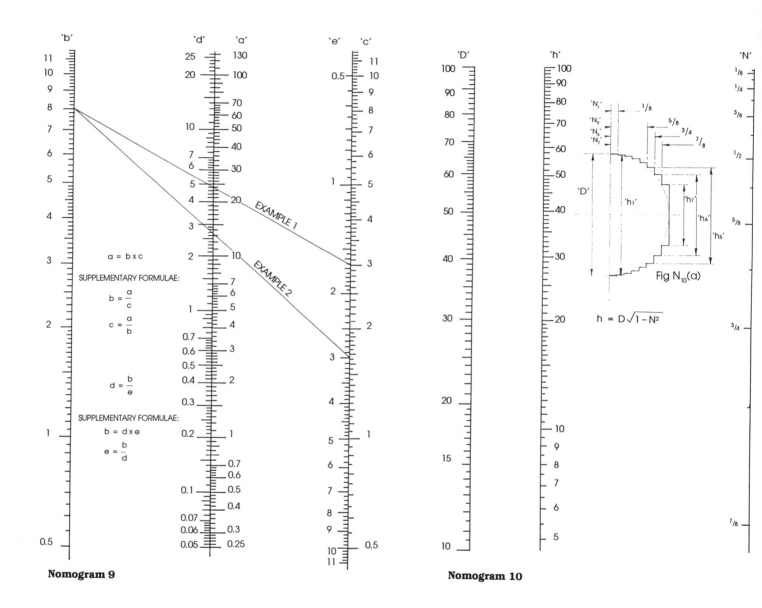

'b'

11
10
9
8
7
6
5
4
3
2
1
0.5

a = b × c

SUPPLEMENTARY FORMULAE:

$$b = \frac{a}{c}$$

$$c = \frac{a}{b}$$

$$d = \frac{b}{e}$$

SUPPLEMENTARY FORMULAE:

b = d × e

$$e = \frac{b}{d}$$

'd'

25
20
10
7
6
5
4
3
2
1
0.7
0.6
0.5
0.4
0.3
0.2
0.1
0.07
0.06
0.05

'a'

130
100
70
60
50
40
30
20
10
7
6
5
4
3
2
1
0.7
0.6
0.5
0.4
0.3
0.25

EXAMPLE 1

EXAMPLE 2

'e'   'c'

0.5   11
       10
       9
       8
       7
       6
1   5
       4
       3
2   2
       1
5
6
7
8   1
9
10   0.5
11

Nomogram 9

'D'

100
90
80
70
60
50
40
30
20
15
10

'h'

100
90
80
70
60
50
40
30
20
10
9
8
7
6
5

'D'   'h₁'   'h₇'   'h₆'   'h₅'

'N₁'   1/8
'N₅'   5/8   3/4
'N₆'   7/8
'N₇'

Fig N₁₀(a)

$$h = D\sqrt{1 - N^2}$$

'N'

1/8
1/4
3/8
1/2
5/8
3/4
7/8

Nomogram 10

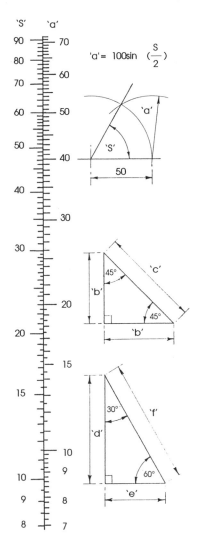

Nomogram 11

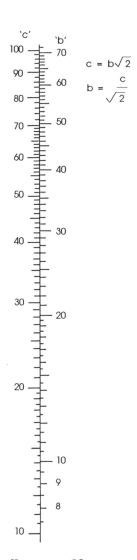

Nomogram 12

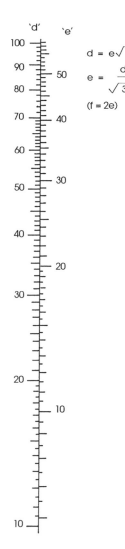

Nomogram 13

5. SAWING TECHNIQUES

Segmented work, by its very nature, implies the handling of small pieces of timber which need to be accurately sawn in some way, usually by machine. It is frequently necessary to carry out the work freehand, against a marked line, without the aid of push-sticks, fence or mitre-block, and perhaps with the saw-table set at some angle other than 90° to the plane of the saw. It follows that, for the sake of the safety of both the workpiece and the operator, the sawing arrangement chosen should be inherently as safe as possible. It is suggested at the outset that a circular saw of any kind is not the best choice, regardless of the nature of the work undertaken, and in any event, for curved-segment work it is out of the question. Personal experience suggests that the bandsaw is the best choice for segmented work, with perhaps the power fretsaw (within its capacity limitations) as an acceptable alternative.

It might be as well to consider the action of the two basic forms of sawing device. First, the circular saw in its 'table-saw' mode will inevitably have two unwanted elements of motion: there is the forward motion against the direction of feed, and there is the upward motion generated by the back edge of the saw if it happens to come into contact with the workpiece. Both components will tend to project offcuts towards the operator (and the guard may not help), particularly if the table is tilted such that the offcut falls towards the saw (Fig.53). A further disadvantage lies in the fact that the saw will tend to cut the bottom face of the workpiece before the top (which will normally bear any guide lines). This imposes visual difficulties in alignment of the workpiece, particularly if the table is tilted; it will also give rise to an instinctive reaction on the part of the operator to attempt to 'correct' a cut whilst it is in progress, and thereby risk jamming — not a particularly good idea where small workpieces are involved. Agreed, the use of a radial-arm saw will tend to eliminate the problems mentioned, with the possible exception of the handling of small pieces of timber close to the sawblade.

The bandsaw, on the other hand, has only one component of force generated by the sawband; this is always downwards towards the saw-table. Further, given squared-off timber, the sawband may be guided to enter the work in whatever relationship to the marked guide lines is desired; in addition, any errors in presentation may be manually

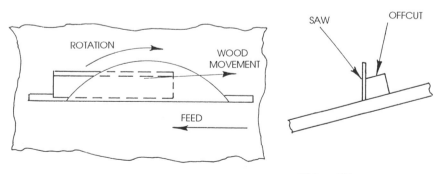

Figure 53

corrected, at least to some degree, as the cut proceeds. The power fretsaw possesses similar advantages, with the exception that the return stroke tends to pull the work away from the table; a tendency fairly readily (and generally instinctively) corrected, even in work of substantial thickness, by firm downward pressure. When cutting plain segments, tapered in plan view but with flanks square to the plan-face, it is normal to saw them by flipping the work from one face to the other, thus saving timber. Where tapered coopered work is involved, it is not possible to carry out the operation directly with a mitre-fence, since the table-tilt necessary to provide the mitre angle will not allow more than one flank to be machined at the same setting of the fence, although the task can be accomplished freehand (Fig.54). It is also possible with the bandsaw to machine parallel-stave coopered work successfully against the normal fence. In this case, each length of basic stock to be

Figures 55 & 56

used must first be machined to the required angle on one flank (Fig.55), after which the fence is set to the required stave-width (plus a small sanding allowance) and as many staves as possible extracted from the stock (Fig.56). Where the stave-width is sufficient to maintain a respectable width of flat surface against the table, the operation presents no particular problems. On the other

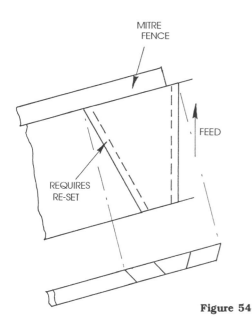

Figure 54

hand, narrow staves, which give virtually no real bearing surface on the table will tend to tip towards the saw as the cut is completed. On the bandsaw, this occasions no real problem, the only effect being to cause the sawband to bend slightly (Fig.57). On a circular saw it is likely to cause, at the very least, severe damage to the workpiece, and may even throw the free stave into the guard, or even at the operator. The effect is undesirable however, even with a bandsaw, but can be fairly easily eliminated with the aid of a stick, attached to the stave to be cut, with a dab of hot-melt glue. The action here is not so much one of feeding the work into the saw, but rather that of maintaining alignment of the stave as the cut is completed. There will, however, be a point at which the parent stock is itself of insufficient width to maintain angular accuracy due to lack of contact area with the sawtable. A piece of stock of the same thickness may, however, be temporarily attached with hot-melt glue to maintain an adequate bearing surface.

Curved-segment cutting of precise circular arcs demands either a bandsaw or a power fretsaw,

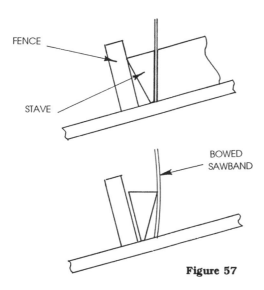

FENCE

STAVE

BOWED SAWBAND

Figure 57

necessarily accompanied by a turntable jig of some kind, in order to maintain the necessary accuracy in terms of radius of curvature. Both machines do however, share a common problem. In bandsaw terminology the effect is termed 'band-lead', and is evidenced by a tendency for the sawband to wander off the intended line of cut, with a marked preference for one side or the other. For example, when cutting freehand to a marked line on the face of the work, it is often quite obvious that the workpiece needs to be fed into the saw at an appreciable offset angle, in order to maintain the intended cutting-line. When cutting against a fence, there will be either a tendency for the workpiece to be pulled away from the fence, or to be pushed ever more firmly against it, the latter effect often leading to jamming the cut and stalling the machine. The problem is caused essentially by the sawband being sharper on one side than the other, causing it to produce a genuine cut on the sharp side and more of a rubbing effect on the other, with a resultant drift in the direction of the sharp side. When cutting relatively thick timber freehand with such a saw, it may appear that some success is being achieved by forcing the saw to follow the intended line at the point of entry into the timber. Things will be very different inside the workpiece however, since the sawband will assume a progressively greater bend inside the work (Fig.58(a)). This will be quite evident when the saw exits the workpiece, since it will visibly flip back (b) into its normal cutting position — that is, if it can be persuaded to leave the workpiece at all, since it is quite common for the machine to stall with the sawband firmly jammed inside the work, and almost impossible to remove. The only real cure for the problem is to make sure that the sawband is acceptably sharp before attempting the task, although a very gentle feed, allowing the sawband plenty of time to remove its kerf on both sides, will alleviate matters somewhat.

All this is quite well-known among workers who regularly use a bandsaw or power fretsaw on relatively thick timber, and is mentioned here only as an introduction to a similar but rather less obvious effect which occurs when cutting curves. The general nature of the problem is illustrated by Fig.59(a) which shows how the rear edge of the band can be impeded by the receding work, causing it to twist slightly and thereby cut off-line. The net effect is essentially that of 'band-lead', but it can quite easily occur with a brand-new sawband. The use of a turntable jig may well lull the user into a false sense of security in this respect, since a well-made jig might reasonably be expected to produce an accurate result, but the sad fact is that it won't necessarily. It is possible however, to set the work up in relation to the saw in a way that extracts the best result from a given situation, although one cannot expect a vast improvement. From (b) it is evident that the 'obvious' position for the saw in relation to the work, with the teeth on a line passing through the pivot and at right angles to the sawband, isn't necessarily the best. If the pivot is moved towards the rear of the saw by some amount (usually best determined by experiment and inspection on a number of trial pieces), the rear of the band will tend to clear the workpiece, with consequent relief of pressure and a truer cut. Thus the method makes best use of the available kerf-width,

but does of course depend on the fact that an appreciable kerf (with respect to the band depth) exists to begin with. It is normally a reasonable assumption that the 'finer' the saw (ie. more points per unit length), the better the result, but in curved work this is not necessarily the case, since a saw will normally possess a 'set' related to the size of its teeth; a fine saw will therefore cut a narrower kerf

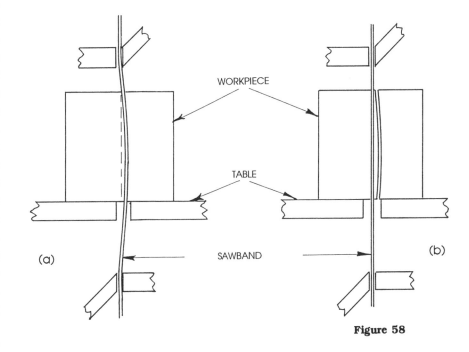

Figure 58

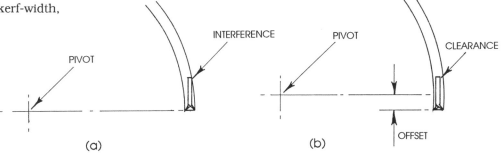

Figure 59

than a coarse one, with increased risk of interference and consequent 'band-lead' propensities on curved work. It is thus preferable to use a coarser grade of saw (of minimum possible depth), with a very slow, even feed. It is also important that the sawband is not kinked in any way, since this will produce the ribbed finish characteristic of bandsaws, however slowly the work is fed.

The power fretsaw does possess the distinct advantage that the blade depth is small relative to the kerf-width and may therefore be expected to produce acceptable results. In general this is a valid assumption, but the 'band-lead' effect can still occur, particularly if the cut is forced. There is also a tendency with oily timbers, such as teak, for sawdust to 'pack' in the kerf behind the saw, giving rise to somewhat unpredictable behaviour on occasion — another good reason for the use of a coarse grade of sawblade. The nature of the timber is in fact a fairly significant factor, and a set-up which works well for a hard, close-grained timber may be quite unsatisfactory for a more fibrous or oily material. It is sensible, therefore, to cut a couple of practice pieces *in the chosen timber*, and check them for finish and fit, before commencing a serious project.

At the risk of over-stating the obvious, it pays to keep the sawteeth clean. Sawbands in particular can become clogged with residue from oily timbers on the sides as well as between the teeth and, whilst they may still be sharp in themselves, they will not perform properly if they are coated with timber residues. A fairly stiff brass brush, used regularly, will be of great benefit. There is no need to alter the set-up to do so; plenty of room will be provided for cleaning simply by raising the sawguard. The operation must be performed with the machine switched off (and preferably with the mains plug removed), and the sawband pulled

through by hand in a series of steps. It is possible to draw the brush across the teeth at a slight angle and by so doing, to move the band upwards or downwards, thereby rendering the entire operation both swift and simple.

The turntable jig can be quite a simple affair; all that is necessary is a plywood disc, of radius slightly less than that chosen for the segment, pivoted on a metal pin of about ¼" diameter, which is itself fixed to a flat baseboard (Fig.60). It is important that the turntable is made as large as possible, both to give support beneath the workpiece, and to enable the longest possible turntable fence to be used. It follows that, if a range of work is undertaken, more than one turntable is desirable, since the turntable radius must obviously be rather less than that of the segment being cut. It is also highly desirable that a scrap piece of

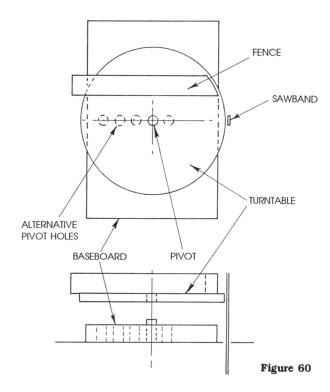

Figure 60

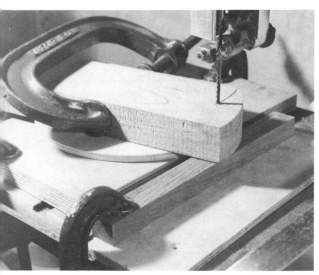

Figure 61

workpiece should be cramped to the turntable fence wherever possible, to eliminate movement between the two; this is of particular importance with the fretsaw, since the vibration of the machine can cause movement without the operator being aware of it.

It is most important that placement of the fence is achieved with the maximum possible accuracy. Since the formula given in Chapter 2, Fig.34 determines the fence position relative to a line passing

wood, of the same thickness as that used for the turntable, is placed on the other side of the saw, to support the segment being cut. This may be held in position with a cramp if dimensions permit (Fig.61), but may otherwise be attached with double-sided adhesive tape. The position of the baseboard is normally made adjustable relative to the saw, in order to set-up the pivot point relative to the sawband; in its simplest form, this may be effected by cramping the baseboard to the machine table. It should be possible to cope with work up to about 10" radius or so in this way, dependent upon the size of saw-table. Power fretsaws tend to have rather smaller tables and it will almost certainly be necessary to fit some form of outrigger. Fig.62 depicts such an arrangement, fitted to a popular make of machine, which in the form shown is set to a fixed radius. The inherent depth-of-cut limitation of the power fretsaw makes it desirable to mount the outrigger flush with the machine-table rather than on top of it, in order to maintain the capacity of the machine as far as possible. Figs.61 and 64 show the bandsaw and fretsaw systems in use. The

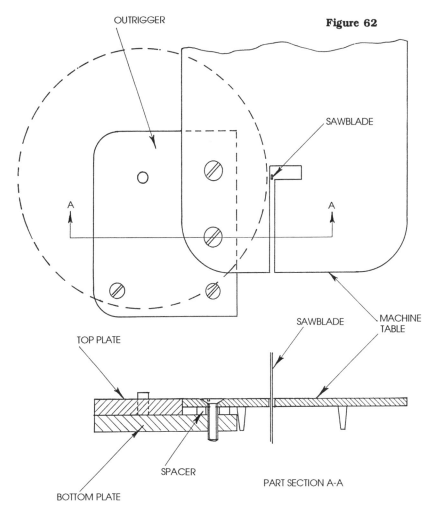

Figure 62

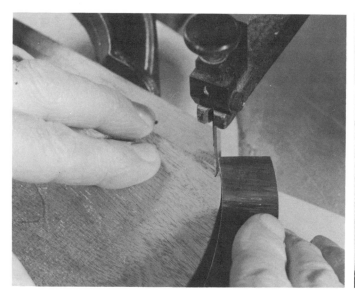
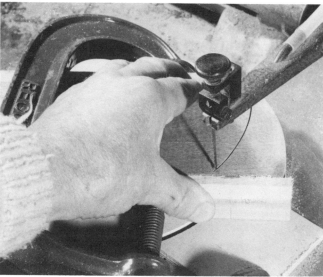

Figures 63 & 64

through the exact centre of the turntable, it is as well to mark such a line at the time the turntable is made, and before the centre hole is drilled. This line may be subsequently used as a reference as many times as required, to determine the fence position 't', which may be transferred from a rule to the turntable with a pair of dividers, and a pencilled line drawn at the precise position of the fence (Fig.65). The fence is then cramped firmly to the turntable and fixed by means of a pair of pins driven into it from beneath the turntable. The arrangement permits easy removal of the fence when it is required to change its position.

It will be seen from Fig.66 that a successive series of segments taken from a single length of stock will be cut 'pointed-end-first'. Whilst this is quite easily the most convenient way of producing a number of segments, there is some tendency, when starting a cut, for the saw to slip away from the intended cutting line on to the previously cut face. The initial feed should therefore be very light

until the saw has established its line of cut, and is effectively supported by the work on both sides. In extreme cases, ie. when cutting narrow segments, (which are necessarily of acute centre-angle), it may be necessary to use a scrap segment as a 'lead-in' block (Fig.63 and 67(a)). Note also the lead-out block held at the exit point of the saw (Fig.64). It will be found that this keeps the saw 'on-track' at the moment of exit, thereby avoiding the

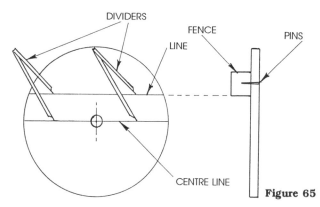

Figure 65

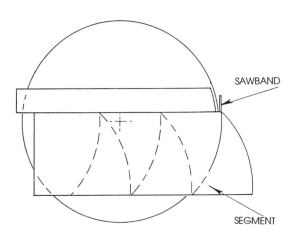

Figure 66

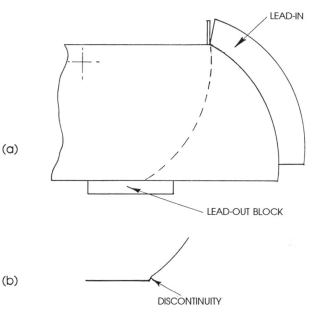

Figure 67

small discontinuity shown in Fig.67(b). Given that the stock timber is cramped to the fence, the turntable may be easily rotated with one hand, whilst applying the lead-in and lead-out blocks with the other, at the same time maintaining the slow, even feed necessary for a good finish. Incidentally, in work of this nature, it is sensible to cut at least one spare segment whilst the machine is set up, and in any case, all offcuts bearing a convex edge should be saved as cramping blocks.

It is also worth part-sawing a number of scraps of timber (ideally of the same thickness as the work in hand) for subsequent use as concave cramping blocks with built-in end-stops as shown in Fig.68. The use of these will be seen in Chapter 7. In this context it is sensible to leave the sawing set-up undisturbed during all stages of subsequent construction (if convenient), so that cramping pieces, and indeed spare segments, may be produced as desired. In many cases, a length of timber may be

too short to cramp to the fence with accuracy, but may well have a useful segment left in it. Given that the stock is squared off to begin with, and also that a straight-edged length of squared off timber of approximately the same width is available, a temporary joint with hot-melt glue may be effected by applying the glue and then pushing both pieces of timber smartly together against a straight length of material previously cramped to a worktop (Fig.69).

Figure 69

Figure 68

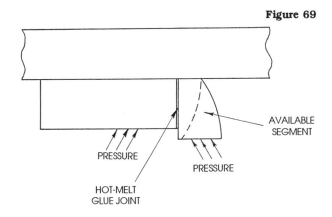

This may be extended to extract more than one segment, but in this case the 'extension-piece' must be of the same width and thickness as that being cut, due to the need to flip the work over.

It has been previously noted that a wide saw-kerf is an advantage with regard to controlling bandsaw behaviour on curves, but this brings its own problem in that the radius of curvature on the concave side of a segment will necessarily be slightly less than that on the concave side. The effect becomes progressively more pronounced as the radius of curvature is decreased, and is shown, highly exaggerated in Fig.70. The effect may be dealt with in either of two ways. First, it is always possible to insert strips of contrasting veneer between segments, such that the kerf-width is effectively taken up; this can lead to quite acceptable decorative effects (Fig.71). Secondly, the convex face may be disc-sanded to increase its radius of curvature slightly. Since the amount of material removed is likely to be small, the operation is quite effectively performed freehand on the sanding table, and is discussed more fully in the chapter dealing with sanding operations.

It is always worth considering the possibility of using segmented work as an inlay for the centre of bowls or platters. Such centre-pieces, although they may be of quite respectable diameter, can

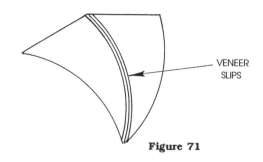

VENEER SLIPS

Figure 71

usually be fairly thin (Fig.72). A useful trick is to make up a segmented ring considerably thicker than required. When assembled, the ring may be turned to a plain parallel-sided cylinder, faced-off dead square at the free end, and then sawn into slices against the machine fence. The technique is particularly useful where matching pairs or sets of turned work are required, or even to provide a common central motif or design for pieces which are not themselves matched for size or shape but which nevertheless may be combined to form a group of some kind. The sawing arrangement is shown in Fig.73, where a deep vertical sub-fence is cramped to the existing fence, and the table adjusted if necessary such that the sub-fence is precisely parallel to the sawband. The work is then sliced into as many pieces as necessary. Note, however, that the work may tend to roll slightly as

Figure 70

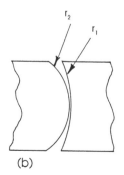

KERF

r_1

r_2

(a)

r_2

r_1

(b)

Figure 72

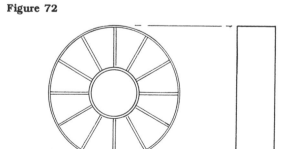

it is sawn, and it may be sensible to temporarily attach a small piece of plywood to the free end of the work with hot-melt glue, to obviate the tendency. In any event this job is positively *not* one for the circular saw, on safety grounds. Fig.74 shows the set-up in use with a bandsaw although, in view of the size of the workpiece, a sub-fence is not used in this case.

Many of the projects to be described feature a 'laminated-stave' assembly made up from a succession of triangular strips, to be used as a 'workpiece-blank'. As with all stave work, accuracy in construction of the blanks is of the utmost importance, and manufacturing methods will generally benefit from a little preliminary thought. The basic problem in this instance is the cutting of the triangular cross section strips. These must be accurate in terms of cross-sectional dimensions and angles, and general straightness and smoothness along their length, if subsequent handwork after gluing (with attendant risk of loss of accuracy) is to be avoided.

The sawing-jig described has proved its worth over a period of several years, and is well worth the trouble of making, not only for the production of laminated turnery blanks, but also for any kind of work which requires triangular beading of any kind (given that the cross-sectional profile is a symmetrical 45° quadrant. As a first thought, it might be imagined that the simplest way of tackling the task is to provide a number of strips of square cross section, followed by re-sawing into triangular strips, after tilting the saw table appropriately. In principle there is absolutely nothing wrong with the idea. The only real drawback (in the small home workshop anyway) lies in the possibility that the demands of other work or the re-thinking of the project itself may require re-setting of the saw table from 90° to 45° and back again. Not

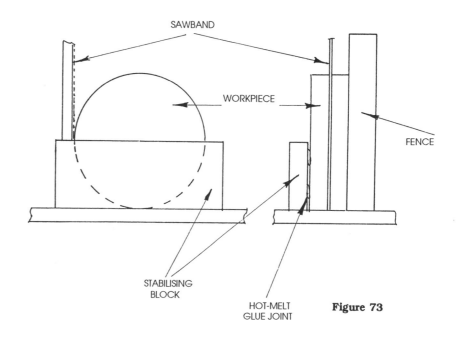

Figure 73

Figure 74

only is this a time-consuming nuisance, but the possibilities for angular error are bound to be increased in proportion to the number of such alterations made.

Given, therefore, that it is required to produce a fair number of triangular strips of this nature, a jig becomes worthwhile. The basic design is illustrated in Fig.75, the main body being constructed from a single length of hardwood, with both flanks machined to 45°. This is the only occasion where the saw table needs to be set to any angle other than 90°, both for the jig and for subsequent work employing it. Since the jig is essentially a device for producing subsequent work as accurately as possible, its manufacture warrants just that little bit of extra care. It is not strictly necessary to machine both flanks; one will suffice for a perfectly usable jig. It would seem sensible however, to make the device double-sided whilst the saw is accurately

set up, thereby allowing the jig to remain usable if one side is subsequently damaged in any way. The design offered has the minor convenience of having the fence in slightly different positions on the two sides. This can be useful when handling a wide range of work, but is by no means essential. It is desirable to make the jig initially about an inch longer than necessary, for reasons which will become clear later. There will also be a use for a spare length of timber, machined to 45° on one face, of about the same length as the jig, but about 3" wide. The dimensions given for the jig are to be taken only as a guide, by the way. As it stands, the device will allow a sawn face of 2" depth; this relates to an assembled square of about 1.4" side-length. It is a relatively simple matter to increase the capacity of the device by tacking a strip of plywood of appropriate thickness to the underside. It is essential that plywood or similar material is used, to ensure

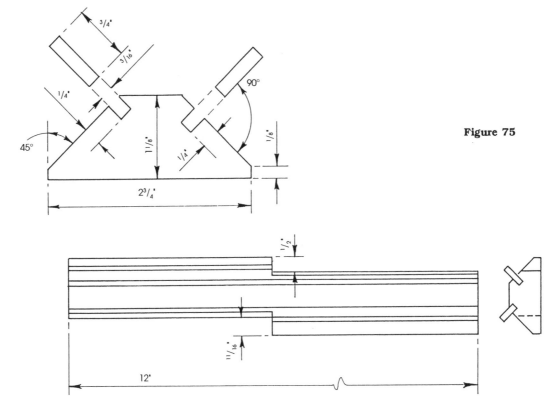

Figure 75

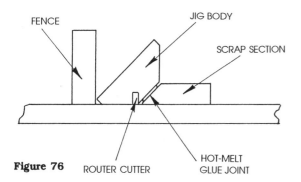

Figure 76

FENCE

JIG BODY

SCRAP SECTION

ROUTER CUTTER

HOT-MELT GLUE JOINT

parellelism of the faces; any error in this respect will be translated to the jig. The machined slots in the jig may be cut with either a router mounted beneath a table (essentially, therefore, a spindle moulder) or by a table saw set to cut a blind kerf of the required width and depth. In this way, it is possible to machine a slot which is square to the working-face. Some form of 'face-down' machining position is to be preferred, since it is considerably more difficult to provide an accurate set-up for use with 'overhead' machining methods. Even so, there is some difficulty attendant upon the machining of the slot, particularly with regard to operator safety. The essential problem lies in the fact that the workpiece is non-square, and is therefore at some risk of tilting during machining.

The problem may be eliminated with the aid of the extra length of stock which was machined at the same time as the jig body. This is now attached to the jig body by holding the jig down flat and simultaneously hard against a straight fence. The spare length of stock is now given a dab of hot-melt glue at each end of the angled face and rapidly pushed against the jig body. The operation is far simpler than it sounds and is well within the capacity of one pair of hands. The 'spare' thus effectively becomes a temporarily fixed push-stick (Fig.76). A further strip of scrap material is necessary to hold the work down firmly against the

worktable, but the entire slot cutting operation may now be carried out with safety, after which the two ends bearing the dabs of glue may be sawn away. It is sensible to cut the slots in the body first, and to tailor the insert-strips to fit them afterwards, since a firm push fit is required, with glue applied to the bottom of the slot only.

It is suggested that jigs of this type are best used as fixed devices forming an integral (albeit temporary) part of the machine, by cramping the jig to the machine table. This allows attention to be concentrated on the workpiece only, and eliminates errors which might arise if both the jig and the workpiece were moved against the machine fence. For this reason, the jig is cut away for about a third of its length, leaving a small portion of the internal corner generated by the junction of the body and the insert-strip to provide guidance for the workpiece as it leaves the sawband. In use, the jig is positioned, with the aid of the standard machine fence,

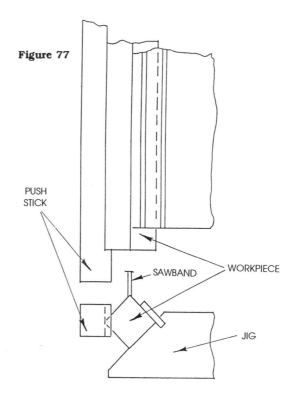

Figure 77

PUSH STICK

SAWBAND

WORKPIECE

JIG

such that the sawband is aligned correctly with respect to the workpiece (which must be square-edged to begin with). The only remaining implement is a further push-stick, made as shown in Fig.77, to enable the workpiece to be held firmly against the sawband for the entire cut. The push-stick is not essential. Its purpose is not so much to ensure operator-safety as to relieve operator discomfort; sideways finger pressure on the sharp corner of a length of stock, over the period of time required to saw the full length can be a distinctly painful experience. In its simplest mode, the jig may be used to cut a pair of identical triangular-

section strips from a single square-section strip, which has previously been machined to the required dimensions (not forgetting the kerf width). In passing, it should be remembered that each laminated construction requires four triangular strips per layer, and thus requires *two* square blocks to begin with — a simple, obvious point, but one which is all too easily forgotten, often resulting in considerable annoyance and re-setting.

It might be thought that the sole purpose of the jig is to saw squares into triangles, and that work of this nature requires square-section stock to begin with, thus leading to a limitation of size imposed by

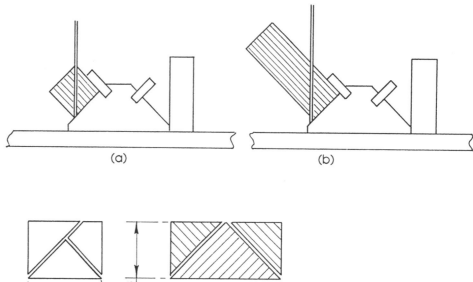

Figure 78

both width and thickness of available stock. This is by no means the case; the only limitation on size is imposed by the thickness of available stock, since it is always possible to saw the material as shown in Fig.78(b) and Fig.79. There are two points to be considered here: firstly, if the basic stock is sawn to a known required width to begin with, the effective thickness can be left to take care of itself, and may end up rather less than its original value (c). It is, however, also possible to be slightly more cunning, and to maximise timber utilisation by cutting a main triangular section which uses the full thickness of the timber and also to save the two triangular offcuts for use in a further piece. The only snag with this arrangement is that the offcuts cannot be used in the same assembly as the main section (given that two contrasting timbers are used) since they occur 'in the wrong place'. Fig.78(d) demonstrates the problem far more effectively than words. They can, however, be used in a second piece of similar dimensions which is assembled in reverse order to the first, or with an assembly which utilises the same timber type throughout, but with contrasting veneer slips between joints. Another, minor problem is that an arrangement of this nature does tend to put the cart before the horse somewhat, in that it is then required to cut some of the inner sections to match the previously-cut outer sections, whereas in general, it is rather easier to work from the centre outwards; nevertheless the possibility exists and the usefulness of the jig in this respect should not be overlooked. Fig.80 demonstrates what might be termed the 'acid test' of jig accuracy. In this case the 90° angle which has been formed indirectly from two successive sawing operations is being checked against a light-source.

Work of this nature inevitably involves calculations based upon the square-root of two (mathematically indicated as $\sqrt{2}$). Although the round-

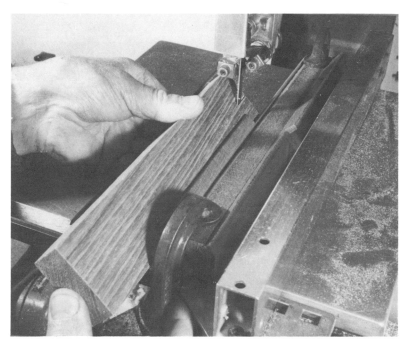

Figure 79

Figure 80

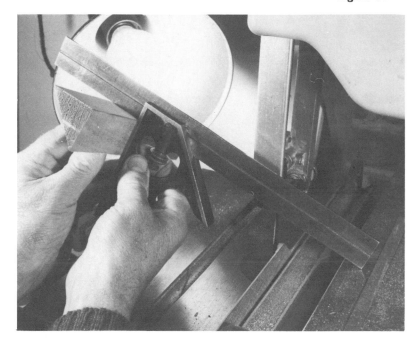

figure factor of 1.4 is useful and reasonably accurate, Nomogram 12 makes life rather easier. This Nomogram comprises only a single pair of adjacent scales sharing the same vertical axis, and does not require a ruler or pencil. All that is necessary is to locate the known value of one variable (say 'c') on the left-hand scale and read the corresponding value of 'b' on the right-hand scale. The Nomogram does of course work in reverse and will give the value of 'c' if 'b' happens to be the known value.

One final word with regard to the use of the jig may be in order. The standard fence is used to align the jig to begin with. Certainly, it does require a little 'fiddling' to get the sawband into precisely the correct position relative to the workpiece, (but most machine-setting processes, particularly those involving home-made jigs, have some element of this nature). Once the position of the fence is established, it is cramped to the machine table at front and rear. One should only be satisfied with the final position of the fence after a trial cut has been made in a scrap piece of exactly the same cross section as that to be finally used. It is not altogether wise to rely entirely on the stationary position of the saw, since even the best of sawbands will tend to wobble slightly and may give a kerf which is thereby slightly offset one way or the other, dependent upon the position of the sawband at the time of measurement. If further adjustment is required after a trial cut, the end of the workpiece should be cleaned off flush before a second cut is made, since the sawband will always have a tendency to feed itself into any previously-formed kerf. In view of the fact that the saw is required to make only straight cuts, a fine-toothed band with a slow feed will produce a finish which requires little or no extra work to furnish a good gluing surface. If the basic stock material is not unduly long, the same set-up can be used in conjunction with a power fretsaw. This machine is, however, necessarily limited not only by depth of cut, but also by throat depth, since it is not possible to 'out-feed' the work beyond the pivot point. In view of the fact that power fretsaws tend to vibrate somewhat, there may also be some difficulty in keeping the workpiece in its correct position in the jig; the power fretsaw is therefore very much a 'second-best' choice as far as this particular jig is concerned.

6. SANDING TECHNIQUES

In general, surfaces intended to be glued together should be brought to a smooth finish, and to their final linear and angular dimensions, by disc sanding (or equivalent in terms of accuracy). In the somewhat special case posed by the concave faces of curved segments this is clearly not possible, and in the absence of appropriate drum-sanding facilities, as good a sawn finish as possible should be aimed for. Segmented work depends very heavily upon the quality of its joints, and sub-standard work will be all too obvious. Any machine sander used will, for some classes of work at least, require table-tilt facilities. If an accurate sliding mitre-fence is also available, well and good, but this is not essential. It is also relatively unimportant if table-setting protractor facilities are not available, since card templates, as described in Chapter 2, are inherently capable of a very high order of accuracy in terms of machine-setting. A plain tilting table may not be enough by itself, however. If one considers a fairly narrow coopered segment, be it straight or tapered, it is quite clear from Fig.81 that the normal method of resting the work on the machine table is potentially inaccurate, partly due to inadequacy of the supporting surface, but also due to the fact that an angular machining process which should be made with reference to the outer face of the work is actually being made with reference to the inner face. This problem will also be encountered in a number of projects, and will generally take the form shown, where a segment requires an accurate mitre angle to be machined on two or more faces; it is therefore worth dealing with as a general principle.

It is a fairly simple matter to attach a home-made sub-table, of the form shown in Fig.82, to the main machine table. This allows the outer face of the workpiece to be pressed against the underside of the sub-table, thereby machining with reference to this face. It is, of course, helpful if the sub-table is arranged to be exactly parallel to the main table, but this is not essential, provided that angular template checks may be made with reference to the sub-table. It is, however, vital that the assembly is solid and does not flex or move in any way under load. It will be found helpful if the sub-table is made in clear acrylic sheet, not less than ¼" thick;

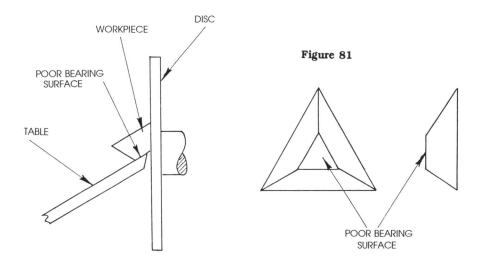

Figure 81

this enables the workpiece to be seen whilst it is being manipulated, and can indeed minimise inadvertent sanding of the fingers, (which is more likely to occur if working by feel alone). It also allows the edge of the sub-table to be placed close to the sanding disc, and still provide a fair indication of the approach of any machining limit-lines marked on the workpiece. Fig.83 shows a typical static set-up, and Fig.84 demonstrates its use. A major snag with a sub-table of this kind is that its position relative to the sanding disc will alter with table-angle; for a given setting, an increase in table-angle will give an increased gap between the sub-table and the disc (Fig.85); a reduction in angle will cause fouling. Therefore, any attempt to make a 'high-class' adjustable job of the sub-table may be self-defeating unless one is prepared to cut substantial slots in the work table. In any event, a sub-table suited to fairly long 'stave' work may give rise to handling difficulties when machining small multi-sided segments, leading to a requirement for more than one sub-table. Thus, there is a strong case for

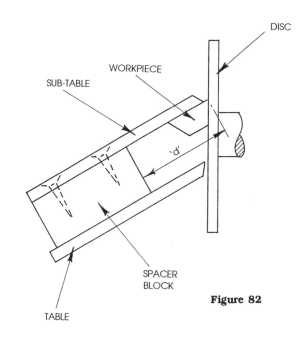

Figure 82

Figure 83

Figure 84

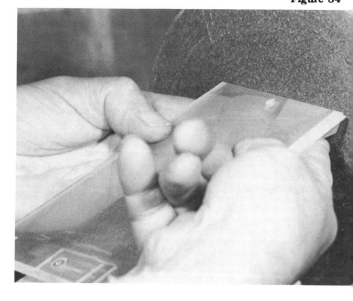

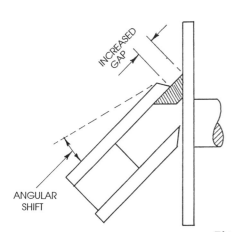

Figure 85

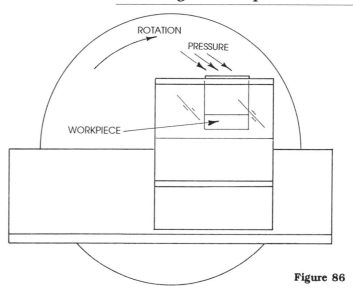

Figure 86

the use of G-cramps to hold the sub-table, since these allow plenty of adjustment whilst retaining firmness of grip. The distance between sander and supporting block (marked as 'd' in Fig.82) should be as short as possible, consistent with freedom of movement of the workpiece, in order to minimise any flexing tendency. If it is made unduly short, difficulty will be experienced in inserting or withdrawing the work sideways, and the disc may actually knock the work free. Incidentally, if this does happen, one should not attempt to fish out the workpiece with the machine running, since this procedure is a fairly prolific source of finger-sanding. It will generally be found that because the sub-table is raised above the main table, and therefore fairly high up on the disc, the disc pressure on the workpiece will have a distinct sideways tendency. The fact that the workpiece is beneath the sub-table will tend to push the work away from its support if working on the 'normal' side of the disc (Fig.86). Working on the other side of the disc will cause the work to be pressed against the support, but may also obscure the working area with sawdust unless substantial dust extraction equipment is in use.

There is a strong case for lines indicating sanding limits to be marked with a thin craft knife in addition to a pencilled line. The drawn line will permit the limit to be approached fairly boldly; the cut line (which will not be visible normally) will reveal its presence only at the last moment, as a minute sliver of timber breaks away from the workpiece. Usually, just prior to this point, a small gap will open up at the cut line, making it easy to see. Knife marking should, however, be undertaken with due consideration of the angle being sanded. If a plain right-angled cut is made, angular sanding will cause early breakaway of the waste, leaving a face which is rather less accurately 'machined-to-dimension' than it appears, to a degree dependent upon the depth of knife-cut (Fig.87(a)). If the knife-cut is made at an angle comparable

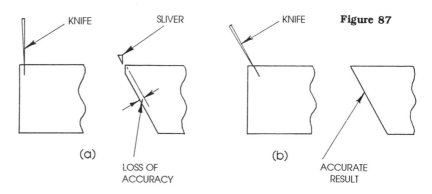

Figure 87

with the sanding angle, this error will become negligible (b). When sanding in this way, it is a distinct advantage to move the work from side to side against the disc. This helps in the application of selective pressure at one end of the work or the other, to ensure that, on completion, the final 'breakaway' occurs simultaneously along the entire length of the piece. It also tends to reduce clogging of the abrasive, which can cause burning of the workpiece, a constant problem if the work is simply pushed against the disc and held there in a more or less stationary condition. Burning is far more than a nuisance incidentally; it is mainly caused by wood particles embedded in the abrasive, which can quite easily score the workpiece and produce a poor finish.

Sanding narrow staves can often pose a problem, since they are frequently difficult to hold. Moreover, the use of the sub-table may be of limited use, since the bearing surface may not be adequate to ensure angular accuracy. If the staves are fairly short (as they are likely to be if they are also very narrow), the following method may be used. In view of the fact that machining is carried out directly

with reference to the centre angle rather than the mitre angle, the set-up is potentially highly accurate. The essential ingredient is a scrap block of wood, sawn and sanded to provide a bevel to suit the required angle. The centre angle is 30° in the case shown; thus the block is mitred at 60° (Fig.88). This particular operation should be carried out with special care, since it forms the basis for the accuracy of the staves. The block is cramped to the sander table, the latter being set at exactly 90° to the disc. It is important that the block is set on the 'upward-moving' side of the disc and that its base is almost touching the disc along its entire length. To try out the arrangement, a scrap stave is sanded on one of its flanks. This can be done freehand without the guide block, since the angle made by the flank with the face (nominally the mitre angle 'B') is not required to be particularly accurate for this exercise; all that is required is that the flank is dead flat, and thereby provides a straight edge at its junction with the outer face (Fig.89). A combination-square is now set to provide the required edge-length 'l', and used to pencil a straight line, parallel with the sanded edge. Ultimately this line will be used to determine the edge-length precisely, by sanding down to it, but for the moment the stave doesn't require to be dimensionally accurate; all that is required is that the line be parallel to the sanded edge. The stave is now placed in the vee-groove made by the bevel and the sanding disc, and sanded down to the line (or sufficiently close to be

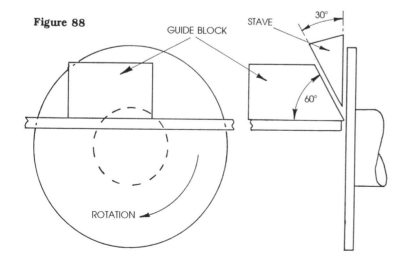

Figure 88

GUIDE BLOCK

STAVE

30°

60°

ROTATION

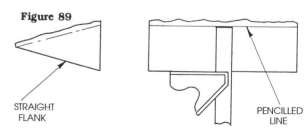

Figure 89

STRAIGHT FLANK

PENCILLED LINE

sure that the second sanded edge is dead parallel to the line). The block should also be sufficiently long to allow movement from side to side, thereby reducing clogging of the abrasive and burning of the stave. With the set-up as described, there will be an 'upwards' component of movement transferred to the stave, which will tend to push the stave away from the 'vee'; this is exactly what is required, since it may be resisted by downwards pressure with the fingers, applied selectively to one end or the other of the segment until parallelism is achieved (Fig.90). In passing, it may be noted that if the block were placed at the downward-moving side of the disc, the tendency would be for the abrasive force to jam the stave into the 'vee' and there would be little or no control available.

The price to be paid for the arrangement is the fact that the sawdust will tend to fly upwards also, and may therefore be out of range of any dust extraction equipment in use. In any event, a respirator or some means of avoiding inhalation of the dust is desirable. There will be a tendency for sawdust to collect on the top face of the segment, thus rendering observation of the sanding line somewhat difficult; it can also be quite puzzling to try to blow the dust away when wearing a respirator. The only real solution is to tap the stave on the sander table from time to time. Accuracy of the centre angle is determined by trying it against a sliding-bevel which has been preset with the aid of a card template. (Fig.91). Given that the bevelled guide block has been prepared accurately, this should be little more than a formality. Should an angular error be apparent however, the set-up may be corrected by slight adjustment of the table itself, or by the insertion of 'shims' under one end or other of the guide block.

One may now prepare the staves proper, the only difference being that, in addition to the pencilled

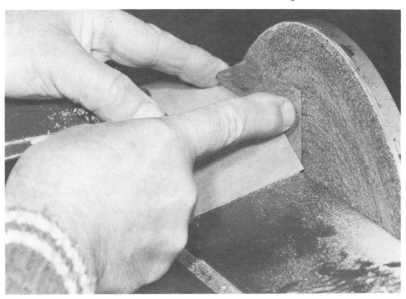

Figure 90

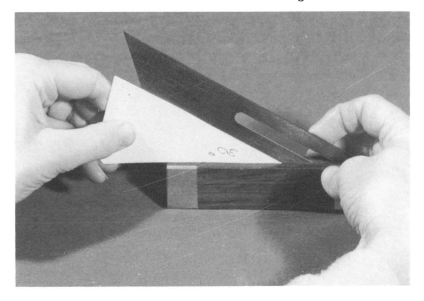

Figure 91

mark, the sanding line should also be knife-cut, which will allow the final line to be determined by break-away of the last sliver of waste from the segment. One advantage of the set-up is that the sliver will tend to be thrown upwards and away from the work and is thereby less likely to jam itself into the abrasive and cause a particularly severe type of clogging. If the staves are too long to be contained within the upward-moving half of the disc, matters become a little more difficult since, although the method works well as shown, any downward movement of the disc will cause the jamming effect previously mentioned. In this case, perhaps the best that can be done is to set the worktable as high up the disc as convenient, such that the downward component of movement is reduced. Even so, some form of holding device may be required; a piece of scrap timber and a dab of hot-melt glue may well do the trick, but it is difficult to offer a really satisfactory solution to this particular problem. The snatching effect of the abrasive, once it occurs, can be quite severe.

Sanding of convex or straight surfaces may be carried out quite easily freehand with a disc sander.

Figure 92

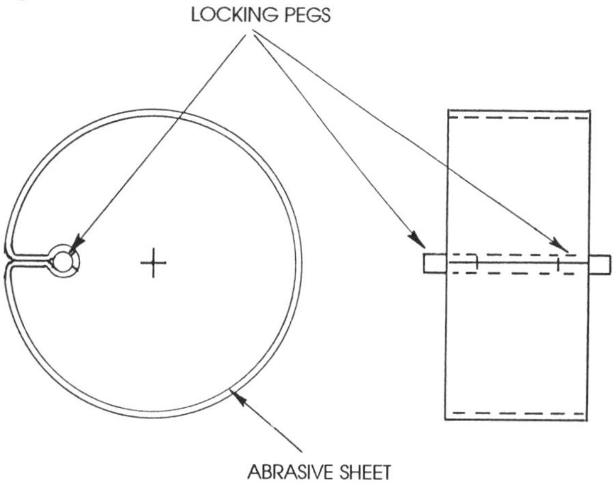

LOCKING PEGS

ABRASIVE SHEET

Indeed this method is perhaps the best, all things considered, for the matching of the convex faces of curved segments to their mating concave faces. Concave surfaces cannot be dealt with in this way and require a drum-sander of some kind if they are required to be dealt with accurately. The use of the lathe as a power source for certain types of drum-sanding should not be overlooked. By its nature, the simplest form of drum-sanding produces a profile in the workpiece which is determined by the diameter of the sanding-drum itself. As a consequence, it can be necessary to produce drums of various diameters. Obviously it is easy enough to turn a drum from scrap timber, and to hold it in the lathe either between centres or by means of a combination chuck, but attachment of the abrasive to the drum can present one or two problems. A very common way of holding a strip of abrasive on such a drum is that shown in Fig.92. The method has perhaps three disadvantages: first, since there is no adhesive contact between abrasive and drum there is some tendency (particularly with narrow drums) for the abrasive strip to slide off the drum. Secondly, the presence of the slot and the hole does rather waste the timber, since it would be difficult to find a further use for it once it has performed its primary function. Finally, the very fact that the periphery has been broken by the slot will, in a material which is inclined by nature to 'move' a little, increase any tendency for the drum to lose its true circular shape. For the foregoing reasons, it is suggested that a better way of attaching abrasive to a wood former is to use 'glue-film'. A strip of abrasive of the required width and rather more than the required length is cut with a knife and steel straightedge, together with a strip of glue-film of the same dimensions. The glue-film is first ironed on to the back of the abrasive, the backing removed, and the strip rolled around the former such that both ends overlap, the strip lying flush with the faces of the drum all round. The assembly is then placed upon the surface of an upturned domestic iron at the 'man-made fibre' heat setting, with the overlap at the top, and allowed to rest momentarily until the glue melts. The assembly is now rolled gently and slowly to gradually allow the glue-film to melt and re-set (Fig.93). It is important to proceed slowly, and to make sure that the abrasive strip is not kinked in any way (it is equally important to be quite sure that the drum has been turned accurately, ie. with its sides straight and parallel, otherwise the strip will not seat on it properly). Final closure of the strip is made by holding the drum in a vice and making a knife-cut through both free ends simultaneously, then discarding the waste and ironing down.   It is positively *not* necessary to apply significant pressure to the abrasive strip whilst it is being glued to the drum; this serves no useful purpose and only tends to damage the abrasive surface. It is merely necessary to allow sufficient heat to reach the glue-film to melt it. The abrasive strip may be removed for replacement or change of grade, by re-heating and pulling it away from the drum, starting at the join in this case. Note that drum-sanders of this type are not particularly suited to curved segment assemblies where concave flanks need to be

matched to their convex counterparts, unless some means is also provided for keeping the sanded flank precisely at right angles to one face of the segment. Nevertheless, the system outlined will be found most useful for general hand-operated processes as it stands, given that the required drum diameter is within the capacity of the lathe. A larger radius of curvature will require special measures. As an example, consider the plain bowl shown in Fig.94. It is required to sand a curve in the rim of the bowl to present the appearance shown, but the radius of curvature demands a drum of unacceptably large diameter.

In this case, it is necessary to provide a jig to mount the workpiece, of the form shown in Fig.95. The side cheeks of the jig are cut to the required radius of curvature by means of a bandsaw or power fretsaw, and hand finished to the required degree of accuracy. They are made as a pair from two pieces of plywood of about ¼" thickness pinned together. At the same time, a pair of holes are drilled to provide a fairly precise fit for a couple of lengths of dowel of about ½" diameter or so, for registration purposes. The two cheeks are separated and re-assembled the required distance apart, with the aid of the dowels and a number of squared-off matching lengths of timber, held in place with generous fillets of hot-melt glue. The workpiece is

Figure 93

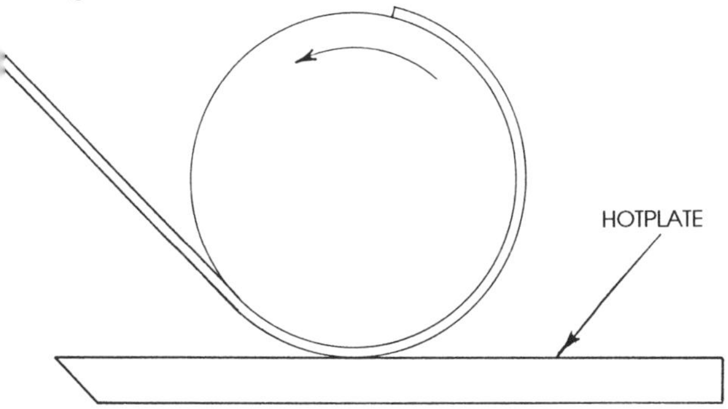

HOTPLATE

Figure 94

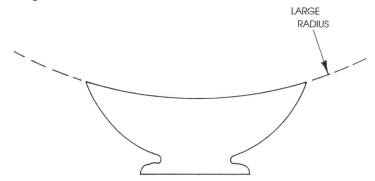

LARGE
RADIUS

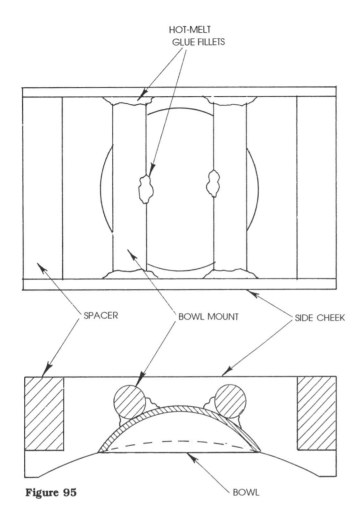

HOT-MELT
GLUE FILLETS

SPACER　　　　BOWL MOUNT　　　SIDE CHEEK

Figure 95

BOWL

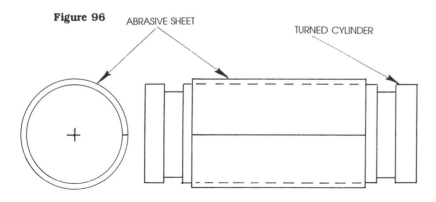

Figure 96

ABRASIVE SHEET

TURNED CYLINDER

located within the jig as required. It should be placed such that the sanding limit imposed by the side cheeks is slightly proud of that required on the workpiece; ie. they should leave a little to be removed. The workpiece is held in position, again with fillets of hot-melt glue, against the dowels and/or spacing bars; it is important that mounting is positive and rigid.

The drum-sander should take the form shown in Fig.96. The length of abrasive surface may be created from more than one strip of abrasive, if necessary. It is important that the length is sufficient to allow the workpiece to be moved from side to side a little, whilst remaining on the abrasive surface — a precaution necessary to reduce the risk of clogging and burning. The set-up may be used initially as it stands; the assembly is simply held against the revolving drum, and moved from side to side a little, until the bare wood of the drum just touches the profile of the jig cheeks along their entire length, indicating that the permitted limit has been reached. The precise final sanding limit may now be approached by turning a couple of matching recesses in the drum to accommodate the jig cheeks, and also to permit the necessary sideways movement. The recesses in the drum may be turned down as a pair, a little at a time, applying the workpiece for further sanding, until the required profile is achieved. It would be an extremely tedious business to change abrasive grades on a drum of this kind. It is suggested therefore, that a fairly coarse grade is chosen and final finishing carried out by hand. Sanding pressure must always be fairly light where glue-film is used to hold the abrasive; any heating of the abrasive will tend to re-melt the glue and cause puckering due to slight movement. Figs.97 and 98 show a practical application of the system.

A jig of the form shown in Fig.99 will prove to be

invaluable when used in conjunction with any lathe-mounted sanding device, be it drum or disc. The home-made device shown is a successor to an initial wood 'lash-up', which had decidedly limited capabilities, but which proved so useful that a more permanent device appeared to be called for. The essential requirements are shown in the drawing. The jig should be suitable for mounting in the lathe toolpost, in place of the toolrest. This allows its base to be positioned anywhere that the toolpost can reach. The pivoted arm, which normally carries the workpiece, should be capable of location at any point on the vertical rod, and constrained to remain at this point whilst being free to pivot horizontally. It is most important that the vertical

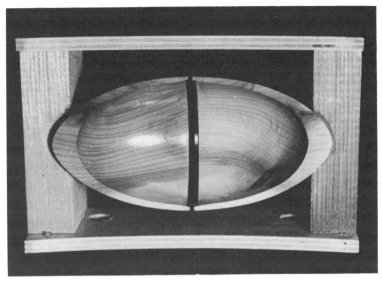

Figure 97

Figure 98

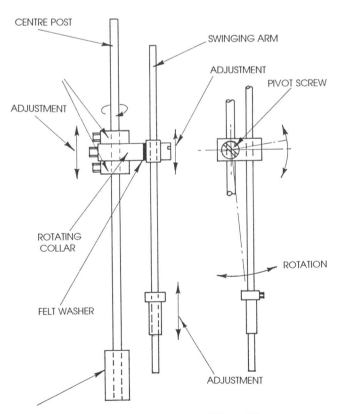

CENTRE POST

SWINGING ARM

ADJUSTMENT

PIVOT SCREW

ADJUSTMENT

ADJUSTMENT

ROTATION

ROTATING COLLAR

FELT WASHER

ADJUSTMENT

Figure 99

movement is restricted in both directions, since there is otherwise a tendency for the movable collar to ride up the main post during sanding, giving rise to inaccuracies in the workpiece. A second pivot allows the arm to swing up and down as desired. Finally, the length of the arm should be adjustable and capable of being locked at any desired length. Regardless of the materials generally used to construct the device, the arm intended to carry the workpiece should be $^3/_{16}$" diameter steel rod. The reason for this particular requirement is that it is quite easy to make suitable wood attachments as desired for the end of the arm, and fit them simply by drilling a $^3/_{16}$" diameter hole of about an inch or so in length in them. Moreover, it is a simple matter to fit a sliding collar which may be locked in position in order that a number of identical workpieces may be fed on to the arm such that all are machined exactly alike. It is appreciated that metalworking practice may not be entirely appropriate in a book intended to deal with essentially woodturning topics, but the addition of a little light metalworking capability to the repertoire can pay-off handsomely, particularly where jigs and fixtures are concerned.

It is by no means necessary to own a metalworking lathe, but a pillar drill (or stand-mounted hand power drill) capable of taking twist-drills up to about ¼" diameter (plus a small collection of such drills) will be a big help. One set of taps of about 2BA or ¼" BSF (metric equivalents roughly M4 or M6) will also be useful. For the rest, a hacksaw, a few files, a scriber and a centre punch will normally suffice. It is fortunate that light metal stock comes in standard stock dimensions, invariably to a high order of accuracy. Thus a ¼" diameter hole made with a standard twist drill will freely accept a piece of ¼" diameter stock rod, but without undue sloppiness (mainly due to the fact that twist-drills will tend to cut just a trifle oversize on their nominal diameter). Given, therefore, a pillar drill and a small vice, one may quite easily prepare a metal part in light alloy by sawing, filing and subsequent drilling. Tapping demands the small extra outlay of a set of taps plus some means of holding them. Generally speaking, one requires little more than this to make quite respectable fixtures.

Tapping into light alloy is not normally to be recommended but, for work of this nature, one can 'get by'. The tapping drill sizes given on the drawings should be adhered to however, in order to obtain a reasonable result without too much bother. When tapping, binding of the tap in the workpiece may be eliminated by rubbing the tap briefly over a stub of an ordinary paraffin-wax candle. Taps are normally available (for any one size) in sets of three, denoted 'taper', 'second-cut', and 'plug', for obvious reasons (Fig.100). It is by no means essential to buy all three for light work, particularly in light alloy. A second-cut and a plug will normally be sufficient, the latter being made necessary by the requirement to cut a full thread right to the bottom of its pilot hole (d). The jig described (or its equivalent) will be needed for a number of projects. It is also worth investing in at least one centre-drill (e), with perhaps the BS.2 and BS.3 ($^3/_{16}$" and ¼" body-diameters respectively) as the most generally useful, not only for starting off holes in metal, but also in wood. Figs.101–103 show the jig in use; it will also feature in the 'candlestick' project series.

Figure 100

 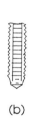 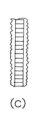 

(a)   (b)   (c)   (d)   (e)

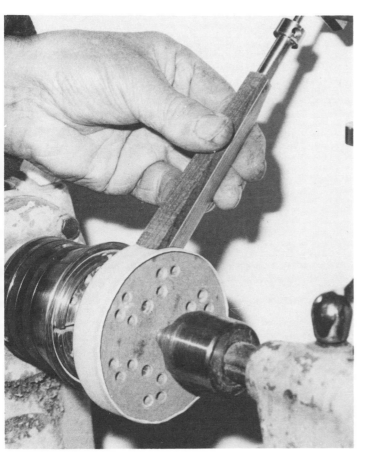

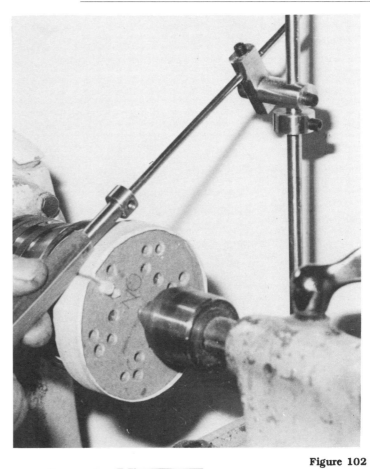

Figure 101

Figure 102

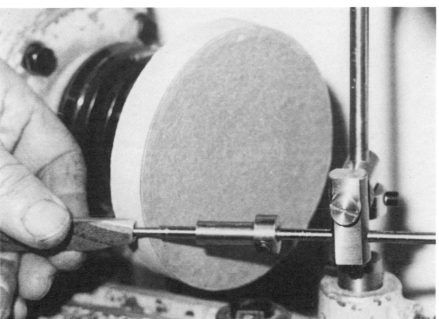

Figure 103

7.   ASSEMBLY TECHNIQUES (Flat)

The notion of 'flat' assembly work is defined here for convenience as that where the height of the assembly is small compared with its planform. The distinction is made between this type of assembly and the more 'three-dimensional' construction of coopered, laminated and multi-layer segmented work, together with solid, faceted assemblies as will be encountered in one or two of the projects. Non-flat assemblies of this kind generally require rather different assembly methods, and will therefore be dealt with in a later chapter.

The assembly of a closed ring of straight-sided radial segments will often be undertaken with some form of band-cramp. The device can come in a number of forms, perhaps the simplest being the hose grip or 'jubilee clip' style. The main compo-

Figure 104

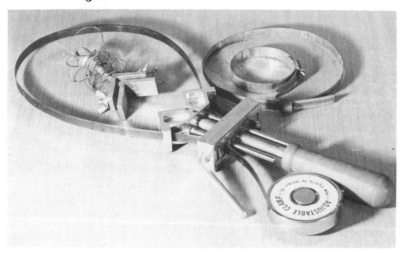

nent of this device is a length of steel strip with shallow crosswise grooves in its outer face; these engage with a grub-screw which is itself trapped in a fixed housing at one end of the strip. When the loop is closed, the screw permits adjustment of the effective length of the strip. Another device employs a loop of high-tensile steel wire, with its ends attached to a screw-operated cramp, which is used to tighten the wire around the assembly; a similar device employs a steel strip in place of the wire (Fig. 104). Both the last-named devices are primarily intended for the assembly of rectangular frames, and are normally provided with corner pieces for this purpose.

A more specialised turnery implement (not illustrated) employs a wide, heavy-gauge steel band of substantial strength, again fitted with a tightening device at its ends. All devices operate on the 'tourniquet' principle of reducing the enclosed area of the loop and thereby exerting pressure on the segmented assembly contained within it.

The cramping mechanism is worth a slightly closer look. Fig. 105 shows a portion of a 12-segment assembly, with a cramping wire in place. It is inappropriate to go into great detail here with regard to the 'mechanics' of the action, but it is perhaps sufficient to state that the tensile force which must be applied to the wire can be considerably greater than the compressive force which actually operates on the segments at the joints. Moreover, the actual pressure is along the line of the joint, and it is only the presence of the remaining segments, applying indirect pressure via the wire, which allows the joint to be closed at all. In practical terms, the pressure is also intensely localised at the corners of the segments, which is extremely bad news for the wire itself, since it will tend to become kinked at these points, and thereby subject to a great deal of wear and tear. The latter effect may be largely eliminated by sawing the outer edges of the segments into an approximately circular form (b). The method has however, some potential for inaccuracy, since the notion of 'segment-length' is thereby rendered meaningless; this can lead to apparent angular errors, as will be seen. If used at all, the technique should only be applied after the segments have been 'dry-fitted', numbered, and some form of alignment mark made on each mating pair of joints (and strictly observed on final assembly). The essential 'indirectness' of the method remains, and it works only by virtue of the fact that the pressure exerted by the cramp is more or less uniform all round. This may be readily demonstrated by a simple experiment: a ring is dry-assembled and cramped as tightly as possible, and the joints inspected for accuracy. A sash cramp or similar device is now applied across the diameter of the work at any convenient point, and tightened a little. It will be found that some joints will open-up at the centre, even with quite light pressure on the sash cramp. Under some circumstances, opposing joints will also open-up a little at the outside, but this is by no means guaranteed, because the tendency to open is positively resisted by the band-cramp, and the wood may compress slightly instead.

Cramps of this type can also present a problem at the point where the tensioning is applied, since the band or wire is not necessarily in direct contact with the workpiece in this area, and the segment position may therefore be somewhat indeterminate

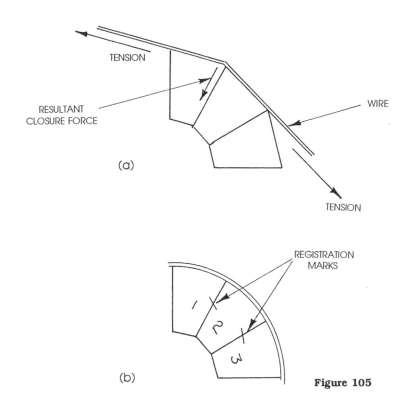

Figure 105

(Fig. 106). In these circumstances, it can be useful to employ a strip of mild steel, about $1/2$" wide by $1/8$" thick, bent around a circular former, to form a gapped ring; this is fitted over the assembled ring of segments, and the band-cramp tightened around it, thereby providing some degree of pressure equalisation. Fig. 107 shows the general idea, and Fig. 108 shows the system in use.

The method is effective, but can give rise to some degree of user-irritation associated with the difficulty of ensuring that the cramping band or wire remains on the hoop whilst the device is tightened. There is also some loss of cramping efficiency due to friction, but by and large, the arrangement has its uses. If a fair amount of segmented work is undertaken, there is some advantage to be had from a collection of such rings of various sizes.

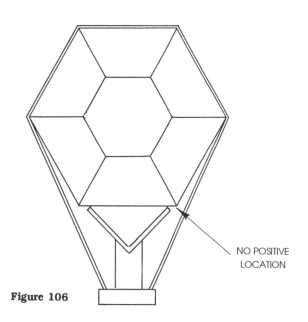

Figure 106

NO POSITIVE
LOCATION

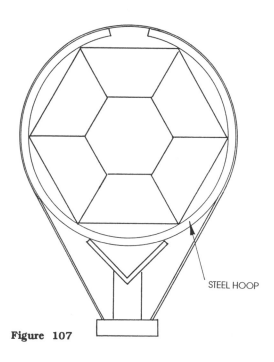

Figure 107

STEEL HOOP

Figure 108

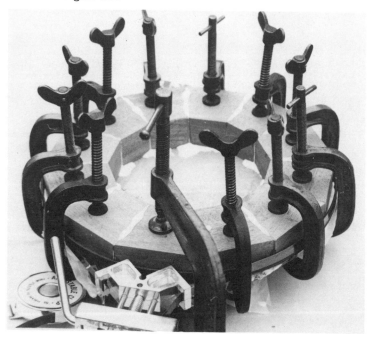

Fig. 109 shows a ring being made; the operation is quite simple and may be carried out by hand. It is not possible, however, to ensure that the extreme ends of the strip assume the required circular form so it is normally necessary to bend the strip into rather more than a complete circle and cut the ends off afterwards. It will be necessary to experiment somewhat; the natural elasticity of the steel strip will cause it to open out considerably after release from the bending forces (Fig. 110).

One or two other potential problems exist: if the segmented ring itself is fairly thick, it can be very difficult indeed to determine joint accuracy by the normal method of viewing the assembly against a strong light-source. Perfect closure also depends very heavily upon the accuracy of the segment length 'l' as well as that of the mitre (or centre) angle. This may be readily demonstrated by Fig. 111. A set of twelve segments is shown in (a), all with perfectly accurate mitre-angles, but with one segment slightly longer than the remainder. If the

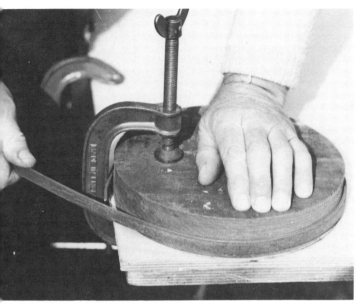

Figure 109

Figure 110

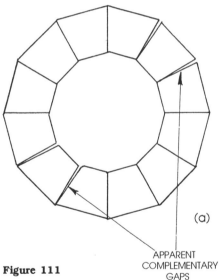

(a)

Figure 111

APPARENT
COMPLEMENTARY
GAPS

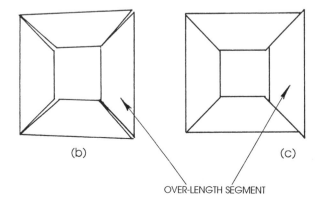

(b)   (c)

OVER-LENGTH SEGMENT

assembly is made with all outer corners in perfect aligment (as would normally be dictated by a band-cramp), then the net effect is to upset the angular accuracy of the assembly. Matters are unlikely to be as bad as shown, but can be sufficient to turn a hairline joint into a visible one. The mechanism may be understood more readily from (b), which shows a four-segment assembly. In this case the over-length segment is quite obviously forcing the assembly apart, thereby creating bad joints. Adjustment of segment position to accommodate the extra length (c) allows perfect closure on all four joints. Unfortunately this is the very condition that a tourniquet cramp will do its best to eliminate, particularly where the number of segments is large. Indeed the condition can be extremely puzzling on multi-segment assemblies, particularly if dimensional errors are present in more than one segment. A further difficulty is imposed if the segment length 'l' is large relative to its width 'w', since this can give rise to inadvertent mis-alignment of the segments both linearly and angularly (even though the segments are themselves perfectly accurate in all respects). This, however, is essentially a matter of manipulation, and demands extra care.

It was mentioned earlier that the well-being of the band-cramp (and to some extent its effectiveness) can be improved by sawing the periphery of the segments into an approximately circular form. This can rarely be done with complete accuracy, bearing in mind that the segments are loose individual pieces, and are difficult to arrange such that a perfect circle may be scribed on them in the correct position. There is consequently some risk of the cramp causing segments to slide relative to one another, particularly when gluing. The fact that the relative positions may have been previously indicated by registration marks is of some help, but getting the segments to stay thus aligned may be a different matter.

The foregoing observations are by no means intended to imply that the tourniquet cramp has no place in segment assembly work; far from it. In some cases, particularly in coopered assemblies, it is the only really convenient method. Indeed, for tapered coopered work, or certain 'three-dimensional' assemblies, it is often necessary to employ a far more crude form of band-cramping, using adhesive tape, (which becomes very highly stressed at the joint lines) simply because the angular relationship between segments will not permit any other type of cramp to bear upon the problem; this is a technique which will be discussed in more detail later. The foregoing points are made only because it is as well that the user is aware of them. It *is* reasonable to suggest however, that the band-cramp is not particularly suited to non-radial assemblies, whether the segment joint lines are straight or curved, because such assemblies, by definition, have serrated outer profiles and, as will

be seen in one or two projects, it is sometimes desirable to retain these. Figs.112 and 113 demonstrate the problem and, incidentally, show that a radial assembly can be made non-radial quite easily, by applying a linear offset between segments.

Fig.114 demonstrates that perfect closure is still possible even if the offset between segments is not constant. Even if the serrations are to be subsequently removed, the initial assembly problem remains, that of the tendency for the mating faces to slide under cramping pressure, thereby destroying the desired relationship between segments.

Sawing the outer faces of the segments into a circular form is likely to fail for two reasons: it is not at all easy to predict the precise 'available diameter' of a closed non-radial assembly, and very difficult indeed to actually achieve it by preliminary sawing; some unwanted movement of the assembly under pressure is therefore likely. For similar reasons, it is difficult to predict the size of any central plug inserted to limit unwanted movement and, with the best will in the world, minor dimensional discrepancies between individual segments will tend to reduce the effectiveness of such predictions anyway. For this reason, it is as well to consider other forms of assembly on occasion, based upon the assembly of selected groups of segments into sub-assemblies, and to finally assemble these groups into a complete ring. The technique works well for both straight-sided and curved segments, and may also be used for plain radial asssembly work, although it is at its most effective when used on non-radial assemblies. Two such methods are described and illustrated, one involving pressure pads in an enclosed environment determined by light alloy angle 'stops', the other a more free-form arrangement employing a fixed sash cramp in association with other odds and ends. The two

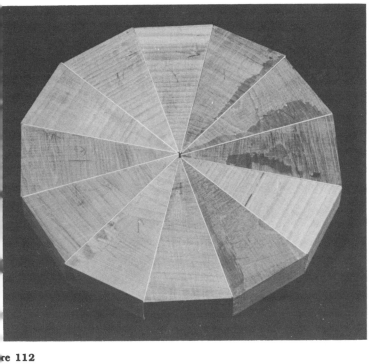

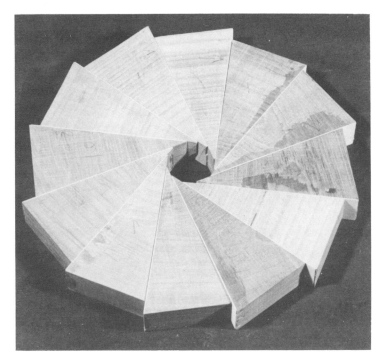

Figure 113

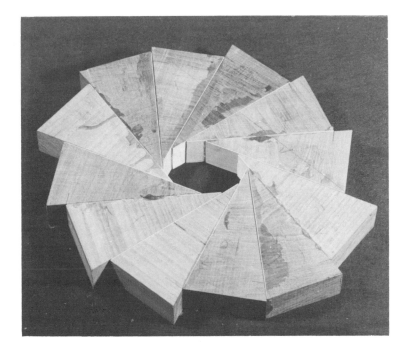

Figure 114

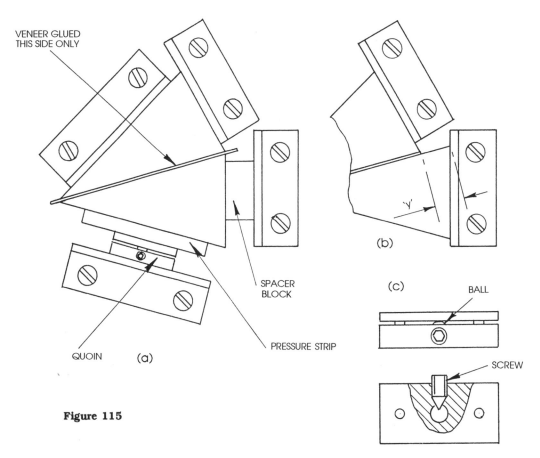

Figure 115

methods may be regarded as interchangeable to some degree, but it will be found that the first-named system is perhaps more suitable for straight-sided segments, and is therefore described in this connection.

The method employs a baseboard of suitable size, which may be an offcut of MDF or plywood of about ³/₄" thickness, in conjunction with a number of short lengths of light alloy angle, 1" x 1" x ¹/₈". The simplest arrangement is designed to accommodate two segments as shown in Figs 115 and 119, and may be used to glue two segments together, or to glue a veneer slip on one of them, using the other as a convenient pressure pad. The angle-pieces (and

spacer block where necessary) are arranged to stop the segments from sliding laterally against one another as cramping pressure is applied. Polythene sheet is used on the baseboard and around the spare segment, to ensure that the glue adheres only where required. The use of polythene sheet for this purpose is quite essential for segment gluing and, although it will be mentioned further in specific cases, its general use for this purpose will be assumed from now on. With regard to Fig.115, it might be argued that a simpler means of arranging segments for veneer-gluing purposes is the more 'rectangular' arrangement illustrated in Fig.116, since this would undoubtedly improve the efficiency of the cramps. There is indeed nothing against the method, other than the fact that the arrangement as drawn is rather more versatile, in that it will cope with offset segment assemblies as well.

Assembly pressure is effected with the aid of expansion blocks, as used by printers to set lines of type-face, together with such packing strips as necessary. The blocks themselves are marketed as 'quoins', their construction being shown in Fig.115(c). They are quite invaluable in light assembly work of this nature, but do however, have a limited range of adjustment, and should be inserted into the assembly in the fully closed position, with sufficient packing added to give a fairly tight initial fit. The same effect may be achieved by a couple of nuts and bolts operating through the light alloy angle against a (preferably) metal pressure pad, which should itself be of sufficient thickness to apply the pressure evenly, to obviate the risk of bruising the woodware. The veneer slip should be pressed firmly down against the baseboard with the fingers, as pressure is applied to the joint; if this is not done, the veneer may ride up the segment face slightly, leaving a gap at the bottom. There may also be a tendency for the veneer to move laterally with respect to the segment face; this too should be carefully watched and dealt with as necessary When the glue has set, the work is removed from the jig, and excess veneer and adhesive trimmed away.

When all veneering activities are completed, the jig may now be used as it stands to assemble the segments into sub-assembly pairs. It may also be modified to deal with offset non-radial pairs, by removing (or altering) the spacer block (Fig.115(b)). The required value of offset 'y' is marked on the top face of every segment, against the *non-veneered* edge. The choice of this edge is

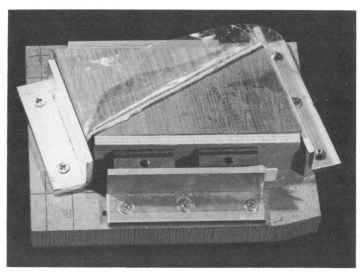

Figure 116

very important: in the event of minor angular modification being necessary when the complete ring, comprising perhaps three sub-assemblies of four segments, is finally closed, it will make a non-veneered edge available for a little light machine sanding, an operation which would clearly be fairly difficult on the other free edge (Fig.117). In passing, it may be noted that the controlled pressure available from the use of assembly jigs ensures that good hairline joints are consistently obtained; indeed, the method has a nasty habit of

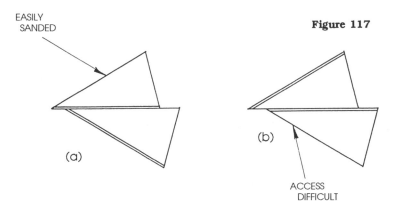

Figure 117

EASILY
SANDED

(a)

(b)

ACCESS
DIFFICULT

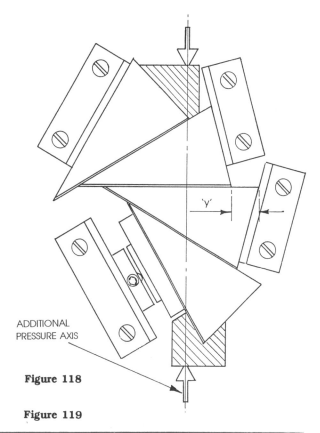

ADDITIONAL
PRESSURE AXIS

Figure 118

Figure 119

revealing minor errors in segments which were initially considered to be accurate in terms of dimensions and angles.

When all six sub-assemblies have been glued, a further modification to the cramping jig is made as shown in Fig.118. This too provides an arrangement whereby the offset 'y' between sub-assemblies is maintained accurately without adjustment. Pressure from the quoins is not sufficient by itself in this case, since the direction of pressure is far from being in the ideal direction, ie. at right-angles to the joint line. This does not necessarily mean that the joint cannot be closed up satisfactorily as it stands; rather, it means that the pressure applied needs to be far greater than might be imagined. For this reason, extra pressure from a sash cramp, via a pair of shaped cramping blocks, is applied at right-angles to the joint line as shown in Fig.120. A very simple experiment will demonstrate the efficiency of the additional pressure thus applied: the glued joint is initially closed with only pressure from the quoins applied; excess glue is now wiped from the joint. The sash cramp is now applied with very light pressure and it will be readily apparent from further glue squeeze-out that the joint was not really fully closed initially. Fig.120 shows the practical application of the arrangement, but without the essential cramping of the segments to the baseboard, omitted in this case for clarity. Fig.121 shows 'the full treatment'. This is not overdoing things by any means. To conclude this section, it is perhaps of interest to note that offset straight-segment work need not be confined to segments of identical size. Fig.122 is an example employing segments of two sizes.

Regardless of 'best-intentions' on the part of the worker, there is bound to be some slight variation between segments. This is likely to be particularly true of curved-segment work. Moreover, if veneer strips are used, there is the possibility that the final width of the segments will be slightly different from that intended, and this in turn will, in curved work, alter the effective centre-angle slightly. None of this need cause despair, since any assembly comprising three or more segments will have at least one position where perfect closure may be achieved. Such closure may, however, be at the expense of some modification to the offset distance 'y' on one or more joints. It is as well to bear in mind that a small angular error is likely to require an appreciable linear correction; this is a fact of life, and may therefore be regarded as another good reason for working as accurately as possible. Whatever the variation, initial assembly should assume that the value of 'y' is that calculated and is constant for all segments. The position of the offset mark is made on the first segment with a pair of sharp pointed dividers set to the required value, followed by a

pencilled mark to make the position obvious. Having dealt with the first segment, it is a simple matter to set a combination square to the pencilled line from the outer edge, and use this setting to mark the remainder. In this context, it helps to place strips of 'peel-off' gummed white label at the points where the marks are expected to occur, and make all necessary registration marks on these. This operation should be followed by a 'dry-fit' of the complete ring although, if veneer slips are used, these should be glued in place beforehand. Where more than six segments are involved, this can be a tricky business in terms of handling. Matters can be eased somewhat by assembling on a disc of fairly thick MDF or plywood, thereby allowing a little judicious cramping of individual segments to the baseboard as required. The dry-fit will almost certainly reveal that some modification to the value of 'y' is called for, and will manifest itself

Figure 120

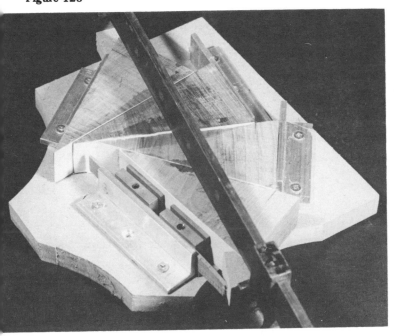

Figure 121

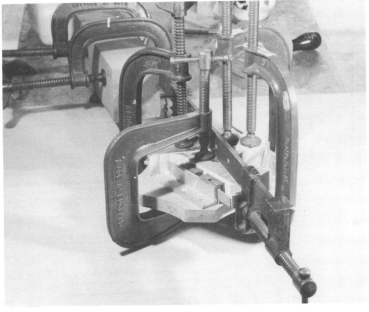

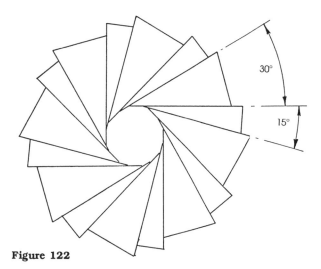

Figure 122

in either of two ways: first, the combined mitre-angles will be insufficient for complete closure, leading to a gap at the outer edge of the last pair of segments, necessitating an *increase* in the value of 'y'; secondly, the gap may occur at the inner edge, denoting excessive angular offset, calling for a *decrease* in 'y'. Variations between individual segments may well result in the value of 'y' being slightly different for some parts of the assembly. This stage of the process is undoubtedly the most tedious and demands a steady hand, a clear head, and above all, a well-controlled temper! Upon completion, any revised positions of 'y' are marked on the label, and all segments numbered, together with an arrow indicating the direction of rotation of the numbering system. Gluing and cramping also demands a little thought. It is somewhat unwise to attempt to assemble a complete ring of five or more non-radial segments in one operation, regardless of the sophistication of the cramping system available, since they will inevitably slide out of position. Assemblies of this kind need to be 'crept up on' with a fair degree of low cunning, using a sub-assembly technique similar to that employed on straight-

segment work.

It is one thing to dry-assemble, and quite another to glue-assemble, since the presence of the glue will, at least initially, cause the segments to slide against one another as cramping pressure is applied, leading to mis-registration of segments. It is therefore worth examining assembly techniques in a little detail, beginning with the application of veneer strips. In straight-segment work, they are pre-glued to the segments, always to the same relative face. In curved work, much the same applies, with the additional proviso that they are always applied to the *concave* face. In this case, it is necessary to press the veneers into position with a cramping-block of radius of curvature comparable with that of the segments themselves — an obvious use for convex offcuts, as suggested in Chapter 5 (Fig.68). It is most important to ensure a good 'cramping-axis' also, to ensure that the veneers do not slide laterally relative to the segment; this explains the purpose of the partially cut concave cramping blocks, since these can now be modified to assist matters. The essential requirement is that the axis of the cramp is at the centre of the face being glued, and is at right-angles to the tangent to the curve at that point. The cramping blocks can fairly readily be arranged such that the requirement is met (Fig.123). It is important that the cramping-block remote from the glued surface is sufficiently long to support the thin end of the segment, since this may give slightly under pressure, resulting in a poor joint. It is also important that glue 'squeeze-out' is not allowed to contaminate the interface between the veneer and the adjacent cramp, thereby gluing them together. A polythene strip stretched over the cramping block and fastened at the rear with a strip of adhesive tape will deal with the problem. The stretching process will cause the polythene to bend back over the block, giving a reasonably safe working area; the corners of the block should be slightly rounded however, or the polythene may break (Fig. 124). As a minor digression, electricians' plastic tape is an excellent choice in this context, since it will adhere to more or less any reasonably-clean surface (even polythene). It will *not* however, deal with dusty wood surfaces; these should be cleaned, preferably with a tack-rag before applying the tape.

It would appear on the face of it that, if the veneer strips are cut 'cross-grain', they will bend into the required curve more easily; true enough, but they will also break more easily, and are generally rather more difficult to cut. They will in any case invariably look better in the finished item if cut long-grained, bearing in mind that the particular appeal of this type of segmented work is greater in plan than elevation. The slightly springy nature of long-grain veneer presents no real problem, and is well within the holding capacity of any adhesive likely to be used. If two or more veneer strips are used in any one joint, they should be glued and assembled in a single operation. Assembly is best carried out on a flat baseboard. This allows both the segment and the cramping-block adjacent to the veneer to be cramped flat against the base-board; this is a most important operation, since lateral cramp pressure, coupled with essential tolerance requirements in the operating parts of the cramp itself, can sometimes cause the work to lift slightly, with some risk of slightly open joints between veneers and segment faces, and also loss of joint squareness, leading to problems when joining one segment to another (Fig. 125). Vertical cramping, if applied fairly gently to begin with, is also of great help in reducing any tendency for lateral slide.

Choice of adhesive is obviously a matter of personal preference. It might be worth mentioning

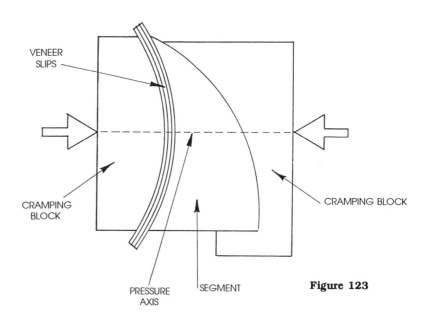

Figure 123

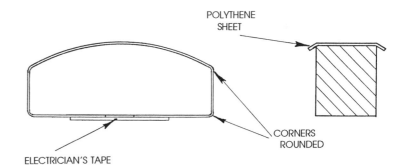

Figure 124

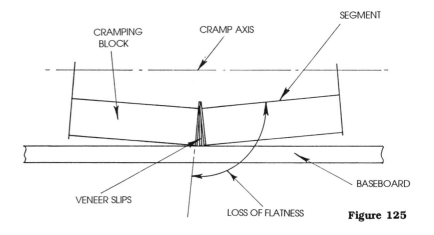

Figure 125

however, that the 'fast-grab' characteristics of aliphatic-resin adhesives (otherwise very similar in general behaviour to PVA adhesives) will permit a fairly cautious initial closure, during which procedure, the veneer strips may be pushed gently down against the baseboard. Once the 'grab' has occurred, the joint may be given a little more pressure, the glue itself then tending to restrict lateral drift. On the matter of cramp pressure: this should be only firm enough to remove excess adhesive; given the general end-grain characteristics of this type of segmentation, the last thing one wants is a glue-starved joint. After the glue has set, the veneer may be trimmed all round, preferably with a chisel, to ensure that continuity of outline is maintained.

Figure 126

The concave veneered surface is then scraped clean of surplus adhesive.

It is equally important to maintain a good cramping-axis when assembling sets of segments, since the tendency for lateral sliding under pressure is present here also. The main problem is that the cramping-block arrangements tend to become ever-more complex, and blocks which work well for one set-up may be quite useless for another. No hard-and-fast designs can be offered therefore, since the nature of the cramping system will depend upon that of the work. One or two general hints might be in order however: first, it is important that the operator is permitted as much hand-freedom as possible; one certainly does not want to cope with a recalcitrant G-cramp in addition to the other handling problems. The simple 'lash-up' shown in Figs. 126 and 127 is extremely useful in this respect, and really has to be tried to be fully appreciated. The bar of the sash cramp is itself cramped to the worktop, via a substantial wood block, such that the jaws are poised over (but do not quite touch) the working surface. The assembly may then be arranged beneath the jaws, and pressure

Figure 127

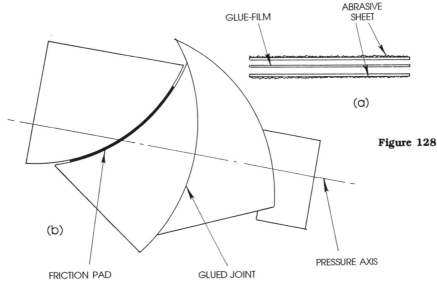

GLUE-FILM   ABRASIVE SHEET

(a)

Figure 128

(b)

FRICTION PAD   GLUED JOINT   PRESSURE AXIS

applied, with no risk that the cramp itself will slip off the work; indeed the cramp may be tightened with one knee if necessary (the use of a knee as an extra hand is a common-enough trick among workers used to working alone). Secondly, although the glued joint may well be arranged that the segments have no serious tendency to slide laterally, the same cannot be said for the interfaces between the segments and the cramping-blocks. Although there is no glue at these points, their less-than-perfect relationship to the cramping-axis may cause them to slide (and it is a very tedious business indeed to be obliged to fashion a special cramping-block, complete with end-stop, for every situation that occurs). A simple and highly-effective palliative may be fashioned from a couple of strips of medium-grade (eg. 180) abrasive, and a strip of glue-film. The film is ironed on to the back of one abrasive strip, the backing-paper removed, and the back of the second abrasive strip ironed down on to the first (Fig.128(a)). The resultant 'friction-strip' is inserted between segment and cramping-block, and will obviate slippage without damaging the work (b). Again it is highly important that the

segments are cramped firmly to a flat worktop whilst the glue sets. It is not essential in this situation, to hold down the cramping-blocks also, other than as necessary to minimise lateral movement. With all these precautions, there may still be a tendency for unwanted lateral movement. This can be minimised by stops, formed by lengths of timber, cramped to the worktop at strategic points.

Ultimately, it will be necessary to close up a complete ring of three or four sub-assemblies, whether these be straight or curved-segment types. The assembly is first made 'dry', and adjusted until the desired fit is obtained. Any angular errors appearing on straight-segment assemblies *must* be corrected by a little light sanding (preferably distributed between as many segment flanks as possible); there is no other way. Curved segments cannot be dealt with in this way; angular errors must be corrected by adjusting the offset 'y' between sub-assemblies, followed by correction of the 'y' registration marks. The assembly may then be broken down for final gluing. At this point it is helpful to take rather special cramping measures in the form of a simple jig which may be made from

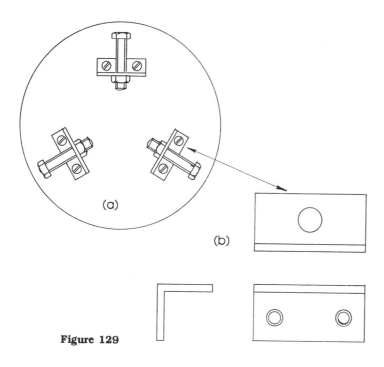

Figure 129

Figure 130

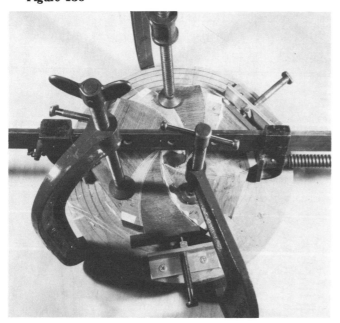

three or four pieces of light alloy angle, together with the same number of fairly substantial bolts (say ³/₈" Whitworth or metric equivalent), each with a nut. The arrangement is illustrated and detailed in Fig.129, and is shown in use in Fig.130. The lengths of angle may, of course, be those used for the assembly work previously described, since the bolt-holes will in no way impair their use in this respect. All joints are glued, and the final assembly made on a flat worktop, with hold-down cramps applied. It may be found, even with this set-up, that perhaps one joint isn't cramped as firmly as it might be, in which case, a sash cramp applied across the entire assembly in an appropriate position will generally add the finishing touch. It is repeated here without apology (because it is important) that pressure on the joints should be firm but not heavy; the joints are substantially end-grain, and a starved joint is a potentially weak joint. Fig.131 shows a group of sub-assemblies awaiting final assembly, and Fig.132 shows a pair of completed rings.

Straight-sided non-radial segmented work has a great deal in common with curved work at least as far as assembly is concerned. All the fitting and cramping techniques outlined in the foregoing may be applied to both kinds, with one important difference: in straight-segment work, the combined centre angle of the group of segments forming a ring must be exactly 360° to achieve perfect closure; no amount of lateral repositioning will make the slightest difference in this respect. Curved-segment work, on the other hand, permits a good deal of adjustment and it will be seen from Fig.132 that segment sizes and offset values may be varied a great deal. It has been stated (perhaps *ad nauseam*), that a closure position may always be found for a ring of three or more curved segments, but this is not particularly easy to demonstrate geometrically. It is suggested, therefore, that the reader experiments with a small number of segments (of fairly large centre angle) in order to gain confidence in this respect. These may be cut from card using the geometric technique demonstrated in Fig.133(a). Initially, a plain straight-line segment of the required centre angle 'S' is drawn. A pair of compasses is then set to the desired radius of curvature, and a pair of arcs struck from points 'A' and 'B', to give an intersection at 'C'. A further pair of arcs are struck from points 'A' and 'D' to give an intersection at 'E'. With the compasses at the same setting, arcs may now be drawn from points 'C' and 'E' to give the outline of the required curved segment. It is often easier to actually cut the segments from thin sheet material (eg.hardboard), using the bandsaw or fretsaw, with the turntable fence set to the appropriate position. One should use an old sawband in this case however, since 'band-lead' is rarely a problem in thin material, and man-made laminates tend to blunt sawteeth rather rapidly.

Sub-assemblies, comparable with those shown in the practical examples, may be made by taping two or more segments together with the required degree of offset (b). Curiously enough perhaps, a plain radial arrangement, with the segments meeting at the centre, is actually the most difficult to achieve with accuracy; this is simply due to the additional restriction imposed by the need for all the segments to meet at the centre, and for the value of 'y' to be precisely the same (ie. zero) for all segments. This in turn requires all segments to be *exactly* the same in terms of dimensions and effective angle.

Many of the turned projects decribed later are made up of assemblies which are strictly segmented work but, in the finished piece, tend to bear more of the characteristics of inlay work and would indeed, if carried out on a flat surface, present a case for the form of veneering known as 'parquetry'. The techniques to be outlined essentially produce sub-assemblies, in the sense that

Figure 131

Figure 132

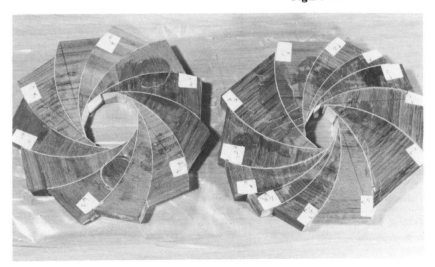

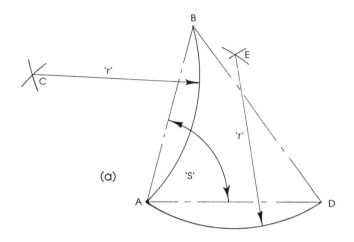

(a)

(b)

Figure 133

each completed piece is itself a segment in a larger construction. Moreover, since the design on one segment is normally intended to precisely match a similar design on its neighbour, a high order of accuracy in cutting and assembly is demanded at all stages. As a case in point, the cutting and assembly of a square block, subsequently intended to form one face of a cube, will be described: the basic form is quite simple, and is shown in Fig. 134. It comprises four triangular blocks, and three strips of contrasting veneer. As a single piece it presents no problems; as one of an accurately-matched set of six, it requires a little preliminary thought. The three essential requirements are: that the finished block is truly square, the veneer slips bisect the corners, and the junction of the veneers occurs at the centre of the assembly. Substandard work in any of these respects will cause discontinuities in the final piece that may well escape the casual glance but will not 'get by' the discerning observer. The number one rule is to make the triangular segments rather larger than demanded by the final dimensions. About $1/8''$ on the length 'l' is about right, regardless of the actual value of 'l'. The segments may be bandsawn and sanded to their basic triangular shape but slightly

Figure 134

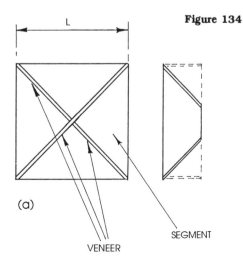

(a)

VENEER

SEGMENT

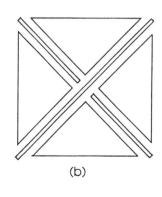

(b)

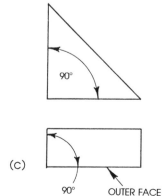

(c)

90°

90°   OUTER FACE

oversize, by freehand methods, or with the aid of a 45° mitre-fence, as preferred. Upon completion the internal joint should be examined and checked at precisely 90° against a strong light-source, and corrected where necessary on the sander. At the same time, the joint-faces should be checked for squareness against the intended *outer* face of the complete assembly (c). The essential reasoning behind the operation is that the internal (90°) joints are the important ones and must be made as accurately as possible, leaving the 45° angles with respect to the edges to take care of themselves. The three veneer slips shown in (b) are now cut with a knife and steel straightedge. They should be made rather longer and wider than finally required, to allow for trimming, with one important proviso that, on the two shorter pieces, one end must be cut dead square to one long edge, and that this particular attribute is identified at the appropriate corner by a light pencil mark. It is now necessary to make up a compression-jig as shown in Fig. 135(a).

The important feature of this jig is that the two segments shown are pressed firmly against the veneer slip between them, and that the entire assembly is pressed flat against the metal-angle face marked 'A'. The intended outer faces of the segments are laid face down, with the square edge of the veneer against the fence, and its pencilled corner at the bottom. Assembly pressure is effected with the aid of quoins or nut and bolt methods, as previously outlined. As pressure is applied, the central veneer strip is pressed firmly downwards and also towards the fence, to ensure that the underside face and 'long edge' of the assembly present continuous unbroken surfaces. Both the MDF base and the metal angle should be covered with polythene sheet to avoid unwanted adhesion of the workpiece to the jig. When adjustment is judged satisfactory, both segments should

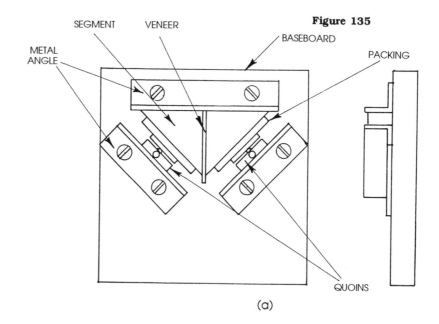

Figure 135

(a)

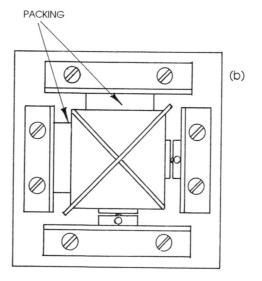

(b)

Figure 136

be cramped to the baseboard to eliminate any tendency to buckle. After gluing, the assemblies should be trimmed free of surplus veneer and glue and, if necessary, the long edge very lightly sanded, to present a clean gluing surface. On no account should the sanding be sufficiently heavy to modify the angular relationship of the veneer slip to this edge, or to affect the existing squareness between face and edge. The jig may now be modified to the form shown in (b) and the work assembled and

glued such that the two short lengths of veneer form a perfectly straight line. The initial tendency of the glue to allow the two parts to slide is of some benefit in this instance, since selective pressure on one or other of the quoins will promote the tendency to slide in the required direction. Once again, the veneer is pressed firmly down against the baseboard as pressure is applied, and finally, the two halves of the assembly are cramped to the baseboard. After gluing, surplus glue and veneer are trimmed away and the underside face very slightly sanded flat to produce a smooth surface, suitable for marking with both pencil and craft-knife. At this stage, the most important point on the assembly is the dead-centre, easily located at the junction of the veneers. The point should be marked with a single light indentation with the point of a scriber. Fig.136 shows a typical sub-assembly.

The next task is the preparation of a template, which must be dead-square, with a ¹⁄₈" dia. hole at the exact centre (Fig.137(a). Ideally, the template is made from light alloy or brass plate, of at least ³⁄₁₆" thickness (it should most certainly not be made of

Figure 137

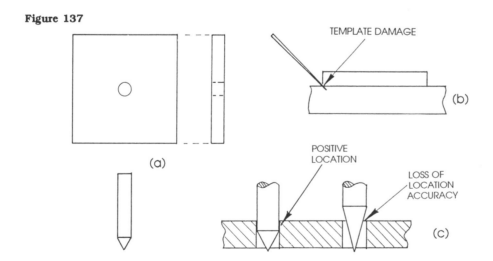

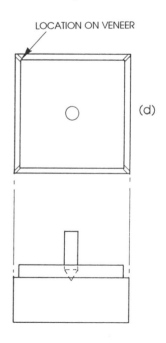

wood). It is appreciated that many woodworkers will not possess extensive metalworking facilities, but it is usually possible to find a hacksaw, a pillar drill of some kind (which may perhaps be a power hand drill in a stand), a few files, and maybe a handful of twist drills in most workshops. Also, given that a bandsaw or power-fretsaw is available, it is possible to acquire saws for light metal-cutting for either machine; this will not only remove the labour associated with hand-sawing, but will inevitably make available the inherent accuracy of machining processes. It is perfectly possible to use acrylic sheet for templates and this material has the advantage of allowing the disc-sander to be used to provide straight edges with accurate corner angles (whether these be square or some other angle, as required). The only real disadvantage

Figure 138

with acrylic is that, in view of the necessity to knife-mark the timber beneath the template at an angle (Fig.137(b)) there is some risk of the knife cutting into the template and impairing its accuracy. Even this potential problem can be overcome however, with a little extra effort: the workpiece is first marked all-round against the template with a very sharp pencil of not less than 2H grade, to give as fine a line, as close to the template as possible. The resultant shape may now be knifed at the required angle with the aid of a steel straightedge, cramped to the workpiece to avoid inadvertent movement, thereby furnishing the required visible pencil line and the invisible knifed line (Figs.138 and 139).

Whatever material is chosen for the template, a little light 'draw-filing' is necessary on each edge, to take out the roughness inevitably arising from either cross-filing or disc sanding. The object here is not to remove significant amounts of material, since this will impair template accuracy, but rather to provide a smooth edge to assist easy passage of

Figure 139

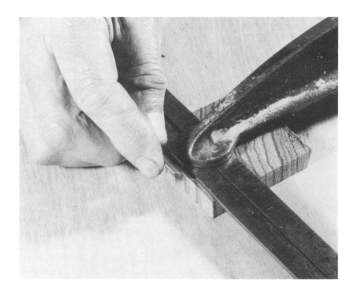

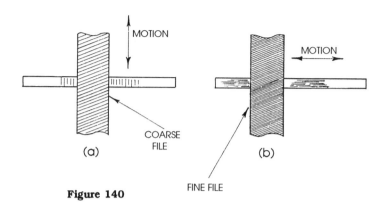

Figure 140

Figure 141

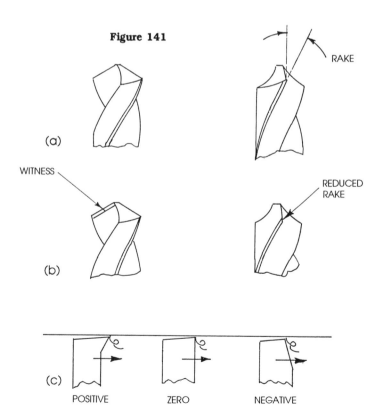

pencil or knife. The two forms of filing are indicated in Fig.140. Cross-filing is used, where necessary, to bring the work down to a previously scribed line, the grade of file being chosen in relation to the amount of metal to be removed, moving to finer grades as the line is approached. Whatever the means of producing the template edges, the marked or reference face should be that which is eventually placed in contact with the segmented workpiece, since it is likely to be the more accurate of the two. Draw-filing is essentially a cosmetic process, and should be carried out with a fine file. For users unfamiliar with metalworking processes, it is worth mentioning perhaps that light alloy can be a fairly tricky material to work, even with simple hand-processes, since it is generally quite soft, and tends to clog files. It also has a propensity for 'galling', which is a kind of unwanted scoring of the worked face caused by rubbing two pieces of the same metal together. Since a clogged file will, by definition, cause such an effect, it pays to keep the file as clean as possible. First, rubbing ordinary blackboard chalk into the file prior to use will tend to eliminate the clogging effect whilst leaving the cutting-surfaces free to perform their task. Secondly, the file should be cleaned regularly with a 'file-card' which is to all intents and purposes a wire-brush pad with very short bristles, mounted on a semi-rigid backing. Finally, persistent clogging may be dealt with by digging-out the offending material with the point of an old scriber or similar implement (tedious, but effective). In passing, brass and acrylic do not exhibit the effect to the same degree.

The next task is to drill a hole of $3/16$" diameter in the exact centre of the template. As a slight digression, the behaviour of metalworking twist-drills must be mentioned at this point, since it involves a very important potential safety hazard. In view of the fact that most woodworkers will need to drill holes in metal at some time or another, the problem rates special mention. A normally sharpened twist drill is shown in Fig. 141(a). In this condition, it will deal cleanly and efficiently with steel, light alloy, and certain grades of brass, producing characteristic spiral lengths of 'swarf' (the metal equivalent of shavings). The grade of brass known as 'free-cutting' does however, present a serious potential hazard in that a twist-drill, sharpened as shown in (a) will tend to snatch at the work as it progresses, and will in all likelihood bite sufficiently deeply to cause the workpiece to rotate with it, with consequent hazard to the operator. The effect is at its worst when an existing hole is being enlarged, and is sufficiently powerful to lift a small machine-vice off the table, even with a $^3/_{16}$" diameter drill (Fig. 142).

A secondary hazard arises from a simultaneous tendency to produce a shower of small slivers of brass, which fly off the workpiece for considerable distances. Acrylic possesses similar tendencies, and although the danger to the operator is somewhat reduced, simply because the material is inherently rather weaker, the end result will be, at best, a poor, splintered hole. The solution is quite simple, and involves 'backing-off' the cutting lips of the drill with a few strokes of a small medium-grade slip-stone. The effect is to change the effective 'rake-angle' of the cutting edge of the drill from positive to zero, or even slightly negative. The process may be done freehand, evidence of a successful operation being readily visible in the form of a bright 'witness-mark' at the cutting edge. Fig. 143 shows the operation being performed, and

Figure 142

Figure 143

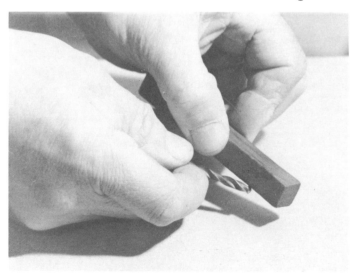

Fig.141(b) shows the result, together with an indication of the meaning of the term 'rake-angle' (c). A drill modified in this way will still cut light alloy and even steel, but with markedly reduced efficiency, and should be re-sharpened for continuous use with these materials. Whilst on the topic, it is also extremely unwise to attempt to clear swarf by hand, even with the machine stationary, since it is invariably razor-sharp, and will cause severe cuts. When drilling material which tends to produce long continuous spirals of swarf, the drill should be fed into the work in a series of gentle steps, rather than one continuous motion; this will cause the swarf to break up into shorter lengths, thereby eliminating the problems caused by a long length of swarf flying around and lashing at everything within reach. Finally, although it is perhaps unlikely that copper will be used for woodworking jigs or ancillaries, the material possesses one characteristic not shared by the others in that it tends to close-up slightly as it is drilled, and will cause the drill to 'bind' in the hole, again with some attendant hazard to the operator.

To return to the template: given that it is accurately made and drilled, the next task is to provide a short length of $^3/_{16}$" diameter mild steel rod, with a pointed end (Fig.137(c)). A metalworking lathe is not necessary for this purpose, despite the fact that the point needs to be at the axis of the rod. It may be produced by hand-filing with the work rotating in a drill chuck in the lathe (or at a pinch, in a pistol drill suitably mounted in a fixed horizontal position). The point must not be too acute, or the rod will lose its positional accuracy with respect to the template hole (Fig.137 (c). The rod should be a light push-fit through the template, with no appreciable side-play It is first tapped lightly into the central indent in the workpiece, and then pushed partway through the template, and the point located in the 'pre-spotted' indent in the centre of the workpiece. The template may now be pressed flat against the workpiece and located such that its corners line up exactly with the centres of the veneers, thereby ensuring that the veneers are located precisely at the corners of the finished workpiece. It is then cramped firmly to the workpiece. The purpose of the initial oversize cutting of the workpiece segments, and the suggestion to allow the 45° angles to look after themselves, is now evident in that a perfectly-centred square may be marked against the workpiece, with the veneers in precisely the required position, regardless of any angular error produced on the outer faces during the initial cutting and assembly processes.

8. ASSEMBLY TECHNIQUES (Non-flat)

Non-flat assemblies are defined here as those which cannot be carried out solely with reference to a flat worktop, since they demand some consideration of depth in addition to length and width. They embrace all classes of coopered work, and include the assembly of solid three-dimensional blocks, such as the five polyhedra which form the basis of the 'Platonic Solids' project. They necessarily include one or two lathe-mounting methods, although many others will be dealt with in Chapter 9. They also include the stacking of rings of segments, which have been previously assembled by one or other of the 'flat' techniques, and it is this procedure which will be dealt with first.

Assembly of stacked rings of segments, and the provision of plywood shrinkage-protection methods will inevitably require the use of the lathe at some point or another (about time, perhaps!). Since lathes, chucks and other fitments vary widely from one make to another it is only possible to give generalised methods, hopefully applicable to most home-owned equipment, but at some point the reader will be obliged to adapt the ideas offered to the machinery available. To begin with, the final assembly of pre-assembled rings of segments will be discussed. The basic lathe requirement here is simply a faceplate, possessing at least one set of pre-drilled holes enabling work to be fixed, removed, and replaced with accuracy. A second requirement is that of an MDF or plywood sub-faceplate of substantial thickness, easily home-made, by screwing a sawn disc of material to the machine faceplate and turning the periphery to an accurate disc. Some kind of registration mark should be made on both disc and faceplate, to facilitate removal and replacement of the disc in the same relative alignment, It is imperative that the outer face of the disc is perfectly flat, with no appreciable lateral wobble when the lathe is running. Man-made sheet material is inherently consistent in terms of thickness and this particular requirement is generally met without too much trouble. If problems are experienced, it may be as well to examine the mating faces of both faceplate and sub-plate; even small 'burrs' of material thrown up by drilling the sub-plate, or local swelling caused by screw-pressure, can affect matters. Relief of the holes by lightly countersinking on the mating face of the sub-plate will assist significantly. A major cause of problems of this kind is the use of a faceplate which is too small for the work in hand. The larger the faceplate and the more widely spaced the fixing-holes, the more accurate the assembly.

A series of concentric circles is pencilled on the centre face of the sub-plate with the lathe running. These are made to assist visual location of the segmented rings on the sub-plate. The sub-plate is now removed, ready for fitting the largest segment ring of the project in hand. At this point a little thought is necessary: the segment ring will be attached by countersunk woodscrews fitted from the rear of the sub-plate, and the placement of these must be arranged such that they fall in the waste area of the ring. The initial assembly of the ring will ideally have been carried out with the individual segments cramped to a flat worktop, and the entire ring should therefore be substantially flat on this face. Excess glue (even on the flat face) may cause a slight problem; if it does, it should be scraped or chiselled off, and the ring mounted with this face on the sub-plate. Even so, it is not disastrous if the ring is not perfectly flat; small slips of veneer or even thin card may be inserted between the ring and the sub-plate where necessary, to relieve stresses imposed by the fixing screws on the mitred joints, the only essential requirement being that the ring is perfectly stable on the sub-plate and is not inclined to rock or move laterally in any way during turning. The face adjacent to the sub-plate is actually that which will be the rim of the bowl, and will not in fact be cut in any way until the piece is finally turned.

Given that the segment assembly has been pre-pared to a preconceived plan, and that the profile of the segment is known, it is a fairly simple matter to determine the position and depth of the fixing screws, bearing in mind that, in order to appear in the waste they will, in all probability, be located towards the inner diameter of the ring. Matters will therefore be materially assisted by the presence of genuinely waste material shown shaded in Fig.144. Once the positions of the fixing holes are known, these may be marked and clear-drilled on the sub-plate, and countersunk on the faceplate side. The ring is located accurately on the sub-plate and cramped in position, using the pencilled rings as a guide. The holes are 'spotted-through' the sub-plate into the ring, using a drill bit of rather smaller diameter than that of the screw to be used, and the ring screwed into position with countersunk-head screws. The sub-plate may now be re-attached to the faceplate. The only real requirement here is that the screws used for the ring do not interfere with those used for the faceplate.

It is not absolutely essential for the periphery of the ring to be turned circular prior to turning the face of the work dead flat, but it may help. Much will depend upon the position of the fixing holes. After facing-off, a series of concentric circles is pencilled on to the work to facilitate location of the second ring. In passing, it is worth noting that turning tools are usually pretty straight along their length, and may often be used as a quick guide to flatness. Final checking should, however, be made with a straightedge of known accuracy against a light-source, bearing in mind that, if the ultimate face-to-face joints are not flush all over, it is more than likely that the worst parts of the joint will be in the finished bowl rather than the shavings (there is a well-known engineering 'law' which practically guarantees it!). Intermediate rings are dealt with in much the same way, with the exception that *both*

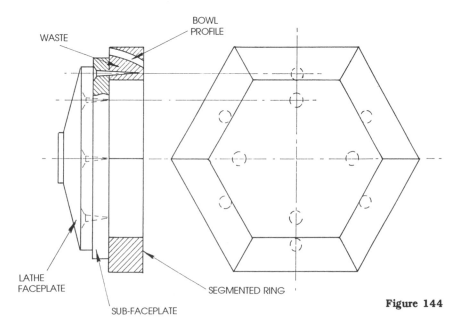

WASTE

BOWL PROFILE

LATHE FACEPLATE

SUB-FACEPLATE

SEGMENTED RING

Figure 144

faces are turned dead flat. The procedure for the second face is similar to that of the first, with perhaps one important difference: if a relatively large number of segments per ring is used, some difficulty may be faced in finding room for the screws on the spare straight-sided parts of the inner rim. In this case it is even more important that the placement and depth of screws be made with due regard to the side profile of the finished vessel, since the screws will almost certainly be on the inner face on one side of the ring and the outer face on the other. It may well be that the profile makes the placement of screws rather difficult, in which case one has little option other than to allow plenty of room on the inner rim, (by initially making the segments rather larger than strictly necessary) and use this area for screw-fixing. Some comfort may be had from the fact that it is rare for this kind of difficulty to be experienced in any kind of vessel with a profile formed by an unbroken curve, since it is likely that only the centre-section of the piece will be substantially flat in elevation profile. This section will require special treatment anyway, since it will incorporate a plywood 'shrinkage-protection' disc. In this case, the flat face of the central blank is mounted on the sub-plate and faced-off. It is then recessed to receive the final plywood disc which will form the true base. At this point it might be appropriate to mention that there is some advantage to be gained by using a sub-faceplate of smaller diameter than the base of the piece, or to arrange for combination chuck mounting. This will allow access for turning the outside of the vessel at the headstock end.

A word about recesses and plugs (or shrinkage-protection discs) might be in order at this point. It is a tempting prospect to turn mating components of this kind with a taper on both components, to ensure a good fit when they are brought together.

The problem here is, that the fit obtained may be more apparent than real, and a joint which looks fine on the side which can be observed, may be in all sorts of trouble on the other, for three reasons: first, the tapers may not match, leading to an annular gap (Fig. 145(a)); secondly, the diameter of the plug may be slightly larger than that of the recess, and even if the tapers are perfectly matched, the face of the plug may not reach the bottom of the recess, leading to a gap between two faces required to be in intimate contact(b). It may well be that neither effect will actually be visible in the finished piece but, in case (b) in particular, the strength of the joint may not be adequate for the turning burden it will be required to bear. Finally, there is a possibility that the plug will not sit squarely inside the recess. This would at best require a final facing-off operation on the plug prior to final mounting in order to eliminate the possibility of lateral wobble on final turning (c). On balance, it is suggested that the flanks of such mating pairs are best turned square to their faces. It is quite easy to do this on the 'plug' member; one merely requires a try-square and a light-source behind the work. The

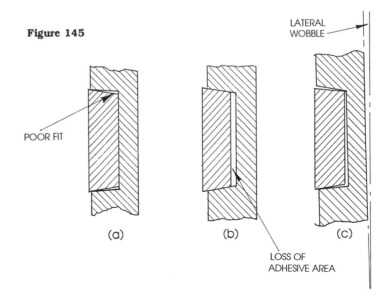

Figure 145

POOR FIT

LATERAL WOBBLE

(a)   (b)   (c)

LOSS OF ADHESIVE AREA

recess may pose something of a problem, since it is not always easy to bring a suitable checking-device to bear on the task, or to observe the result, even if it is. Personal experience suggests that perhaps the soundest approach is to turn the plug first, making sure that it is dead square on the flanks. The recess is then turned almost to the final size with the aid of calipers. Finally, a very shallow initial recess is cut such that the ring fits nicely without lateral movement. The recess may then be carefully taken down to its full depth. As a small practical consideration, the plug should be furnished with some kind of temporary handle, stuck on with hot-melt glue. If this is not done the plug may be impossible to remove, simply because there is nothing to get hold of. When all is well, the disc may be permanently glued in place. It is unwise to design a completely blind fit; at the very least, there should be a small hole in the centre of the plug (or the workpiece), otherwise on final assembly it will be difficult for air to escape, much less surplus glue. Incidentally, the hole must pass through or avoid the handle (which need not be placed centrally). The depth of the recess should be carefully gauged such that the plug finishes dead-flush with the base of the ring; there is little point in finish-turning a piece of plywood which is flat to start with. Wherever possible, the gluing of the plywood disc to the base ring should be arranged such that tailstock pressure may be applied to ensure good closure of the joint.

The plywood disc thickness must bear some relationship to the size of the piece to be turned. Small bowls of about 8" (200mm) diameter are effectively handled by 1/4" (6mm) thick material. From 8" to 12" (200 to 300mm) diameter, 3/8" (9mm) is advisable. Above this diameter, 1/2" (12mm) material would not be overdoing things. The problem here is not so much the strength of the plywood,

but rather of 'resonance', a topic which it is inappropriate to introduce here, but one which will be discussed in detail in a later chapter.

At this point the method of attachment of the plywood disc to the final mandrel or chuck may be considered. This must, of course, be done with due consideration to the equipment available. It is strongly suggested that the use of adhesive mounting methods be seriously considered, although if the user is unfamiliar with the technique, some form of practice should be carried out with small, plain and therefore relatively unimportant pieces, in order to assess the reliability of the joints. The technique is a very powerful one (in more than one sense), as will be seen later, the only real point at issue being that of the strength of the adhesive. Whichever adhesive is employed, it is obviously necessary that the user is happy with the idea, hence the need for a degree of prior experiment. The only snag with normally accepted adhesive-mounting methods is of course that, if the joint is to be strong enough to withstand woodturning loads, then it cannot be easily broken when finished. Some form of parting-off and cleaning-up operation is inevitable upon completion of the piece; but then, the spigots or recesses generally associated with combination chucks would also require subsequent treatment. Indeed, almost the only method which does not require substantial 'after-work' of this kind is that of woodscrew fixing. The snag with this particular method, however, lies in the risk of breakthrough of pilot holes (or even worse, the ends of the screws themselves) into the turned face. Damaged tools can of course be re-ground, but in general no amount of careful filling will completely disguise the presence of screw holes, and any attempt to explain them away as a design feature is inevitably somewhat unconvincing. There is in fact, an adhesive-mounting method, personally developed over a period of about four years, which has proved, after rigorous trial, to be highly-effective, to the extent that it arguably rates considerable discussion in its own right (see Chapter 9).

To return to 'run-of-the-mill' adhesive-mounting, the method requires a turned disc or short cylinder which may be relocated accurately on the lathe at will. This is arranged to fit a shallow recess in the plywood disc of the workpiece, such that concentricity of the latter is guaranteed (Fig.146(a)). The two may now be glued together. As an aside, it is a very simple matter to ensure flatness of a recess (or even an internal shoulder), by knife-cutting a piece of stiff card of width equal to the inner diameter against a reliable steel straightedge, and offering it to the work(b). As a matter of interest, Fig.147 illustrates the holding-power of an arrangement of this kind. It is pointed out however, that the set-up (although perfectly genuine), is intended as a demonstration only; the amount of overhang allowed in this case for photographic purposes is normally neither necessary nor desirable.

Figure 147

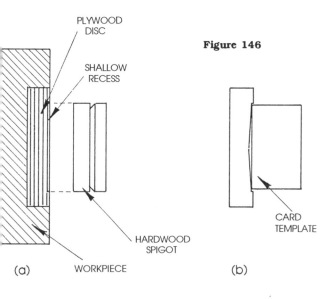

PLYWOOD
DISC

Figure 146

SHALLOW
RECESS

CARD
TEMPLATE

HARDWOOD
SPIGOT

(a)   WORKPIECE   (b)

The completed stack of blanks is now ready for final assembly. Only one pair of rings (i.e. one face-to-face joint) should be assembled in a given gluing operation. This ensures that cramping is adequate and evenly distributed all round and also that the one joint being made receives undivided attention. Concentricity is obviously important and, given the initial tendency for adhesive to allow the pieces to slide out of position, it is also important to be able to make the joint swiftly and precisely. To this end, a pair of rings is assembled 'dry' such that the periphery of the smaller is accurately aligned with respect to that of the larger. The joints are aligned so that they are correctly staggered, brickwork fashion, and a clear registration mark pencilled on both discs so that they may be brought rapidly into their correct alignment after applying the adhesive. This operation should not be neglected on any account. It is all-too-easy during the fairly active period of gluing and cramping, to forget about it

Figure 148

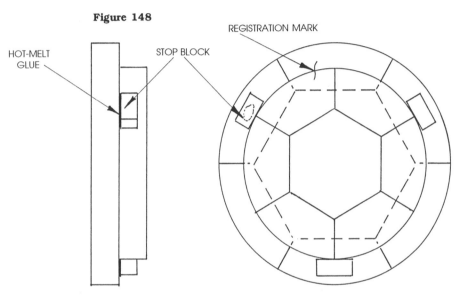

Figure 149

and notice it only when the glue has set, and the only remaining option is to feel foolish.

The rings are now firmly cramped together in the dry state, and a pencilled line drawn around the inner and outer joint limits; this is merely to ensure that the glue is spread only where it is needed. A number of 'stop-blocks' (a minimum of three) is now stuck to the larger ring with hot-melt glue, such that they are in contact with (but not glued to) the periphery of the smaller ring and thereby determine its position precisely (Figs. 148 and 149). The cramps are now released, and final gluing and cramping may be carried out in one simple, rapid operation in the knowledge that the pieces will not slide relative to one another. The entire assembly is dealt with in this way, one joint at a time. Once completed, the entire assembly may now be finally turned and finished inside and out. As mentioned in Chapter 1, the nature of the grain orientation will make turning a positive pleasure, with little or none of the roughness often associated with cross-grained faceplate work.

Parallel-sided coopered work generally requires the application of some kind of tourniquet cramp, although it will normally be necessary to use two or more cramps, dependent upon stave length. Tapered coopered work is an entirely different proposition; a moderate degree of taper will pose severe difficulties for ring-cramping since the cramps will not sit properly on the work, and in any case will tend to slide towards the narrow end. There is at least one solution to the problem but, prior to discussing it, the question of a 'dry fit' must be dealt with. It can be a fairly irritating business trying to persuade a dozen tapered segments to 'stay put' long enough to examine the joints closely. A controlled procedure will do a great deal to alleviate the situation. The simplest technique is to arrange the staves in a circle around a central post, which may be more or less any cylindrical object of suitable size, such as a small bottle; the object of the exercise is simply that of preventing individual staves from toppling over completely (the usual source of irritation). The entire assembly is now encircled with both hands and closed inwards in a single movement. This will almost invariably allow all the joints at the top of the assembly to be simultaneously examined for fit. If the stave joints have been machined accurately, this will mean that, if the joints fit correctly at the top, they will do so along their entire length. In cases of difficulty (usually where the taper is fairly pronounced), it is a simple matter to lay the staves flat and join them temporarily by small pieces of electrician's tape, as shown in Fig. 150. This is extremely effective, particularly since it allows the fit to be examined at both ends of the piece, but does produce the slight

Figure 151

Figure 152

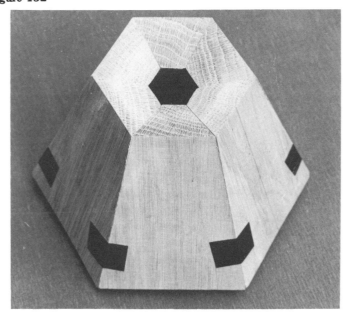

Figure 150

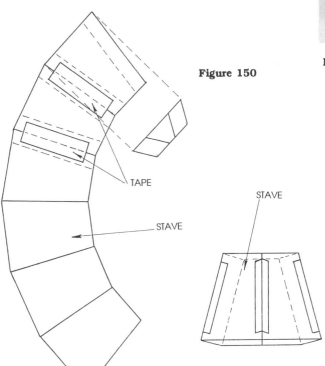

TAPE

STAVE

STAVE

disadvantage of requiring dismantling if machining adjustment is required. There is of course, no objection to employing the same method with parallel-sided assemblies. Figs. 151 and 152 show both.

Given that the fit is satisfactory, the assembly is again laid flat and the joints are firmly taped-up along their entire length ensuring that the edges are in intimate contact but not overlapping. The assembly is now inverted, so that the mitred faces are uppermost, and all mating faces glued. The assembly is now closed up (very slowly and carefully, to allow surplus glue time to squeeze out without unduly stressing the tape). The final joint may now be wiped free of surplus glue and taped; further strengthening strips of tape may be applied across the joints if necessary. Given that the initial taping has been done with care (and the tape is of adequate strength) no further attention is required.

Oily timbers in particular, such as teak, may give rise to tape adhesion problems, even with electrician's tape. In such cases, an excellent solution is the replacement of the tape by strips of plain open-weave gauze bandage (as used for retaining medical dressings), applied in conjunction with glue-film. The glue-film is first ironed on to the outer faces of the timber, close to the edges to be jointed. The pieces to be joined are placed in the required alignment, and clamped to a flat surface if necessary; the bandage is then ironed-on to the glue-film. The resultant hinge-joint is both strong and reliable; indeed the idea is strongly recommended for all classes of segment-assembly work. The method has one minor snag, in that the bandage is very difficult to remove completely when no longer required. If the piece is to be subjected to subsequent turning or other work which results in the removal of the taped areas, this is no problem; on the other hand, if the faces so treated are required

to be left as facets in the final piece, some prior experimentation on scrap timber (of the same kind) is advised, to ensure that the required surface finish is eventually obtainable on the completed workpiece.

A certain amount of part-turning and sub-assembly work is now required in order to fit a base to the body, but first, the coopered piece itself must be mounted in the lathe in order to square-off and recess one end. With parallel-sided work, it is a relatively simple matter to ensure, during initial taping, that the closed ring of staves is at least square at one end, by assembling them against a temporary straight fence (Fig. 153) although, if the staves are cut accurately to matching lengths, it is highly likely that both faces will be acceptably square. Preparation of the lathe sub-faceplate involves the further mounting of a locating-disc on the centre face, such that the coopered ring may be placed over it with no lateral movement.

A number of methods of mounting coopered work to a faceplate have been put forward over the years (some of them quite 'hairy'). The method shown in Fig. 154 has been found to be highly effective. It requires no mutilation of the workpiece in terms of fixing-screws etc., and does not involve metal cramps of any kind; the only material which can come into contact with the turning-tool is wood. The method is therefore, above all, both positive and safe from the operator's point of view.

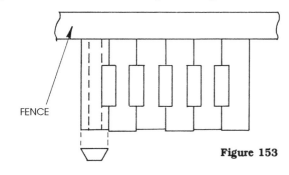

FENCE

Figure 153

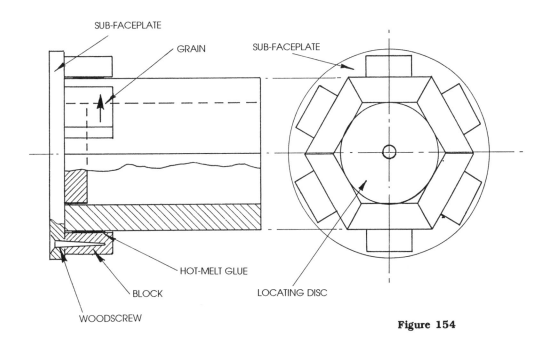

SUB-FACEPLATE
GRAIN
SUB-FACEPLATE
HOT-MELT GLUE
BLOCK
LOCATING DISC
WOODSCREW

Figure 154

The workpiece must first be cramped firmly against the sub-faceplate by means of tailstock pressure. It is then necessary to attach a number of substantial cramping-blocks to the flat faces of the workpiece with a generous application of hot-melt glue, such that they are also simultaneously in firm contact with the sub-faceplate *but not stuck to it.* The blocks are then held to the sub-faceplate by means of woodscrews 'spotted through' pre-drilled holes. The grain of the cramping-blocks should be at right-angles to the axis of the screws, thereby ensuring maximum 'side-grain' strength (Figs.154, 155 and 156).

The method permits unobstructed tool access to the free end *and* both the inner and outer faces of the work. In addition to 'squaring-off', and turning the necessary recess for a suitable base, it is quite possible, if preferred, to part-turn the inner and outer diameters, rendering final turning (after the work is reversed) rather easier. Indeed it will generally be found preferable to finish-turn at least part

Figure 155

of the inside of the piece whilst it is readily access-
ible to turning tools, since deep-turning on the
inside of such a vessel is very difficult. The outer
surface might be best left alone at this point, since
the flat outer facets of the workpiece will assist
further adhesive mounting when the work is reversed. A baseplate *may* be fitted at this point,
either as a solid disc of suitable wood, or a pre-
veneered disc of plywood. It must be noted however
that, if this procedure is adopted, it is necessary to
have the disc pre-centred on a mandrel, to enable
the workpiece to remain concentric when reversed.
The alternative of repeating the original mounting
procedure with the work reversed is perhaps to be
preferred, since it reduces overhang and vibration
when turning the inside of the piece. It will of
course require a slightly larger location disc on the
mandrel to accommodate the slightly larger inside
diameter arising from inside-turning. In passing, it
may be noted that the original blocks should be
sufficiently well glued to resist easy mechanical

Figure 156

removal, but may be turned away after reversal.
Final shaping of the outside of the piece may be
done effectively 'between-centres' with suitable plywood discs at the ends. One of them might easily be
the true baseplate, attached to a chuck or faceplate;
in any event, tailstock support will obviously assist
matters considerably.

Tapered-stave turning is approached in much
the same way, but bears the initial difficulty of
mounting the work satisfactorily on the sub-plate,
the essential problem being the somewhat minimal
contact, as shown in Fig. 157(a). It is still necessary
to provide a locating plug on the sub-faceplate, but
this must obviously be tapered to the flank-angle of
the workpiece. Given that initial taping and assembly of the piece is carried out with due care, the
final assembly should stand upright, on a flat base.
Bearing in mind, however, that the first face to be
lathe mounted is the wider of the two, preference
should be given to this end in terms of stave-
alignment when initially taping up. To hold the
work firmly, a number of angled blocks (which can
be initially bandsawn to the required profile as a
single strip) are glued around the workpiece
and screwed in place as for parallel-sided work.
The resultant assembly will be found perfectly
adequate to hold the workpiece sufficiently firmly
to face-off the free end, and to bore out a hole
suitable for an end-grain plug to fill the central hole
and a plywood disc to provide a good, firm surface
for attachment to the final driving chuck or mandrel (Figs. 157, 158 and 159).

The plywood disc is not necessary for shrinkage
protection in coopered work, and may be dispensed with if other available means of finally-
chucking the piece are deemed to be adequate.
Most of the turning will have to be carried out with
the base mounted on the final chuck. The cramping method described is not recommended for use

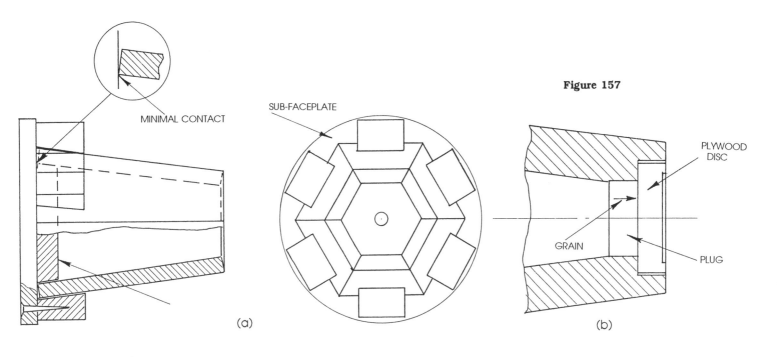

Figure 157

MINIMAL CONTACT

SUB-FACEPLATE

PLYWOOD DISC

GRAIN

PLUG

(a)

(b)

Figure 158

Figure 159

on the narrow end, since the angular nature of the workpiece renders the method a trifle suspect. It is quite in order, however, to turn down as much of the outer surface as can be accessed to a plain cone whilst it is on its initial mount, in order to generally lighten and balance the piece, but quite obviously the inner surface is best tackled from the wide end. Even so, it will be found that the turning operation is pretty much the same as for any other end-grain work.

Assembly of a complete ring of coopered segments which are designed to meet precisely at the centre, can demand something a little special in the way of assembly technique, particularly where the number of segments involved is reasonably large (say twelve). It is one thing to assemble a fairly flat ring of segments in this fashion, and quite another to assemble an essentially coopered construction of appreciable stave-length. The basic problem lies in the tendency of the staves to twist slightly during assembly, and an arrangement which is judged perfect at one end may be found rather less so at the other (one can obtain the strongest indication that something is wrong by examining the centre of the assembly). It is quite possible to get an unwanted non-radial effect (at either or both ends) particularly if it is attempted to glue and assemble all twelve staves in one operation; the tendency of the adhesive to permit the staves to slide against one another will make life difficult in this respect, even if the staves themselves are highly accurate. The problem may be exacerbated by the fact that external pressure caused by a cramping-ring will tend to favour alignment of the outer edges, possibly at the expense of the centre-point; theoretically no problem if all segments have been made exactly the same width, but one likely to have some significance in practice (this is a matter which was discussed

earlier, in Chapter 7). If however, one is genuinely satisfied with accuracy in this respect, assembly becomes a simple matter of taping the whole twelve segments together as a planform prior to closure.

In addition, the twisting tendency carries with it a very nasty little trap, which is that of reducing the effective mitre-angle between segments, albeit by a very tiny amount, but possibly sufficient to cause a slightly open joint somewhere at the centre of the assembly, a fault which may be obscured by the presence of excess glue, and may thereby not be seen until too late. In any event, the following method is offered as a means of reducing the final assembly problem for twelve individual segments to six (or less) sub-assemblies. The method also permits minor corrections if the final closure appears likely to cause an angular gap somewhere; it does in fact possess the advantage of showing up minor angular errors which might pass unnoticed in a full assembly made in a single operation.

The only reason for constructing any fully-solid coopered assembly is that of turning an item which makes a feature of the segmentation from rim to centre. This in turn suggests the likelihood of veneer slips between staves, for which reason, the assembly of these to the staves is dealt with first. Although in principle, any of the methods of assembly discussed in Chapter 7 may be employed, the stave length may make these procedures rather cumbersome; for this reason, an alternative method is given.

Two possible methods of assembling veneer slips to staves are shown in Fig.160. In view of the tendency for one stave to slide against the other in case (b), a friction pad, made from two small pieces of abrasive sheet, glued back-to-back, is placed between them. Pressure on the top block may however be applied via a cramping block, if preferred (a). Pairs of staves may be assembled as

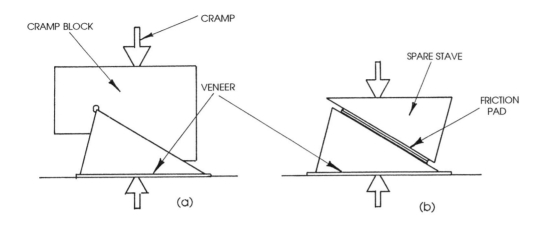

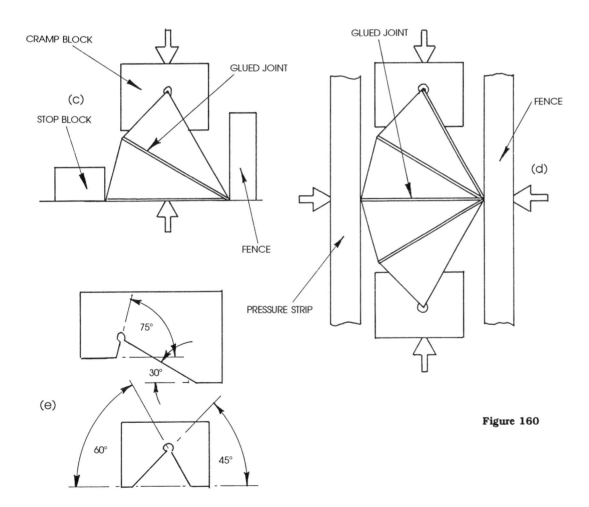

Figure 160

Figure 161

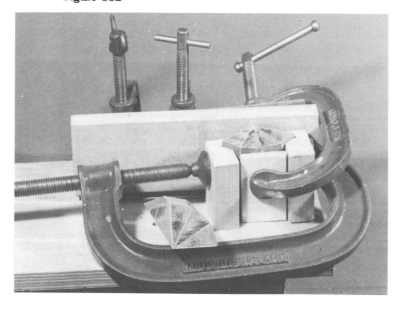

Figure 162

shown in (c), using a slightly different cramping block (see also Fig.161). It is as well to note the angular relationships between the angles of the 'vee' and the pressure face; these are shown for a twelve-segment assembly (e), but are readily applied to other arrangements. The shape of the block provides essentially parallel pressure-faces for the cramps themselves. It is essential that the lateral stop-block is cramped in the position shown, to prevent the lower stave from sliding outwards under pressure. The arrangement will allow the centre points of the staves to be correctly aligned along their entire length, but cramping pressure should be light, since there will be a tendency for the top block to slide inwards and damage the centre point. In fact the best procedure is to apply finger pressure to the top block until surplus glue is squeezed out. The subsequent G-cramp pressure should be very little more than sufficient to maintain the position of the staves thus achieved.

The six sub-assemblies made by this means may be carried a stage further by the arrangement shown in (d) and Fig.162. Note that the cramping blocks used are exactly the same as those used for the initial sub-assembly. It is worth noting also that the natural pressure-axis for two sub-assemblies based upon a twelve-segment construction is exactly at the centre of the assembly. For this reason, this particular operation is very simple indeed. The only further requirement is a cramp applied between pressure pad and fence, thus applying token pressure to the assembly to ensure that the centre-points of the segments are in contact with the vertical fence along their entire length. Finally, it is a very simple matter to assemble the three sub-assemblies into a complete cylinder, using tourniquet cramps (Fig.163).

The next assembly procedure to be described is that of a multi-faceted block. The procedure for

Figure 163

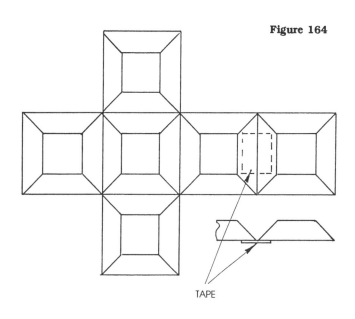

Figure 164

TAPE

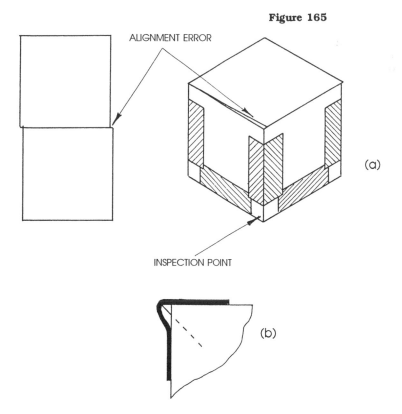

Figure 165

ALIGNMENT ERROR

INSPECTION POINT

(a)

(b)

assembling a cube from six mitred squares (Fig. 164) will now be described, albeit briefly, since the essential major processes have already been dealt with. Any further details, peculiar to individual assemblies, will be dealt with in the description of the projects which require them. The overall assembly is very much a 'three-dimensional' affair, similar in essentials to that of coopered work, but bearing the additional difficulty of top-and-bottom closure, simultaneously with the sides. It is suggested that assemblies of this nature are best tackled in one massive operation, regardless of the number of joints which have to be simultaneously glued, for two very good reasons. First, regardless of how accurately the individual segments are made, any error in registration, however slight, in any sub-assembly, particularly with regard to lateral shift, will inevitably reveal itself as a poor joint on a subsequent assembly (shown in exaggeration in Fig. 165). To be sure, the assembly of a cube may

Figure 166

be tackled by assembling the four sides in one sub-assembly and the top and bottom in another, without too much difficulty in terms of registration, but some assemblies, notably the icosahedron featured in the 'Platonic Solids' project (Fig. 166), requires closure of twenty identical triangular segments; mistakes in registration are very easily made in an assembly of this complexity. In any event, the second problem is not always easy to deal with effectively, namely that of clearing all surplus glue from the joints of a sub-assembly at the points where they must meet a further segment or sub-assembly. Any glue residues here will tend to inhibit perfect closure of subsequent joints, and any over-enthusiastic digging or scraping in these areas is likely to damage the mating surfaces, particularly if, for one reason or another, the initial assembly has been left until the surplus glue is fully-hardened. On balance, it is suggested that the best way of dealing with the problem is to avoid it altogether.

Initially, the dry assembly is made as a taped planform laid out as shown, using transparent tape (eg. Sellotape) initially, to enable the entire length of the joint lines to be inspected. It may then be closed up and taped as necessary, for ease of

handling, and all joints examined for perfect closure. In fully-closed assemblies of this kind, one must be able to trust the angular accuracy of the mitred joints implicitly, since it is possible to observe the outer joint-lines only. Given that the assembly is satisfactory, it is re-opened into the initial planform, and re-taped with electricians' plastic tape, keeping the segments in their original relationship. (In passing, it is to be noted that clear adhesive 'office' tape, ideal though it is for initial observance of dry-assembled joints, cannot be guaranteed to be sufficiently strong to withstand the stress generated at the joint lines as surplus glue is squeezed out, however slowly the closure action is performed — the local stress generated at the sharp corners of mating segments is very high indeed. Moreover, tape of this kind, although excellent for its intended purpose, doesn't always adhere particularly well to wood.) The tape should not be allowed to cover the corners of the assembly, for a very good practical reason: most of the squeeze-out will be driven towards the interior of the assembly, where it will do no harm. Some will, however, be directed towards the corners where it will tend to collect as a small blob beneath the tape, making complete closure unnecessarily difficult. Also, some final inspection of the glued joints is desirable, and this can only be done by wiping away surplus glue at the corners and examining the effectiveness of the complete joints from their observed condition at these points. Electrician's tape will be found sufficiently strong to produce perfectly acceptable joints, without further cramping pressure of any kind, given that they are taped as shown in Fig. 165(a). Any form of taping is susceptible however, to the generation of one particular type of error, usually quite small, but often sufficient to impair the finished piece. It is shown, highly exaggerated in (b). Although rarely, if ever necessary, it is possible in the case of the cube only, to add further cramping pressure with three G-cramps as shown in Fig.167. It is quite easy to organise the position of the cramps such that they do not mutually obstruct one another. Closure of the cramps must be done slowly, a little at a time, otherwise they could do more harm than good by exerting undue pressure on one pair of faces, thereby forcing the others apart.

Finally, the assembly of triangular 'coopered-laminated' strips will be described. Sets of triangular-section strip are readily assembled with the jig shown in Fig.168 (two are required). They are constructed such that the 'vee' channels in both are the same height from the base and parallel to it. With the two jigs lightly cramped to a flat worktop, it should be possible to hold a square-section strip between two triangular-section strips such that its relationship to both is precisely the same; in other words it should be possible to glue both sides

Figure 167

Figure 168

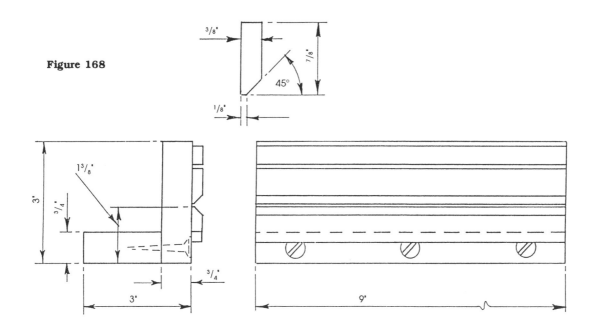

simultaneously with accuracy. Initially the pressure is light, in order to enable the centre strip to be located accurately. Final pressure is applied with G-cramps across the entire assembly (Fig.169). It is important that, when the jig is built, the vee strips are attached firmly to the jig body by gluing as well as by any other means (eg. nailing or screwing) used for initial rapid positioning. This is because in use, the pressure on the flanks of the vee is quite high and will tend to force them apart; if this happens, accuracy is lost. The vee channels are convenient only for work which is of sufficient cross-section to allow the glued joint to stand proud of them (Fig.170(a)). In cases where this is not possible, a further strip may be glued to the jig body members to provide a narrow channel(b). It is likely that this would be necessary only for the first set of strips of any given construction. It is occasionally convenient to use only one of the body members, by holding it in a vice with the vee channel uppermost, and using a flat pressure strip of fairly substantial depth to assist in maintaining an even pressure over the entire assembly, in conjunction with as many cramps as appear necessary ((c) and Fig.171). This particular setup is useful where the parts under assembly are small in cross-section and therefore difficult to reach and manipulate if held between both cheeks of the jig. The jig will, however, allow the second triangular strip to be assembled between both cheeks, since the jig will itself hold the parts in the necessary alignment.

Quite easily the worst mistake which can be made during sawing of the triangular strips is to cut them undersize, so that they do not fully-contain the central square. No amount of subsequent planing or sanding will produce an acceptable pattern; the assembly will merely succeed in looking untidy when it is finally turned. On the

Figure 169

Figure 170

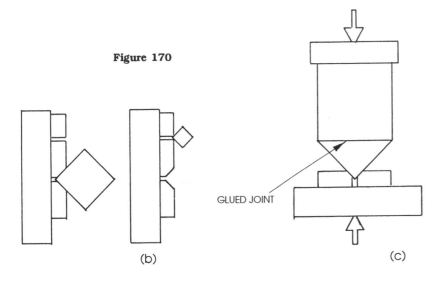

GLUED JOINT

(b)   (c)

Figure 171

Figure 172

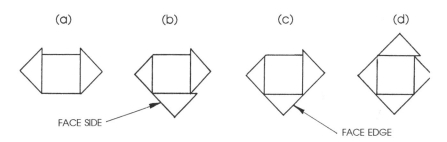

(a)   (b)   (c)   (d)

FACE SIDE   FACE EDGE

Figure 173

VENEER

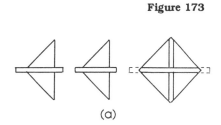

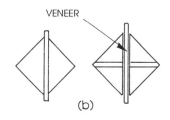

(a)   (b)

(c)   (d)   (e)

other hand, it is quite easy to deal with oversize triangles; in fact a fairly strong case can be made for the idea. In this case, assembly proceeds in the manner outlined in Fig. 172. The first two triangles are assembled such that they both overlap on the same side. The third triangle is then assembled as a singleton, giving the result shown in (b). The arrangement provides one flat face which may be used as an initial reference for dealing with the remainder of the singleton; this is planed and machine-sanded straight and square with the reference face. This provides the traditional 'face-side and face-edge'. These are used to remove the excess from the remaining triangles. Finally the fourth triangle is glued in place, and its excess removed.

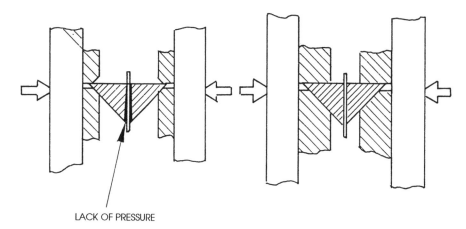

LACK OF PRESSURE

Figure 174

If the overlaps are sufficiently large, they may be sawn away, but the process is perhaps undesirable and should not in any case be necessary. All that is needed is to make the strips sufficiently large in the first place, to provide a small guaranteed overlap.

The jig, together with its complementary sawing-jig (Chapter 5), need not be confined to the work described thus far. A rather simpler lamination comprises four triangular sections with veneeer slips between them (Fig.173(a)). Alternatively, two (or more) sets of laminations of identical cross-section may be made and glued as shown (b). In this case, a square blank is sawn into two identical triangles, and assembled with a veneer slip between them; it is then re-sawn, and a further slip inserted, after which it may be turned as desired. A similar arrangement may be made with two pairs of non-matching timber triangles. These are assembled as shown in (c). They are then re-sawn (d), and re-assembled with one of the pieces turned end-over-end, to provide the pattern shown in (e). Clearly an alternative method of assembly is required for (a); the arrangement described earlier cannot be used directly as it stands, since the pressure is not correctly distributed over the cross-section. It is therefore necessary to make the jig as shown in Fig.174 to allow even pressure distribution; if this is not done, the pieces will tend to topple and leave a gap.

9. LATHE-MOUNTING TECHNIQUES

The lathe-mounting techniques offered in the previous chapter are concerned specifically with the special problems posed by coopered and built-up segmented work. Those which follow are of a more generalised nature, in that the turnery blanks are not necessarily fabricated in any way, and may if necessary take the form of a single piece of timber. They may also be partly turned items, which require re-chucking for one reason or another, or they may be jigs in their own right.

One form of jig which appears in various forms can be adapted for a wide variety of turned pieces of a broadly 'spheroid' nature, including apples, pears, eggs, and the like. The general nature of the assembly is shown in Fig.175, the idea being to trap the object between two end cheeks, described here for convenience as a 'chuck-plate' and a 'clamp-plate' respectively, with the aid of three or four bolts. Such devices are readily home-made in MDF or plywood of fairly substantial thickness. There is one very important safety aspect to be considered in respect of any device of this nature, this being the presence of rotating metal parts which, if inadvertently touched with the turning tool, can cause an accident. Jigs of this type are normally designed for work only on the extreme end of the workpiece, usually for final finishing or end-turning processes, and the major part of the metalwork will not (or should not) be anywhere near the turning tool. It is more likely that the ends of the bolts facing the tailstock will be in a position

to cause a problem. For this reason, excess bolt-length should be arranged such that it projects towards the chuck end of the lathe, and the heads of the bolts are recessed into the clamping plate. In view of the possible resultant difficulty in gaining access to the bolt heads with a spanner, they should be slotted. There is some temptation to avoid unnecessary work, when making the cheeks, to cut them square. In view of the fact that the presence of the corners will be indicated only as a 'ghost-image' when rotating, again providing a potential source of accidents, the small extra effort involved in turning-up at least the clamping plate to a disc is worth making. All this is, of course, common-enough practice, and probably fairly widely known, but there is one further feature

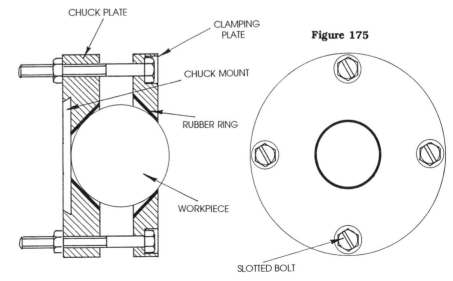

CHUCK PLATE

CLAMPING PLATE

Figure 175

CHUCK MOUNT

RUBBER RING

WORKPIECE

SLOTTED BOLT

which may be added. Work of this kind, particularly if it is a sphere, or a fairly close approximation thereto, can tend to angularly 'walk' a little between the cheeks, presenting a constantly shifting axis to the tool. Whilst this is invariably quite small, and by no means dangerous, it can be annoying, particularly if one is attempting to turn the final 'blossom-end' pip on say, an apple. Angular movement of this kind is readily avoided, provided that a small hole can be tolerated at one end of the piece (generally no problem with fruit, since a stalk is normally required). The trick is to ensure that the chuck is furnished with a small hole (say 1/8" diameter) at its centre, enabling a rod of the same diameter to be fitted, such that it axially locates the workpiece, thereby preventing unwanted angular movement (Fig.176). The usefulness of the idea belies its simplicity; unfortunately only a generalised implementation can be offered, since combination-chucks vary widely in design, and many of them are of 'open' construction at the centre. The Child 'Masterchuck' is very easily modified in this

respect by locking it solid (without a workpiece), and simply drilling a hole through the centre bolt. This bolt is, by design, intended to be fully tight, regardless of the mode of operation of the chuck, and will therefore automatically return to its correct position even after dismantling and re-assembling the chuck. Other chucks, which may not feature any form of 'solid-centre', may require other treatment. This can be effected by designing the chuck plate such that it incorporates an extra central boss, through which the hole may be drilled Fig.176 (b). The hole should be drilled from the tailstock of the woodturning lathe in which the chuck is normally used, thereby ensuring concentricity, and should be started with a No.BS.1. centre drill, followed by a normal metalworking twist-drill of the required diameter. It is essential, for accuracy's sake, to provide a hole of appreciable length in the chuck (or boss) and to ensure that it provides a fit which allows no lateral wobble of the rod in the hole. It is suggested that a hole of 1/8" diameter is entirely suitable, particularly in view of

Figure 176

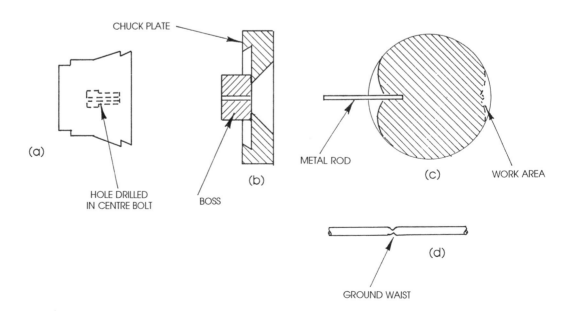

the fact that metal rod of this diameter is readily available. Most metal rod, as sold by suppliers to the model engineering fraternity, will be very close indeed to its stated nominal diameter, but for dimensional accuracy and straightness, the hardenable grade known as 'silver-steel' is difficult to beat. It will however be equalled by a similar type of steel sold by clockmakers' suppliers as 'blued pivot steel'. The material is so-called because it is sold in a hardened and tempered state, which produces a blue colour on its surface. Silver steel is normally sold in the 'let-down' state, ie. as 'soft as it gets'; it is soft enough in this state to be sawn with a hacksaw, but blued pivot steel cannot be sawn in this way (unless it is first 'let-down' by suitable heat treatment). It may however, be ground to the profile shown in Fig.176 (d) and then snapped-off (first covering it with a cloth). The ends may then be squared-off on a grinder.

Twist drills are quite capable of drilling slightly oversize holes, dependent upon how they are sharpened and used. For this reason, the rod should be obtained first, and suitable drilling experiments carried out in scrap metal, to ensure an easy push-fit between the rod and the drilled hole. For ¹/₈" diameter rod, it is suggested that such experiments are carried out with a twist drill of 3.1mm. diameter (strangely enough perhaps, a ¹/₈" diameter drill might give too sloppy a fit, for the reasons given, but there is of course no objection to giving it a try). If it is necessary to attach a boss to the chuck clamping-plate, it is preferable that this particular fitment is *not* made of wood. This is because wood is slightly compressible and an easy push-fit in metal, for example, will be a rather more difficult fit in wood, even though the same size of drill is used in both cases. This is by no means a disadvantage when the hole is drilled in the workpiece, since the rod will tend to stay with the workpiece rather than the chuck. The rod can also be used as a convenient handle for any subsequent hand-finishing operations. It can be a nuisance however, if the rod is an unduly tight fit in the boss. The boss material can be of metal, acrylic, synthetic resin bonded paper (SRBP) or fabric, eg. Tufnol, or even MDF, and is tailor-made for adhesion to the chuck-plate by means of cyanoacrylate or epoxy adhesive.

The chuck and clamp-plate dimensions will necessarily be determined by the nature of the work undertaken, particularly with regard to the diameter and angle of the centre holes, and it may therefore be necessary to make more than one (for either end) although, given that the required working area on the workpiece is fairly small, any one plate will accommodate quite a large range. If the chuck-plate is made such that the bolt holes are accurately located, it is a simple matter to make further plates by spotting-through and drilling matching holes in rough-sawn discs. These may be attached to the chuck-plate by short bolts, and turned to suit the requirement in hand. It is equally important in this case that the bolt holes are recessed to take the bolt heads before turning. In passing, the bolt holes may be counterbored quite easily freehand with a router; the possibility that the counterbore is not perfectly concentric with the hole is of litle importance, provided that it is of sufficiently large diameter to accommodate the bolt heads. It may be noted that the ends of the bolts projecting towards the chuck will normally be out of the way, and will not present a direct hazard. The habit of stopping the lathe after switch-off by grabbing the chuck body, is definitely to be avoided with this jig. The bolts are not easily visible when the lathe is running, and the consequences of a possible accident could be quite serious. From personal experience, it can be stated that this is the kind of mistake which needs to be made only once in order to get the message.

It is important to ensure that cramping jigs of this nature do not damage the workpiece, and therefore that the angled cramping-faces are suitably coated to ensure that this condition is met. It will be found that thin sheet rubber will serve admirably, and may be cut in the form of an annulus (ie. a washer), pressed into place and held with impact adhesive. An old bicycle or light motorcycle tyre inner-tube is about right. A car inner-tube is too thick and will be difficult to mount, in addition to providing too 'spongy' a grip, leading to a form of 'chatter'; a household rubber glove is too thin, and will tend to part company with the clamp-plate and roll-up under load. Self-adhesive flock materials (eg. baize) whilst ideal for their intended purpose, are not suitable for this kind of work, because the adhesive is unlikely to withstand the loading requirements for long, and the flock surface does not really provide a significant friction grip.

Whilst the use of a jig of this kind is obvious enough for 'fruit', there is another, rather less obvious use. One or two of the projects to be described will feature a plain ball, turned to as perfect a sphere as can be managed. If such a ball is to be used as a cruet, for example, it is a fairly simple matter to bore the main hole whilst the work is on its initial chuck in an incomplete state. It may then be reversed on to a pin chuck in order to deal with the other end as desired. The resultant piece will have its grain running axially or crosswise, dependent upon how it was initially mounted, or if segmented, the nature of the initial assembly will be fairly easily determined by inspection. Suppose, however, the piece is first finished to a perfect ball (a means of doing so is given and further illustrated in the series of ellipsoid-turning projects). It may

then be mounted in the clamping plate chuck described, such that its grain (or segmentation) axis is offset to some predetermined position. The ball is now drilled with a single small hole at the 'free end' (it will not 'walk' during this operation since the initial contact with the centre-drill will fix its position). It is now reversed and located by means of the central rod at the chuck end, re-clamped and bored, shouldered etc. as desired. Final mounting of the bored end on a pin chuck will enable such further work as necessary to be carried out. The result of this procedure will be a piece which will (annoyingly perhaps) escape the attention of the casual onlooker, but will invariably catch the eye of the discerning observer, particularly if the latter is a fellow woodturner, and may lead to an enquiry as to just how the piece was mounted or made. Enquiries of this nature are always a very satisfying experience for the maker; most of us like to show-off a little. Figs. 177 and 178 show two aspects of the jig in use.

Choice of adhesive for a given woodworking application is generally a matter of personal preference, doubtless based on experience, coupled with expert information from adhesive manufacturers. It is possible to apply different criteria however, to joints which are intended to be permanent, such as dovetails or segmentation butt-joints, and those designed to be of a temporary nature, such as guide-blocks, faceplate attachments etc. This section is devoted entirely to the latter application, coupled with the use of spigots and recesses as required by combination chucks for faceplate work. The use of spigots and recesses for faceplate turning is generally-speaking an excellent way of mounting a workpiece in terms of strength of grip, and general freedom from vibration or rocking of the workpiece under load. One might argue that modern parallel-shank woodscrews in a faceplate are

Figure 177

Figure 178

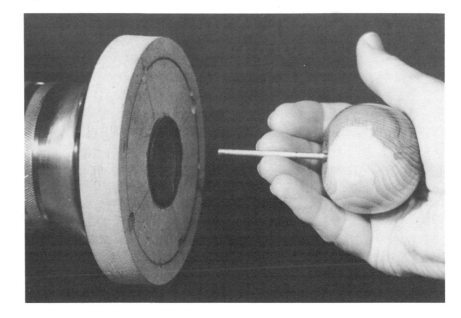

equally effective in these respects but, for work of relatively small diameter, particularly in end-grain, it is not uncommon for a little 'loosening-up' to take place, at the very least. The single, central woodscrew can be particularly prone to effects of this kind, the nature of the timber itself being a prime consideration. As a particular (and perhaps extreme) example, a single woodscrew fixing in a small piece of end-grain lignum vitae will have a pronounced tendency to either strip the thread or split the timber, dependent upon the size of the initial pilot hole; rarely is it possible to turn, say, a chess piece in this way without trouble. The real problem with spigots and recesses however, is that they demand extra work, and in some cases, extra timber. They have to be cut into the workpiece in the first place (which operation itself requires the work to be held in the lathe in some way). Upon completion, the spigot needs to be removed, or the recess must be filled somehow.

As an introduction to an alternative process, the reader is invited to consider Figs.179 and 180. The first shows a Brazilian mahogany bandsawn blank, 6" (150mm) in diameter and 3" (76mm) thick, being roughed-down; the second shows the same piece being attacked on the inside. In passing, a job of this kind would be completed inside and out, ready for final sanding, in about six minutes, giving some idea of the fairly heavy duty imposed by turning. Fig.181 shows an identical bowl being finished in the lathe. The bowl was turned without spigot, recess or woodscrews and, after removal from the mounting system, required no significant work on the base. Fig.182 shows the completed bowl.

So what system is it? In fact it is (and obviously must be) an adhesive system. Nothing new here; the 'glue and brown paper' concept has been around for decades, and many workers employ adhesive methods using PVA, cyanoacrylate, impact adhesives etc. Most of these will readily permit

fairly heavy loading if applied correctly, but removal invariably requires work with tools of one kind or another, with some effect at least, on the mounting face. In fact, the piece shown was mounted with hot-melt glue, used in perhaps a slightly unusual way.

It may be of interest to note that the mounting face of the piece shown was an adhesive 'pallet' (for want of a better term) of only 1³/₄" diameter. From experience it is known that the same pallet will readily cope with work of about 8" diameter and 3" thick. Work of 12" diameter and over 2" thick has been easily turned on a similar pallet of rather less than 3" diameter. In passing, a little schoolboy mathematics will readily demonstrate that, for a given adhesive strength, (and for that matter, any adhesive system), the 'grip' of such a system is proportional to the cube of the diameter of the pallet or the workpiece (whichever is the less). Thus a pallet of 2" diameter will have eight times the grip

Figure 179

Figure 180

Figure 181

Figure 182

of a pallet of 1" diameter. This principle can be looked at in another way, ie., to double the grip of the system, the pallet diameter needs to be increased by only 26%. From this it follows that an 'annular' contact area, as shown shaded in Fig. 183 has exactly the same grip for the dimensions given, as the central unshaded portion, thus opening-up all sorts of possibilities for coopered work, and slender hollow-ware (eg. pepper-mills).

Finally, it is frequently convenient to use a pallet with a central hole to facilitate location of certain types of workpiece. Given, for example, a pallet of only 1" diameter, the presence of a ¼" diameter central hole will reduce the grip by less than 2%. Against this, the load imposed by turning will be only directly proportional to the diameter of the workpiece (ie. doubling the diameter will merely double the loading whether it be torsional (twisting) or leverage (Fig. 184). It must be said, however, that the dead-weight of a turnery disc-blank is proportional to the square of the diameter, ie. a 12"

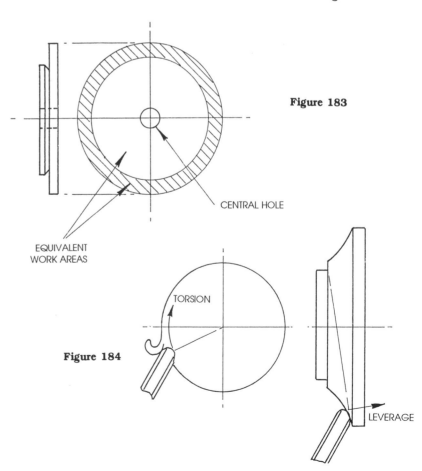

Figure 183

CENTRAL HOLE

EQUIVALENT WORK AREAS

TORSION

Figure 184

LEVERAGE

diameter disc will weigh four times as much as a 6" diameter disc of the same thickness. To this must be added the effect of mounting such a disc a little off-centre. This is a potentially severe effect, regardless of mounting-method. It is dependent upon lathe speed, which must be carefully controlled, if only to reduce vibration to an acceptable level. Whatever chucking system is employed, there is one potentially highly-dangerous (albeit highly unlikely) possibility, namely that of the lathe itself coming to a dead stop with a heavy disc on-board — however sweetly-running to start with. Such an event is only possible by some effect internal to the lathe, such as a bearing seizure, or the inadvertant application of a brake of some kind on the lathe itself, but the initial effect of the rotating workpiece will impose a severe strain on all parts of the attachment system. In fact, the most likely effect of such a stoppage would be to unwind the chuck from the lathe mandrel, and have the entire assembly doing its best to climb up the far wall of the workshop (or the operator who happens to be in the way).

Hot-melt glue applied in what may be described as the 'normal' way (ie. wood-to-wood), is somewhat uncertain in its behaviour, and bond strength may vary from job to job dependent upon working conditions — not a particularly sound arrangement from the safety point of view. Whatever the 'speed-of-setting' of the adhesive, the surface-chilling effect of the wood will certainly reduce the grip of the adhesive to a level well below that of its inherent capabilities. It would also be difficult to get the concentricity or axial alignment dead right

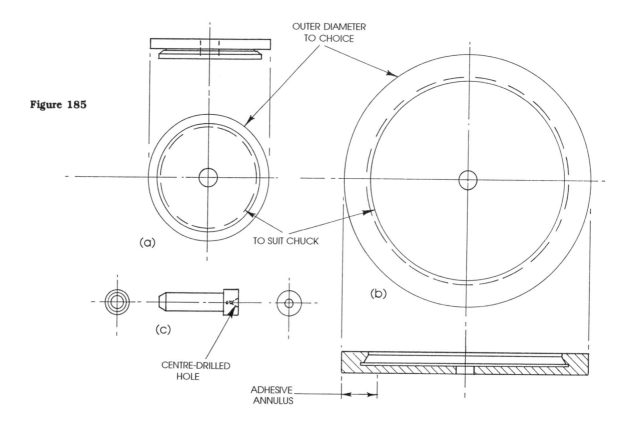

Figure 185

OUTER DIAMETER TO CHOICE

(a)

TO SUIT CHUCK

(c)

CENTRE-DRILLED HOLE

(b)

ADHESIVE ANNULUS

in the setting-time available. Even if this could be managed, there remains the problem of getting the workpiece off the chucking system without attacking one or the other with a tool of some kind. There is one simple way of overcoming all these problems simultaneously, to an extent that final accuracy is essentially that offered by the lathe and chuck in use, both in terms of concentricity and lateral alignment (wobble). The solution is to make the pallet as a metal disc, of good thermal conductivity and moderate mass, both requirements being particularly well-served by aluminium alloy. Two designs, suitable for compression and expansion modes respectively, are shown in Fig.185.

The adhesive face of the pallet is simply a dead flat surface; the remainder of the device is a machined spigot which is made to suit the requirements of the chuck in use. The adhesive material is hot-melt glue either in 'stick' form (the glue-gun itself is not necessarily required), or even more conveniently, in the form of 'glue-film'. The remaining requirement is a flat hot-plate which may be set to about 50°C. An inverted domestic clothes-iron set to the 'man-made-fibre' level is admirable — provided that the implement is kept in the workshop and not returned to normal domestic use, since it can get a little messy over a period of time. The pallet is laid on the hotplate, flat surface uppermost, and a piece of glue-film, sufficient to cover the surface (a roughly octagonal shape will do) is removed from its backing paper and laid upon the pallet (Fig.186). When the glue has visibly melted, the pallet is picked up and laid face-down on to the workpiece, and pressed firmly into contact with any convenient metal implement, ie. a screwdriver, the end of a spanner — more or less anything. In view of the fact that the pallet is, in this condition, rather too hot to handle directly, it is necessary to use a suitable implement. That shown

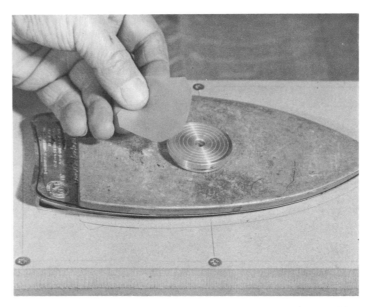

Figure 186

in Figs.187 and 188 is simple to make from a length of $1/8''$ diameter metal rod, and is highly-effective in use. The attachment face of the workpiece, which may be side or end-grain, must of course itself be flat and smooth, at least over the attachment area, and preferably marked with a pencilled circle just a little larger in diameter than the pallet, to enable the latter to be positioned accurately. The stored heat in the pallet itself is sufficient to completely negate the chilling effect of the timber on the glue. It is thus possible to utilise all the bond-strength that the adhesive can provide (which is considerable!). Minor adjustments may be made to the position of the pallet for as long as it can be moved over the workpiece fairly easily (Fig.189). It should never be forced to move, once the real setting process is under way, since this gives rise to a seriously impaired bond, which will if broken, be seen to have a somewhat granular appearance. This can be annoying, although it is easily corrected by gentle re-heating and adjust-

Figure 187

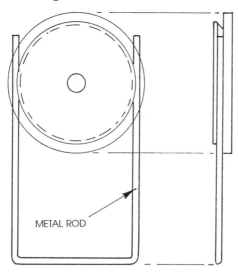

METAL ROD

Figure 188

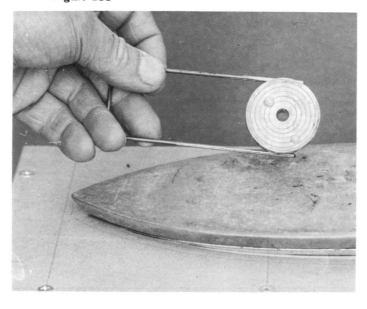

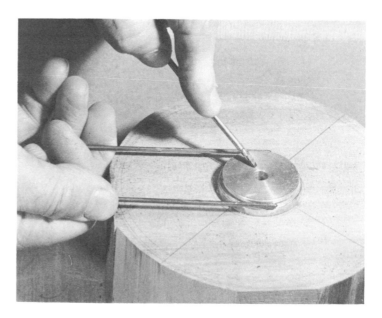

Figure 189

ment. The onset of the condition is easily recognised and, once experienced, should not cause further concern. It must be noted at this point that, if the pallet/timber interface is not level, the pallet will tend to slide a little off-centre of its own accord as it cools. When the pallet is sufficiently cool to stay in place (although still too hot to touch), it may be rapidly cooled by placing the assembly, pallet-down, on a substantial metal surface (eg. – any machine-table). The pallet may now be fitted to the chuck as a normal spigot. After the turning process, the pallet is removed by placing it in contact with the hot-plate for a few moments, until it can be slid off the workpiece using fairly firm pressure (it is neither necessary or desirable to wait until it is hot enough to fall off). Whilst the film of glue remaining on the workpiece is still hot, it can be scraped off with any straight edged, sharp implement, such as a cabinet-scraper or chisel, leaving the base of the workpiece in virtually its original condition. It may be that the radiated heat from the hotplate may cause slight local dulling of a wax-polished 'lathe-finish' in the vicinity of the heat source; this may however be quickly restored by hand, and a harder finish will be unimpaired anyway.

One or two points need to be observed: the melting point of the adhesive, although by no means excessive, is nevertheless such that the temperature of the pallet (and the hot plate) will be sufficient to cause painful burns if either is touched directly with the skin. When melting the glue, the pallet should remain on the hotplate only for as long as it takes for the glue to become visibly melted — an easily detected condition. Prior to this point, full bond-strength may not be achieved; after it, a distinct tendency for the assembly to sizzle will be noticed. Whilst this latter condition will not impair the bond, it is unnecessarily hot, and the foaming of the glue at the periphery of the pallet will tend to make observation and accurate location difficult. If the pallet is inadvertently allowed to remain on the hotplate until the glue goes brown, it is far too hot, and the properties of the adhesive may be impaired. The pallet should be removed from the hotplate, placed on a metal suface, and swiftly wiped clean with an old rag. When sufficiently cool, it may be replaced on the hotplate and fresh glue-film applied. A brand-new unused pallet will cause the first sheet of glue-film applied to break-up and leave areas of the pallet untouched by adhesive. This first film should be swiftly wiped all over the pallet with an old cloth, after which a second film will behave normally. After a period of use, the pallet will tend to become somewhat soiled with excess adhesive, particularly around the rim. Removal should never be attempted by mechanical means, since this may impair the inherent accuracy of the system. If the (cold) pallet is dropped into a vessel containing a small quantity of acetone (or some 'brush-cleaning' fluids), the adhesive will become denatured and rather rubbery after a while, and may be easily wiped away (indeed if left long enough it will fall off). The surfaces which form the spigot, and which are therefore in contact with the chuck, should be kept scrupulously clean (as should be the chuck itself). Any unwanted material in this area will tend to impair the accuracy of the system.

The system outlined has been in constant personal use over a period of about four years, and has replaced the spigot/recess procedure *entirely*. The adhesive has an extremely strong grip, and appears to be unaffected by oily or green timbers. The turning of end-grain-mounted cocobolo for example (a notoriously difficult wood to glue) is well evidenced in many of the photographs, particularly the cruets and candlesticks. As a rather silly experiment on one occasion, a piece of teak (another oily timber) was actually wiped over with car engine oil and then mounted end-grain on a 1" diameter pallet and turned. It stood up to a brutal attack with various turning tools with no problems whatsoever. Personal experience does seem to indicate that hot-melt glue, applied with due regard to its behaviour, is remarkably timber-tolerant, (perhaps the inventor should be awarded a medal).

Obviously the proof of the pudding must be in the eating. The bond-strength of the adhesive will be a variable quantity for any individual worker, at least to begin with. To this end, it is suggested that the system be tried out gradually, initially with small pieces, increasing the work-load imposed on the bonds achieved, and of course acquiring experience in making and breaking the bonds themselves, until a sound working practice has been established. In this respect the system should be treated no differently from any other.

Practically all the work produced and illustrated

in this book has been carried out with the aid of the hot-melt system in conjunction with either the Child 'Masterchuck', or a home-made chuck of rather simpler design. It may, however, be readily adapted to other makes, for which reason no specific dimensions are given. There are two basic possibilities, one to suit the compression mode and the other to suit the expansion mode of the chuck (see Fig. 185). The essential difference between the two lies in the diameter of the workpiece which may be attached to the pallet (a figure which is not necessarily relevant to the diameter which can actually be turned). Basic turning of bowls up to about 12" diameter may be accommodated in the compression mode, since, as previously noted, it is not necessary to use an adhesive pallet of diameter greater than 3" to accommodate work of this size. The real advantage of larger sizes lies in the accommodation of coopered rings, where only an annulus at the periphery of the pallet is actually used. It is not, however, suggested that the method is suitable for large diameter coopered assemblies. It would most certainly be strong enough, but would perhaps be found no easier to use than the sub-faceplate method outlined in Chapter 8, in view of the difficulty of heating and cooling a pallet of large diameter and hence, mass. Small to medium-size assemblies are, however, very easily accommodated. Perhaps the real virtue of the system in respect of essentially tubular work is that the

smaller compression-mode pallet can be used, in conjunction with suitable guide-discs based upon a central locating pin (Fig. 190). The grip of the adhesive is perfectly adequate for example, to allow the bored end of an embryo pepper-mill to be located on a small pallet, and held there with safety and accuracy whilst the other end is bored, shouldered etc. as desired. The only real problem with work of this kind is not so much that of loss of adhesion, but rather that of vibration when working at the free end of a workpiece which is long relative to its diameter (an effect which must be regarded as a 'fact of life', regardless of mounting method). For this reason, shoulder-cutting should be very light, and tailstock support used as soon as possible.

On the subject of tailstock support, it is a very simple matter (given more than one pallet) to turn both matching halves of a pepper-mill, and leave them on the pallets, making such adjustments as are necessary to the fit of the shouldered portion as necessary. The top of the mill may be mounted with a central locating-pin (shown also in Figs. 185 and 190) in the first instance, the head of the pin being lightly countersunk with a metalworking centre-drill. This will provide a 60° included-angle conical countersink which exactly matches the standard conical tailstock centre. The assembled piece may thus be mounted between centres (albeit firmly fixed to the driving-chuck) and turned down as an entity to the desired external profile. An alternative method (and better in some cases) is to plug the tailstock end with a pre-turned wood dowel (which should be a fairly firm fit and of the same form as the metal pin illustrated, including the pre-drilled countersunk hole). By this means, the cap of the piece may be completely finished at the end, since it may be turned until the tool just begins to cut the dowel. Thus the workpiece may be sanded and

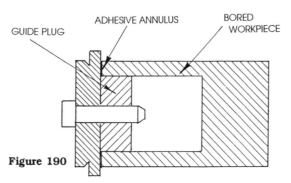

GUIDE PLUG   ADHESIVE ANNULUS   BORED WORKPIECE

Figure 190

finally polished before removal from the lathe. The hole in the top (which is by definition at the dead-centre of the piece, and very cleanly cut) will receive the average peppermill mechanism with no further effort. The basic series of operations to form a complete peppermill by this means is illustrated in Fig.191, which is self-explanatory. Work of this nature does, however, demand that the tailstock and headstock of the lathe are in accurate axial alignment, since the fact that the base of the piece is rigidly attached to the driving face will lead to vibration if they are not. Normal 'between centres' work does not demand this facility, since the problem is taken care of by the fact that the driving and tailstock centres allow some degree of mis-alignment of this kind. The point is made only because it is easily overlooked. In passing, since the two sections of the mill must rotate easily relative to one another, the fit between them will necessarily be rather freer than desirable for turning as a fitted pair. This problem is easily remedied by arranging for a perfect push-fit with a strip of Sellotape wound round the projecting shoulder. After turning, this is removed, and a little candle wax rubbed on the bearing surfaces.

A variation of the idea may be used as a support for the bowl-end of a goblet. In this case, a shaped pre-turned plug is made to fit the inside of the bowl of the proposed goblet, which is then mounted as shown in Fig.192. to turn the outer profile and give plenty of support to the stem, which may be as delicate as desired. To be sure, other devices are commercially available for the purpose, but the arrangement shown is very easy to fit and remove and, given the use of the central guide-pin, may be used with any of a collection of home-made 'support-plugs' which may be fitted in a matter of moments as the occasion demands.

The technique employed for the turning of bowls

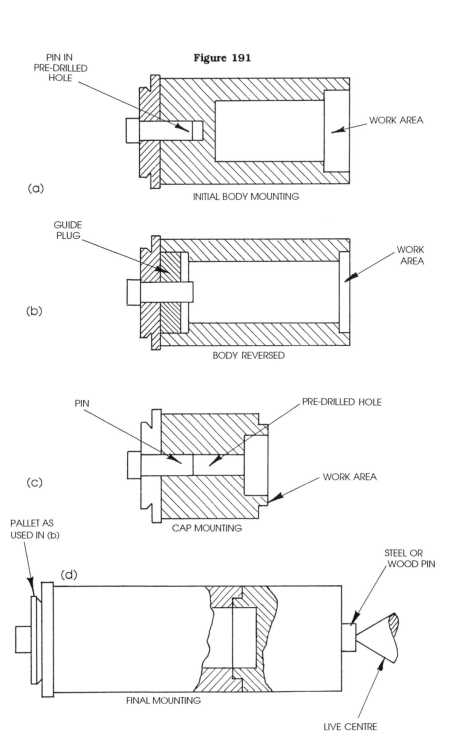

Figure 191

(a) PIN IN PRE-DRILLED HOLE — WORK AREA — INITIAL BODY MOUNTING

(b) GUIDE PLUG — WORK AREA — BODY REVERSED

(c) PIN — PRE-DRILLED HOLE — WORK AREA — CAP MOUNTING

(d) PALLET AS USED IN (b) — STEEL OR WOOD PIN — LIVE CENTRE — FINAL MOUNTING

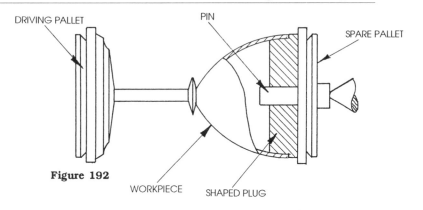

DRIVING PALLET   PIN   SPARE PALLET

Figure 192

WORKPIECE   SHAPED PLUG

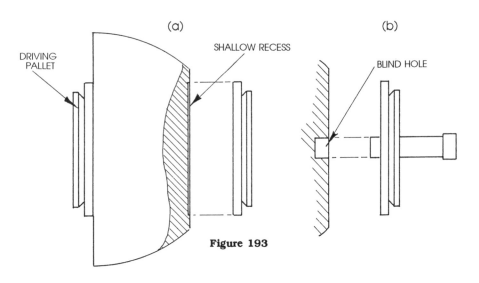

(a)   (b)

DRIVING PALLET   SHALLOW RECESS

BLIND HOLE

Figure 193

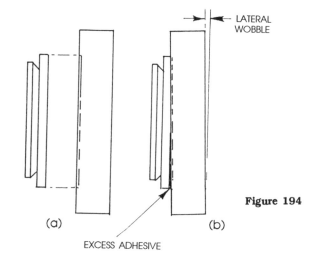

LATERAL WOBBLE

Figure 194

(a)   (b)

EXCESS ADHESIVE

is obviously a matter of choice. Many people will turn the inside and the outside of a bowl at the same working session, ie. with the bowl mounted on its base from start to finish. Others may prefer to turn the outside of the bowl first, and take out the inside separately, reversing the bowl between operations. This can be carried out very accurately indeed by employing either of the techniques shown in Fig. 193.

Firstly the intended outer face of the bowl is mounted in chuck or faceplace, by any desired method, and the outer profile turned to the required shape. The base is then faced-off dead flat, and a very shallow recess, no more than 1/64" deep, turned in the base, to the exact diameter of the intended driving pallet, in the same way as described in Chapter 8 with regard to plywood shrinkage-protection discs. The pallet is then heated, and prepared with hot-melt adhesive, transferred to the workpiece and held firmly in place by tailstock pressure until cool. It may now be reversed in the lathe and the inside completed. This particular method is capable of a very high order of 're-mount accuracy'. An alternative method is that of drilling a small hole in the centre of the base from the tailstock, and using a locating-pin in the pallet to provide the necessary registration with the base (b). There is perhaps one cautionary note to add in respect of these procedures: no amount of accurate re-chucking will deal with the inherent tendency of wood to move slightly as internal stresses are released by the turning process. For this reason, the piece should be dealt with inside and out at the same working session, to minimise the tendency.

Much the same method may be employed to provide jigs and fixtures intended for regular use. In this case, a dimensionally-stable material should be used for the jig, such as birch plywood or MDF.

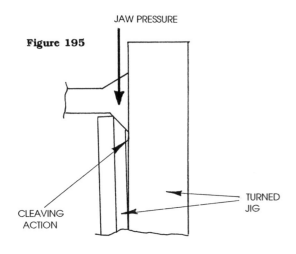

Figure 195

JAW PRESSURE

CLEAVING
ACTION

TURNED
JIG

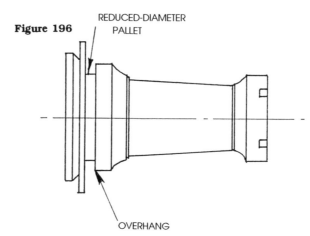

Figure 196

REDUCED-DIAMETER
PALLET

OVERHANG

The jig is prepared by turning a shallow locating recess to the exact diameter of the pallet, which is then fitted by the same means as previously described (Fig.194). Generally speaking, it is best to dedicate a pallet to any jig which is intended for regular use, but in cases of dire necessity it is always possible to remove the pallet and replace it at some future date in the knowledge that concentricity will be retained. Build-up of adhesive must be carefully watched however, since it is possible to introduce a little lateral wobble by this means (b).

A brief word about MDF might be in order: it is an excellent material to use for jigs and fixtures of this kind, which can generally be made from otherwise useless offcuts, but it is essentially a compressed laminated material and should not be used where heavy leverage-type turning loads are likely to be imposed, for the simple reason that the 'delamination-strength' of the material will inevitably be far less than the strength of any adhesive likely to be employed. For the same reason, the material should be used with very great care if it is used to make a fixture complete with its own integrally-turned compression-mode spigot. The

problem here is essentially that of the chuck jaws tending to split the material as they are closed (Fig.195). Expansion-mode recesses are less of a problem, since they are essentially larger in diameter, and the pressure is thus spread over a far greater circumferential length). It is also likely that the expansion-mode angle of the chuck will be less acute than the compression-mode angle, although this depends on the particular make of chuck.

The bond-strength of hot-melt glue will readily permit the use of pallet contact-faces of quite small diameter. This allows small items such as chesspieces to be fully turned at their ends (with no tailstock support, and to be finish turned at the base, since the pallet can be sufficiently small to allow the base of the workpiece to overhang the pallet (Fig.196); thus there is no question of the pallet getting in the way of turning tools, abrasive paper, or polishing cloths etc. Indeed the system will readily permit the turning of small lengths of dowel, fruit stalks etc. and even custom-made pin chucks (these are featured in a number of projects). For light work of this nature, a short stick of wood, which can be as little as ½" square, can be mounted and turned quite easily. Fig.197(a) does, however,

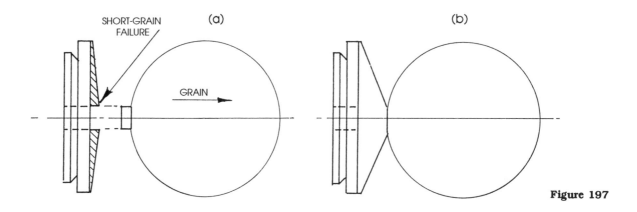

Figure 197

show a potential failure of the adhesive system. In this case, it is not actually the adhesive that fails, but rather the short-grain section of timber in the immediate vicinity of the pallet. The effect only occurs if the pallet itself has a central hole; it is by no means dangerous (although the workpiece might become damaged), but it can be annoying. The cure is simply to allow a little more waste in the vicinity of the pallet (b).

Figure 198

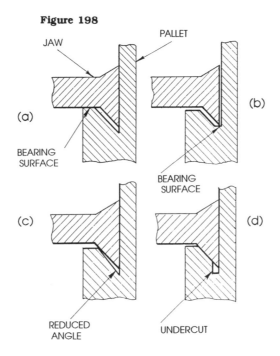

In general, the design of spigots or recesses for a given make of combination chuck will follow the recommendations given by the manufacturer of the device. It may be of some help, however, to examine a couple of possible problems which may occur, together with means of dealing with them (Fig. 198). It must be stated that the effects shown are more likely to occur in metal than in wood, due to the compressible nature of the latter, although the hardness of the wood itself will determine their extent. Effect (a) is caused by cutting the recess too deep, and thereby causing the bearing surface to be formed at the junction between the outer diameter of the spigot and the inner diameter of the jaws, rather than at the angled 'hook'. This may allow a certain amount of lateral or even angular movement, and a possible cause of loss of accuracy as a result of a sudden impact-load (ie. a 'dig') on the workpiece. Effect (b) is simply another means of arriving at the same problem; in this case it is caused by a flat at the bottom of the hook recess. Aside from careful control of spigot dimensions, there is some advantage to be had from either (but not necessarily both together) of the methods shown in (c) and (d). These have the effect of utilising the wedging effect of the jaw angle to force the jaw hard against the shoulder of the spigot.

10. TURNING TOPICS

It might be as well to state at the outset that this chapter is *not* about the 'basics' of woodturning technique; there are plenty of books available which deal with this particular topic. Nevertheless, certain aspects of the work covered herein are perhaps somewhat uncommon, and necessarily involve the personal safety of the individual engaged in them plus, of course, the well-being of the workpiece itself. This applies particularly to intermittent-cutting activities, or the stresses likely to be imposed upon segmented joints by the unthinking or unwise use of turning tools; it thus leads inevitably to matters of technique. The opinions expressed here are entirely personal, and may in some cases provoke disagreement. They do however, represent an attempt to examine the problems (intelligently or otherwise) from the point of view of an engineer, rather than a woodturner, and readers may therefore find them of some interest. This is not however, the prime reason for airing them. Rather, it is that much of the turnery described herein is of a highly-intermittent nature, and will tend, therefore, to reward or punish working practices rather more dramatically than work involving continuous cutting.

As an introduction to the topic perhaps a brief experiment, which may be performed by any woodturner regardless of experience, might be in order. It is necessary, for the most rapid and obvious effect, to select a piece of timber about a foot or so long, and a couple of inches square,

which contains 'hard and soft' patches. More or less any piece of oak will meet this requirement, but it may be equally well-served by a piece of softwood with at least one fairly large, dense knot, extending over an appreciable portion of the length of the timber, and preferably somewhere near the middle. The first task is to turn the piece between centres with a gouge to a plain parallel-sided cylinder, to a moderate degree of accuracy and finish. Now for the experiment: the piece is turned along its entire length with a chisel (plain or skew, large or small, as preferred), with the bevel of the tool rubbing the work as firmly as possible, certainly sufficiently so to noticeably burnish the work. As the knot is traversed, it will be found that the workpiece begins to feel a little bumpy beneath the tool, and the effect will increase as the tool progresses; in other words, the cross-sectional profile of the workpiece ceases to be circular. The experienced turner will instinctively correct the tendency by lifting the tool off the bevel a little but, for the purposes of the experiment, such corrective action should be avoided. It will be found that, by the end of the cut, the workpiece will be anything but circular in cross-section. The reason is, of course, that the bevel of the tool, which is necessarily rubbing the work *which has just been cut,* is following the profile of the workpiece and is taking the cutting-edge along with it; no problem if the cut is producing a perfect circle, but too bad if it isn't. In view of the fact that 'error-stimulus' is imparted by the uneven density of the timber, and therefore remains for as long as this timber condition exists, matters are bound to get progressively worse. In fact, they are likely to get worse anyway, since the bumps imparted to the tool by the workpiece may cause it to bounce off the work slightly at the high-spots, thereby progressively increasing the effect. The only cure is to take another cut *off the bevel*, and this is what most people do instinctively, whether they realise it or not. The foregoing is by no means an attempt to denigrate the 'bevel-rubbing' concept, (which has been around for a very long time for the very good reason that it does in fact work), but rather to demonstrate (a) an unwanted side-effect of having too much of a good thing, and (b) carrying out an accepted turning practice without thinking about it too hard. Readers remaining in doubt might try turning a square-to-round pummel. The procedure may follow normally-accepted practice, ie. with very little more than the point only (Fig.199(a)), but also with the bevel of the chisel very firmly rubbing the work (this is not normal, and may be found a little difficult, but it is not impossible). It will be found that the tool gets a very

bumpy ride (b). This particular action is not, incidentally, the same thing as presenting a significant length of the cutting-edge to the work, a practice which will provoke an instant 'dig' (c). To return to the first experiment: the progressively-increasing nature of the effect as described is an example of a phenomenon known to engineers as 'positive-feedback' which, despite its rather fearsome label, is very easy to understand. The process is essentially an action which, once stimulated, gets progressively greater, even if the initial stimulus is removed, by 'feeding on itself' to an ever-increasing extent. The effect as related to this particular experiment is in a sense trivial, in that it is within the power of the worker to correct it at any time by lifting the tool off the bevel. It will be found in the projects which feature the intermittent cutting of a number of separate pieces spaced around the periphery of a mandrel, that the tool must be off the bevel at all times, or the final shape of the pieces will be nothing like that intended.

Some forms of positive-feedback are perfectly capable of building-up to destructive levels very rapidly indeed. One of the most violent examples occurring in woodturning is the 'dig' of a chisel which causes the tool to suddenly reverse direction along the workpiece, leaving a deep gash as evidence of its passing (a similar effect can occur with a gouge, particularly when starting a cut on the inside of a bowl). It is no respecter of persons or degree of proficiency and will attack without warning (which is why it happens). The usual explanation of the this decidedly exasperating occurrence is that of 'showing too much of the tool to the work'. By and large, the lower part of the chisel (ie. that in contact with the toolrest) is regarded as safe, and the remainder as correspondingly unsafe. It is worth examining this particular phenomenon in a little more detail: Fig.200(a) shows an acceptably

Figure 199

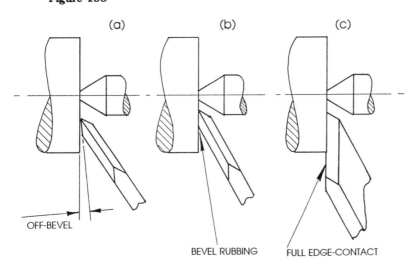

(a)   (b)   (c)

OFF-BEVEL

BEVEL RUBBING   FULL EDGE-CONTACT

safe mode of operation for the tool, where only the lower half of the chisel is actually cutting the timber, with the leading edge or 'point' just a trifle clear of the wood, in order to avoid the slight scoring or feathering which it would produce if allowed to be in contact. If the attitude of the tool is changed such that the upper half of the cutting edge begins to bite into the work, it is quite common, even with experienced workers, for the tool to suddenly dig deeply and thereafter become quite uncontrollable. Note that it is not the top corner of the tool that is the root cause of the damage; the dig may well occur without this part of the tool coming into contact with the work at all. It may be however that the severity of the dig does cause such contact, in which case the tool will most likely be slammed firmly down on to the toolrest by the revolving work. In 'cage' work, (see Project 8, for example) the risk of this part of the tool catching in the workpiece must be regarded as a very serious one. The phenomenon is certainly real enough, but the act of using the 'wrong' half of the chisel is by no means a guarantee of its occurrence; after all, the 'correct' half of a large chisel may well be more than the entire edge-length of a small one (b). The real problem is the unexpectedness of the occurrence. The experienced turner will be able to determine this too by experiment, by deliberately trying to induce such a dig, whether it be in parallel-turning, or the shaping of, say, the outside of a goblet bowl. It will almost certainly be found that, although it is possible to produce a gash of some kind by deliberately mis-using the tool in some way, it is by no means the same effect as the true dig, for the very simple reason that it is, by definition, expected by the turner, and is therefore a controlled action (whatever the result). The feedback, in the genuine unwanted dig, is started by the unexpected increase in load caused by slight overcutting, which

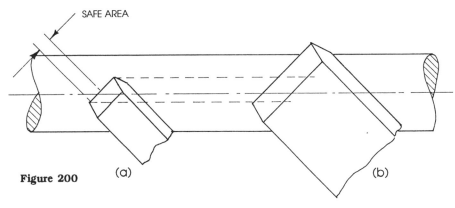

Figure 200   (a)   (b)

makes the tool tilt slightly. The tool movement gives it a slightly deeper bite, which imposes a little extra loading upon the tool, causing it to move and bite a little more deeply, and so on. The process is cumulative with each part of the action 'feeding' on its immediate predecessor, with the whole business getting totally out of hand almost instantly. It is as well to be aware that, if the operator knew beforehand in some way that the action was about to take place, it could be readily inhibited, either by a change of tool attitude or simply by offering a little more resistance to the movement of the tool in the unwanted direction. This is in fact what happens in practice; the experienced worker instinctively reacts to the general feel of the tool and applies the necessary control before the unwanted action can really get under way. In fact there is one way (positively *not* recommended, even by way of experiment) of practically guaranteeing a genuine unwanted dig, and that is to use a chisel to finish-off the outside of a large bowl. This is the sort of trick that it would be most unwise to try, but it is as well perhaps to examine the reasons why the use of a chisel on large-diameter work is not regarded as good practice. First, the power of the lathe motor may be regarded as unlimited in this context, since there is generally no way the operator can stop it dead from the toolrest. It follows that, whatever happens as the result of a dig, the unpleasant consequences will occur to the workpiece, the tool, the worker, or possibly all three. Secondly, the margin of error in terms of 'presentation angle' for the tool is considerably reduced as the diameter of the work is increased, since a given angular motion of the tool will present a considerably larger cutting surface, ie. it will take a much larger shaving (Fig.201); the effect is considerably enhanced as the tool progresses towards the base of the bowl. Plain (more or less) parallel-sided work of appreciable diameter is a little easier to control, but requires care, together with the largest, heaviest tool that can be conveniently managed. This particular point is made because, as will be seen, the cutlery-handle project described later involves the turning of a 'cage' of individually-small pieces, which collectively present a fairly large diameter. Fig.202 shows an attempt at a deliberate 'dig'. It is very difficult indeed to do this sort of thing to order for the benefit of flash photography, and the result is therefore a little contrived.

It is now perhaps worth considering the action of cutting tools in some detail, beginning with the

Figure 202

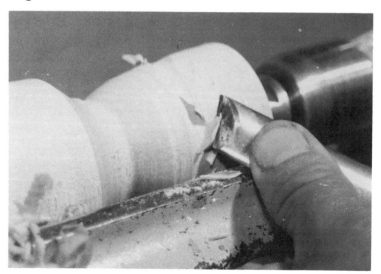

Figure 201

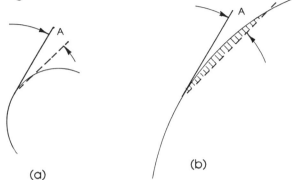

(a)   (b)

scraper, despite the fact that it is unlikely to be the first tool likely to be picked up when beginning a project. Many turners profess utter disdain for it; others see it as having its place in the tool-rack, particularly where the safety of the workpiece might otherwise be compromised. Be that as it may, the scraper is positively *not* the tool for intermittent cutting of any kind. Turning tools rely heavily upon the support offered by the workpiece itself. A scraper pushed straight into a revolving workpiece which allows continuous contact will cut, and will even produce shavings, for as long as the shavings are suported by the work just in front of the tool (Fig.203(a)). If this is removed, as in the case of intermittent turnery, the tool will tend to break the wood away rather than cut it (b). Matters are no better on the leading edge of the workpiece, but for a slightly different reason. In this case, the full length of the operational portion of the cutting edge meets the work at the same instant and, since the top edge of the tool is more or less parallel to the leading face of the workpiece at this instant, the tendency is for the timber to be crushed and torn away rather than cut (c). The net effect is for the workpiece to end up with rather ragged leading and trailing edges, regardless of what happens in between them. Matters are somewhat improved if

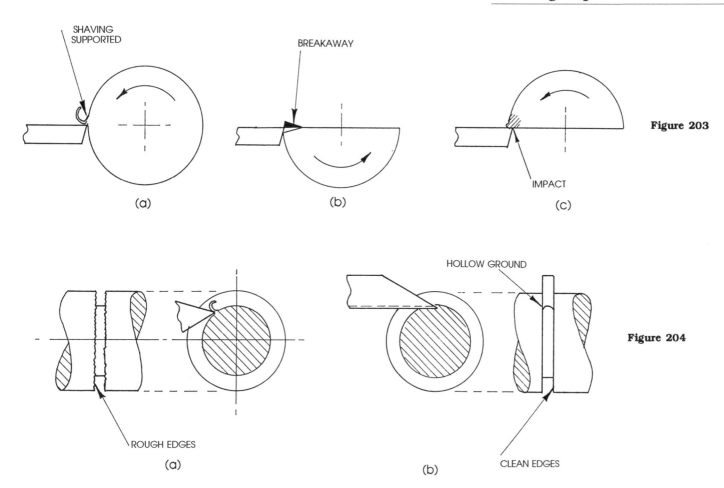

Figure 203

Figure 204

the tool has a fairly acute bevel, and is presented more or less tangentially to the work (Fig.204(a)). This is more of a genuine cutting action, and is in fact that of the parting-tool. However, it works only by virtue of the fact that the cutting edge is fairly short, since it represents a fairly high energy-input; in fact a large chisel presented in this way could well knock the work clean out of the lathe. As it is, the edges on either side of the cut tend to suffer somewhat since the fibres are torn away at these points rather than cleanly cut; an exception to this is of course provided by the hollow-ground parting tool, which slices through the fibres on either side prior to removal of the centre portion (b).

The use of the plain parting tool or a very narrow chisel can in fact be quite useful in intermittent work, but the action must be a side-to-side motion, to provide more of a slicing cut.

The slicing action produced, for example, by a gouge or a chisel as it is moved along a cylindrical workpiece is vastly different (Fig.205). In this case, the cutting edge has essentially two components of motion relative to the workpiece: there is the motion at right-angles to the lathe axis, produced by the rotation of the workpiece, and there is the lateral motion provided by the operator, which moves the tool along the work. The resultant motion allows a smooth slicing cut to be made, due to the

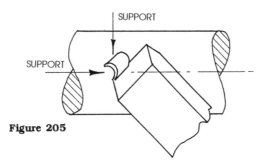

SUPPORT

SUPPORT

Figure 205

fact that the shaving is being supported by the workpiece. A similar effect occurs when squaring-off a shoulder, or even more to the point, when turning a square-to-round pummel, the only essential difference being that there is rather less motion of the tool relative to the toolrest but, in both cases, the shaving receives support. Thus, for intermittent turning, the gouge and chisel are to be preferred over the scraper. On the face of it, the use of these tools may appear to be somewhat unsafe, but in practice this is not the case, given that much the same precautions are observed as for plain turning. It has been shown that the use of the chisel becomes rather more risky as the workpiece diameter is increased, due to the reduced margin of error in tool presentation thereby caused. For this same reason, the larger the diameter of the workpiece, the larger the tool required (in the sense of length of cutting-edge). Aside from the damping effect available with a more massive chisel, the risk of catching the work with the top edge of the chisel is considerably reduced. This latter attribute is of considerable importance in 'cage' work, since an accident of this kind could, in extreme cases, actually prise one or more of the components out of the cage, and would in any case severely damage the work.

The difficulty in starting a cut with a chisel at the extreme end of a cylindrical workpiece is well-known; the reason is of course that there is initially nothing to support the tool, apart from the toolrest, and the start of the cut must be made very carefully, with close observation of the tool-point. A similar operation when performing intermittent turning in a cage formation is that much more difficult, in view of the fact that the true profile of the workpiece cannot be seen clearly, and the cut must therefore be started by 'feel' rather than observation. It is perhaps better in such cases to start the cut somewhere near the middle, by gently lowering the tool onto the work, and then progressing right-and-left to each end. In this connection, it is generally accepted to be bad practice on tapered work to cut 'uphill' (ie. from the smaller diameter to the larger), since the direction of the grain of the timber is not necessarily being used to best effect. It is suggested however, that the method outlined is, for intermittent work, the lesser of the two evils. The gouge is generally a safer implement, and is to be preferred wherever it can be used successfully in terms of a smoothly progressing cut, essentially for the reasons already given, since its curved edge-profile tends to keep the back edge clear of the revolving workpiece and thereby inhibits any tendency to dig. The price to be paid is generally that of difficulty in producing a surface free of ripples; this latter problem may be considerably alleviated by the use of a wide, shallow gouge.

Convex surfaces, as presented by the outside of bowls for example, do not in general present undue difficulty when using a gouge. Inside-turning of such vessels is a different proposition, and it is quite common for the beginner to experience really savage digs, particularly when entering the wood to begin an inside cut. The point is made here because of the vulnerability of end-grain glued joints in segmented work, particularly if the vessel is thin-walled, and the joint area thereby limited.

The effect of any form of turning on the inside of a bowl near the rim is, at least in part, to tend to split the bowl open; even if the tool is cutting well, there is inevitably some pressure on the workpiece. A dig is simply a violent enhancement of this effect. It is in fact at its worst when starting a cut, since the tool will rip across the face of the work from inside to out, placing a great deal of stress on the joints (or for that matter, on any weaknesses or flaws in solid timber). Although the positive-feedback principle still applies, the occurrence is generally much more rapid and is invariably beyond the control of the turner the instant it starts. It is tempting to think of the part of the tool labelled 'B' in Fig.206 as the 'trailing-edge'. As far as the inward movement of the tool from rim to centre is concerned, this is true enough but, in terms of the rotation of the work, it is the *leading edge*. The same may be said for outside turning also (eg. Fig.200). If this edge of the gouge is actually allowed to contact the bowl, one can expect instant trouble in the form of a gash that can split a thin-walled bowl apart, segmented or not. The newcomer to turning is invited to take a bowl of some kind (a plastic one will do), and hold various turning tools in the appropriate positions,

and try to imagine the effect on a real piece of turning. The generally recommended tool for this kind of work is the deep-fluted gouge, ground with a square end, and used with the bevel close to if not actually rubbing the work, as far as can be managed. It is actually quite impossible to achieve this condition near the centre of a deep, incurved vessel, and it is much easier to remove the middle by working from the centre outwards. The square-across gouge is certainly relatively easy to use, although the task by no means impossible with a round-nosed gouge. The problem in the latter case is that it is fairly difficult to distinguish, either by eye or by feel, where the 'danger-point' lies; experience is necessary. One very important safety point regarding the turning of any vessel, is that of paying attention to the *sound* of the tool as it cuts the work. Normally, on plain-turning, this will be a hissing sound. This is fine, but the instant a regular click is heard, the lathe should be stopped immediately, and the workpiece carefully examined. In most cases, a break in continuity will be present, whether this be a failed joint or a flaw in the timber. Either way, turning should not proceed until repairs have been effected (or in extreme cases, the piece discarded).

Another effect which must be watched with some care is that of 'resonance'. This too can have a very powerful 'build-up' effect, to the extent that it can destroy a workpiece, and also place the operator at some risk. It is basically a form of vibration, although not the kind that occurs in a badly-centred or otherwise unbalanced workpiece (although unbalance can initiate resonance elsewhere in the system). Rather, it is a form of natural vibration of the workpiece, or indeed the tool, the toolrest, the chuck, the tailstock, or virtually any part of the set-up, when 'excited' by an input of energy. The *available* energy input in this case is basically that

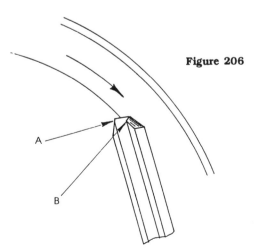

Figure 206

A

B

of the lathe motor, imparted to the driving mandrel and, as previously noted, may be regarded for practical purposes as unlimited; the *actual* energy input to the workpiece will be determined by the action of the tool on the work. Thus, although the tool may be more or less stationary, it can nevertheless be regarded as the controllable energy-source. A simple experiment will demonstrate the resonance phenomenon very effectively: If a thin lath of wood is cramped to a table, and its free end bent slightly and then released, the lath will vibrate or 'oscillate', at a 'frequency' (essentially the speed of to-and-fro motion) determined by the dimensions of the lath ie. its free-length, width and thickness (Fig.207). It will be found that a long, thin lath will oscillate more slowly than a shorter, thicker one, for example. The frequency of oscillation is termed the 'natural' frequency of the system. Given time, the oscillation will die down, since it will be opposed or 'damped' by other factors, such as air-resistance, and other forces within the timber itself. If it were possible however, to continue to impart energy to the system, for example by means of a series of timed blows which aided the existing movement sufficiently to overcome any resistance effects, the oscillation would build up to a destructive level. This may seem to be a somewhat irrelevant lecture, but the effect is exactly that which

can occur in a number of turning operations. To take, for example, the case of a plain turned 'long-and-thin' cylinder: the load imposed by a turning tool somewhere near the centre of such a piece will cause it to vibrate and produce the characteristic 'ribbing' effect well-known to most turners. This is often described as the work trying to 'climb-over' the tool, an effective enough description, but occasionally perhaps a little misleading. For example, it would seem to fit the behaviour of a workpiece with the proportions of a billiard cue, but would be rather less-effective if applied to a fairly hefty table leg. The latter is however, equally prone to oscillation, albeit to a lesser degree (and at a much higher frequency); one could scarcely describe the action in terms of the work climbing over the tool, but ribbing is still likely. It might be productive to consider why the effect is more likely to occur at the centre of the work than at the ends. Given normal turning practice, the tool-loading will be much the same everywhere; the essential difference is that the timber will be more likely to move under pressure at the centre than at the rigidly supported ends. Thus the initial conditions for vibration and hence resonance are more in evidence at the centre. The natural vibration of the workpiece relative to the speed of the lathe will have an effect upon the degree of ribbing produced, and it may well be possible to minimise the effect or indeed eliminate it by altering the lathe speed (usually downwards for safety's sake); this practice by no means guarantees the cure however. Quite often the instinctive reaction of the worker faced with ribbing is to increase tailstock pressure. This is fine if the vibration is caused by slackness of the workpiece between centres rather than resonance but in the latter case, particularly on relatively thin work, the cure may be worse than the disease. There may be some benefit to be had by reducing the length of the

Figure 207

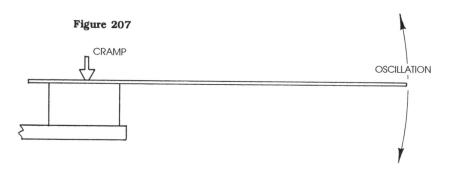

CRAMP

OSCILLATION

cutting edge applied to the work (ie. use a smaller tool in the case of the gouge, and work more towards the point in the case of the chisel). The effect here is to reduce the energy input which, for a given depth of cut, is related to the amount of tool in contact with the work. There may be some advantage also in reducing the depth of cut anyway, for much the same reasons. One should not expect too much however; resonance is too powerful an effect to be unduly bothered by such trifles. Curiously perhaps, a possible cure as applied to metal-turning is (in some cases only) to *increase* the depth of cut, but the essential reasoning behind this procedure can rarely be applied to woodturning. The reader may well wonder where all this is leading: the answer lies in the behaviour of 'cage' or other forms of intermittent turning. It would be surprising indeed if a solid cylinder of perhaps six inches diameter and much the same length exhibited a great deal of resonance-associated behaviour; on the other hand, a cage of equivalent dimensions comprised of half-a-dozen 'sticks' of wood may well do so, simply due to their relatively more slender form. This can be quite a surprise when it occurs, and the cure may be difficult to find; nevertheless, it pays to be aware of the possibility. It does help to remember that each individual component in a cage is under the tool for only a brief instant in any one revolution; change of lathe speed may well be of some assistance therefore.

Bowl turning has its own particular brand of resonance. In this case, it is the change of shape of the bowl which can cause severe problems to the turner. The same effect causes a bell to ring when struck; in this case, the frequencies of vibration (invariably more than one) are within audible range, and the bell-tone is heard as a result of air movement caused by the oscillation. In the turned bowl case, the effect can also be heard, quite often in the form of an unpleasant noise, or perhaps even a screech, which can suggest (usually wrongly), that the tool is scraping rather than cutting. The tool may also feel as though it is bumping along the work, despite the fact that is obviously cutting the timber. The final visible effect is generally that of poor finish, although in severe cases it may be possible to distinguish ribbing also. In its ultimate form, the effect can destroy the workpiece. The change of shape which occurs in the workpiece is quite complex, and may be likened in some respects to that seen in a very large free-floating soap bubble but, in simple terms, it may be regarded as a change from a perfect circle to that of an ellipse whose axes are constantly changing; there may also be some lateral wobble, ie. in the direction of the lathe axis. It can be seen that the effect of a cutting-tool on such a surface can be quite disastrous (Fig.208). In general, the thinner the wall of the bowl, the more likely the effect, but turning a bowl with a thin rim which tends to thicken towards the base is unlikely in itself to cause a severe problem; the real culprit is more likely to be a thin centre-portion, since this can give rise to a much greater movement at the rim. By way of comparison, it is most unlikely that one would attempt to

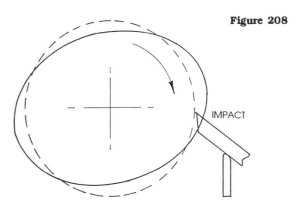

Figure 208

IMPACT

turn a goblet by first completing a long slender stem and then shaping the bowl; such an approach is obviously asking for trouble. On the other hand, one might not think twice about completing a bowl (either inside or outside) in a series of continuous sweeps which thin the wall down more or less evenly throughout its depth, resulting in a need to work on the rim of a piece which has very little 'meat' in the centre. Even worse perhaps is the practice of finishing-off the inside of a bowl with a scraper, working from the inside out. There is nothing wrong here by the way (provided that the base section is of reasonable thickness), if the outside of the bowl has yet to be turned, since the damping effect provided by the bulk timber itself will inhibit any tendency for the piece to resonate. Twenty or thirty years ago, most bowl bases were necessarily substantial, simply in order to prevent the gouge from clipping the fixing-screws. Modern chucking systems have changed all that (but the advantages thus conferred must be balanced by an appreciation of the likely behaviour of the timber).

At this point, it might be advantageous to examine the scraper again. It is fairly common to use the scraper as a kind of 'form-tool', at least to the extent of removing unwanted ripples from say, the inside of a bowl. The problem here is that, for inside work at least, the necessary smoothing action requires the scraper to be shaped to at least some approximation to the general curvature of the work. This means that a relatively long cutting-edge is applied to the work, which in turn means a high energy input. Since the severity of the resonance phenomenon is very closely related to applied energy, one can expect trouble if a scraper with a long cutting edge is applied to the inside of a thin-walled bowl. The thickness of the scraper will also have one or two effects on the work (both good and bad). The good news is that a thick scraper is likely to be massive (ie. heavy) also, and therefore gives the turner rather more control in terms of persuading the tool to stay 'on-line'. The bad news is that, the thicker the scraper, the greater the likelihood of an unwanted deep 'bite', if the cutting-edge is fairly close to the toolrest, since any upward tilting of the handle will cause the edge to move forward also (Fig.209). Agreed the effect tends to disappear as the distance between the cutting-edge and the toolrest is increased, but this brings its own 'leverage' problems in terms of overall control of the tool. One must also be aware of the variation in 'depth of bite' which can occur towards the rim of the bowl as distinct from the base. The effect here is, of course, due to the curvature of the workpiece itself; there is little that can be done about it, but an awareness of the problem is helpful.

There is no intent here to attempt to persuade any turner (even a complete beginner) to turn a bowl in a specific way, if he or she is managing quite successfully already. Rather, it is an attempt to demonstrate what is actually happening to the timber during the turning process. It is perhaps as well to differentiate here between the turning of seasoned and 'green' timber. In the latter case, it is fairly common to leave a tool-finish; moreover, the natural damping effect of a high moisture content in the timber plus the fact that green timber seems (for some reason) to turn much more easily than seasoned timber, will enable the turner to take rather greater liberties. Since segmented work is unlikely to be green (one might say it better hadn't be), the problems associated with turning technique are likely to be as described. It is as well to bear in mind therefore, that the rim area of a segmented bowl will include a number of end-grain timber joints, and the thinner the bowl, the weaker the joints.

All this leads of course to the safety of the turner,

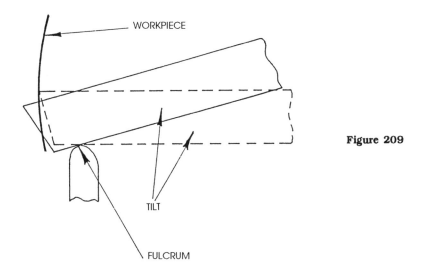

WORKPIECE

TILT

FULCRUM

Figure 209

as well as that of the workpiece. It is generally accepted nowadays that any turner who works in the complete absence of personal safety-gear, in terms of dust and impact control, is asking for trouble to a greater or lesser extent, dependent upon the nature of the work performed. Accidents will happen from time to time, regardless of skill and experience but even so, one aspect of technique can also have a marked effect upon personal safety. It may be summed-up by saying that, perhaps the best way of avoiding the consequences of an accident is to be somewhere else when it happens. This of course relates to the position of the turner relative to the work. It is perhaps as well that the turning of the inside of a bowl automatically positions the worker at one end of the lathe; thus if anything does fly off, the only chance of getting hit is a ricochet of some kind. Outside work, including spindle-turning, and particularly off-centre work, demands rather more care. It is strongly suggested that a working stance which positions

the turner's more vulnerable portions (the head, for most of us), to one side or other of the potential line-of-fire is not at all a bad idea. It is by no means difficult to learn to adopt such a stance, but it must be said that the ability to switch tools from one hand to the other helps a great deal, a technique very quickly learnt if one possesses a lathe with both inboard and outboard faceplate facilities. The working photographs in the book show both left and right-handed turning. This is positively *not* due to any attempt to show-off, or be clever in any way; on the contrary, it is seen as a matter of both necessity and convenience. Nobody is born with the ability to turn wood; it has to be learnt, and ambidexterity is only a matter of further learning. The preference of the individual for left or right-handedness is, in any case, often defeated by the nature of the equipment available. Woodturning aside, there can't, for example, be all that many left-handed pianos about.

PROJECT 1.   OFFSET STRAIGHT-SEGMENT
(Platter)

Figure 210

The project illustrated in Fig.210 is the only example offered for straight-segment work, other than the practice piece given in Chapter 2. The design of such pieces entails little more than deciding upon the profile and segmentation pattern required, and then using Nomograms 1 and 2. It is perhaps worth reiterating however, that this type of segmentation is best displayed in shallow pieces, since it is the plan-view which is all-important.

The project was originally made for a number of teak offcuts from planed boards of constant thickness. Dimensions are given in Fig.211, but these are of no real importance since the technique may be applied to work of any convenient size. The first task is to saw and sand twelve equal segments, ensuring that the centre angle and length 'L' are accurate. A dry assembly is then made to ensure that all joints fit perfectly. Slips of sycamore veneer

between segments are a feature of this design, but may be omitted if desired.

The centre-piece for this project is of particular interest perhaps, not so much for its construction or appearance, but rather because it represents a recovery from potential disaster in the original project. It therefore serves to illustrate that a project of this nature, comprising a great deal of cutting and assembly, need not necessarily be abandoned as a result of an unplanned occurrence during turning (although much of course, depends on the nature of the occurrence). It was originally intended that the centre-piece would be of fairly small diameter, comprising a number of turned rings enclosing a small central plug. In the event however, the need to remove an unsuspected blemish in one of the segments required the platter to be turned more deeply on the inside than originally

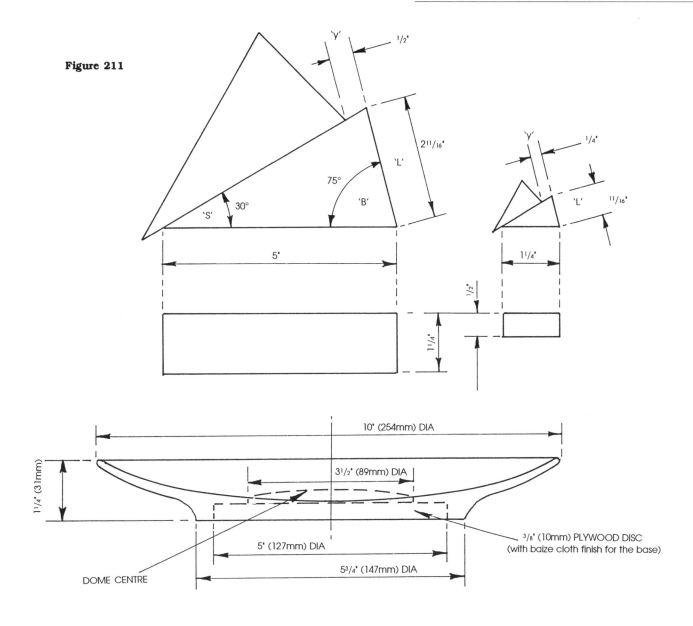

Figure 211

intended, with the result that the final sanding broke through the segment at the centre to reveal the plywood safety-base (Fig.212). In view of the fact that the profile of the bowl was almost flat at the centre, the segmentation was paper-thin over quite a large area. It was therefore necessary to turn away a rather larger central recess than intended and even so, the segment was little more than veneer-thickness at the periphery of the recess. A central plug following the original line (regardless of pattern) obviously carried the risk of further breakthrough, due to the inevitable need for further sanding after fitting the plug. Accordingly it was decided to employ a domed construction at the centre, and to sand both the bowl and the plug dead-smooth before assembly, to ensure that final finishing after fitting the plug didn't involve the removal of a significant amount of material. This in turn necessitated that the depth of the recess and the thickness of the plug at its periphery matched precisely (Fig.213).

The centre-piece is dimensioned in Fig.211 for convenience, but may of course take any desired form. That chosen was a similar non-radial assembly of twelve segments with interleaved veneer slips. It may be mentioned at this point that, given the time and effort involved in a moderately complex centre piece of this nature, it is worth making it two or three times as thick as needed. It may then

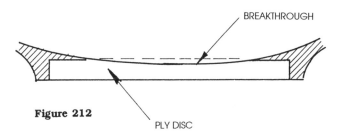

Figure 212

BREAKTHROUGH

PLY DISC

Figure 213

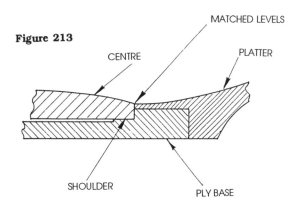

MATCHED LEVELS

CENTRE

PLATTER

SHOULDER

PLY BASE

be faced-off and turned to diameter and then bandsawn into two or three slices for use in further bowls or platters, as described in Chapter 5. This particular design, as it happens, carries a certain degree of risk. Obviously a recess and a plug, both divided into twelve precisely equal segments are bound to match at the circumferential joint between them, since the diameters are equal. Fine in theory, but practical assemblies are inclined to defeat theory by virtue of the fact that precision of this order is difficult to achieve; there is almost bound to be some unevenness between segments due to machining, assembly, or even lack of concentricity when mounting in the lathe. The only real solution would appear to be to attempt to disguise any slight inaccuracies by the interposition of a contrasting ring of timber at the joint. In this particular case, in view of the relatively large diameter of the plug, it was decided to glue a ring of veneer around it. Before this point in the proceedings however, some thought must be given to the method of turning the plug since it is very important that the piece retains its concentricity when it is returned to the lathe after veneering, since a little careful rim-sanding of the veneer is beneficial. Various chucking methods have been given in Chapters 8 and 9. It will be assumed here, for convenience, that a turned dummy spigot is employed, and that it remains attached to the plug until final assembly to the platter.

The plug is turned to the required diameter, ensuring that the edge is both straight, and dead-square to the face (if this is not carefully done, attachment of the veneer will be difficult, and final fitting into the recess of the platter even more so). The central hole in the plug must also be filled in some way. The method chosen in this piece (among others) was to turn a series of plugs in contrasting timbers, re-boring each in turn after gluing in place

(Fig.214). This operation may be performed either during the turning of the centrepiece or after it has been fitted to the platter. A great deal depends upon the equipment available: for example, a double-ended lathe is invaluable in work of this nature, since the bowl itself may be turned on the outboard side and the remaining piece on the inboard side, but given a little careful planning, it is by no means an essential requirement. It is, however, necessary to decide at the outset upon the diameter of all the plug pieces, and to make these as separate items to start with. The remainder of the operation consists of boring the recess and fitting each plug and re-boring as necessary (Fig.215).

The technique for gluing a thin annular ring around the periphery of a disc has already been described in essentials, in connection with the construction of drum-sanders (Chapter 6), and the reader is referred to this chapter for a full description. It is perhaps sufficient to state here that this is one case where hot-melt glue may be used in the assembly of a finished segmented project, as distinct from its many uses as a temporary fixing for jigs and the like. Its use is made possible by the fact that the adhesive may be heated through the veneer and the latter may therefore be permanently glued to the disc with the aid of glue-film and a domestic clothes-iron (Fig.216). Glue-film possesses the distinct advantage in this case, of allowing the gluing to take place piecemeal, rather than attempting to deal with the entire ring in one operation, as would be the case with other forms of adhesive. The veneer may be cut 'long-grain'; over this diameter it will assume the desired radius of curvature quite easily, and even the ends of the strip may be pulled-in tightly, despite the springiness of the veneer. Moreover, it will be less likely to break during assembly and will in any event, take

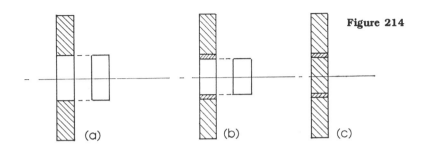

(a)   (b)   (c)

Figure 214

Figure 215

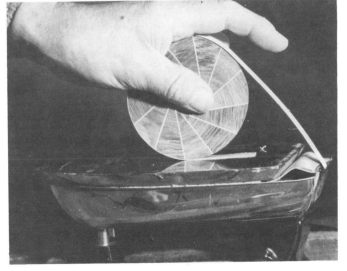

Figure 216

Figure 217

a much better finish eventually. The only real problem lies in the closure of the final joint. This should be carried out with a razor-blade or thin craft-knife, cutting through both the thicknesses at once. The inner scrap-piece may be removed by reheating the joint. It is important that the joint is a perfect butt-joint and does not leave a gap on final closure, since this will be all-too-evident in the finished piece. A useful dodge, particularly when closing a veneer ring, is to have a chunk of cold metal handy (a fairly hefty turning chisel or scraper will do nicely). After heating the veneer and melting the glue, rolling on the cold metal will cause rapid chilling and a practically instantaneous grip. This procedure may of course be carried out at any part of the proceedings, as needed.

The centre piece may be returned to the lathe and given most of its domed profile at this point, regardless whether its central plug assembly has been fitted or not. It is also necessary to ensure that the rear face is turned flush (i.e. with no lateral wobble) at this stage, for at least ¼" inwards from the periphery, in order to ensure that it seats firmly in the recess in the main bowl. The thickness of the ring in relationship to the recess should eventually allow it to sit just a little proud of the main bowl after gluing. Any unevenness in the base of the centrepiece must be accommodated by turning a secondary recess in the main bowl (Fig.213). Final finishing after gluing should need to be little more than a light scraping by whatever means is preferred. A chisel laid flat on the toolrest will do the job admirably and will not give rise to unscheduled deep bites into the work. One of the advantages of segmented work is that the grain pattern will stand for this type of finishing operation without exhibiting any rough patches. Finally the platter is slightly sanded all over, and finished as preferred. As a matter of interest, Fig.217 shows a hand-finishing (scraping) operation being performed. Much of the work illustrated in the book cannot, by virtue of its discontinuous nature, be finished on the lathe. A personal preference in these (and many other) cases, is for a two-part clear plastic coating, applied in several coats, rubbed-down between each with wet-and-dry abrasive sheet. The finish is also used where necessary, as a grain-filler, by applying several more coats in the appropriate places. The teak used in this project required considerable filling, with excess being removed as shown, with shaped scrapers ground from small pieces of high-speed steel hacksaw blade (a material which also furnishes excellent home-made craft knives.

PROJECT 2.   COOPERED WORK
(Biscuit barrel, tapered vase)

Figure 218

There is perhaps not a great deal of point in offering specific designs for parallel-stave coopered projects, since the final turned profile is very much a matter of individual taste, and the nature of the assembly tends to impose its own limit on internal and external profiles. In passing, one should be perhaps conscious of the possibilities of using such constructions for small, essentially cylindrical work, such as salt and pepper-mills, although no projects of this nature are offered here. It is suggested that small-diameter work is limited to about six staves, since anything greater than this number will lead to difficulties in making and assembly.

The large biscuit barrel illustrated in Fig.218 is a fairly typical example of the kind of work that can be extracted from offcuts. This is a twelve-stave construction in teak, with sycamore veneer slips between staves. Essential dimensions are given in Table 3. The parameters given in the table are those used in Chapter 2 and associated Nomograms (1-6). The lid is a birch-ply disc, veneered in teak on the underside and given a parquetry veneer pattern on the top. The rim is also veneered in teak, using the hot-melt technique described in Project 1. The base is of similar construction, but plain veneered on both sides. Both are, of course,

TABLE 3

Dimensions: Inches, Degrees

Parameter	Value
N	12
B	75
o (max)	$5^{7}/_{8}$
q (min)	$4^{7}/_{8}$
l	$1^{9}/_{16}$
i	$4^{23}/_{32}$
w	$5/_{8}$
h	6

Figure 219

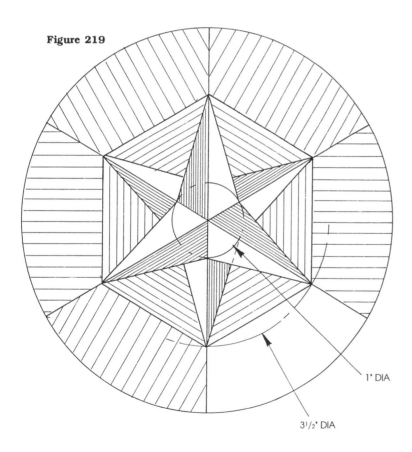

1' DIA

$3^{1}/_{2}$' DIA

recessed into the barrel. It is perhaps inappropriate to go into detailed discussion of decorative veneering of the type shown, but it is suggested that the chosen design is drawn accurately directly on the plywood, and the veneers cut directly over the design (quite easy with designs involving straight edges only), and assembled with glue-film (used for once for its primary purpose). Fig.219 gives details of the lid design.

The tapered stave project illustrated in Fig.220 is perhaps of more interest, since it is not only an unusual assembly, comprising five sides, but the combination of semi-flat and turned surfaces opens up a number of possibilities. Accordingly it is given the 'full treatment'. The dimensions given may also be used as check for a full exercise involving Nomograms 1–6. Before proceeding with the full design however, it may be noted that, where a mixture of faceted and turned work is involved, there may be some benefit in drawing both a plan and elevation, if only to gain some appreciation of the final appearance of the piece. Nomogram 8 will be found useful in this respect, since it aids in the construction of polygons of any reasonable number of sides inscribed within a circle of chosen diameter. It is necessary first to determine the centre-angle 'S', but this can be done from the simple formula included with the Nomogram.

All necessary dimensions are given in Table 4, and the general appearance of the piece in Fig.221. Note, however, that, in order to provide a flat base, the stave-length 'v' must be arranged to give a height 'h' rather greater than that finally required, since there is a need to turn away the inevitable waste at both ends, arising from the taper; this explains the difference between the values of 'h' on the drawing and the table. Stave construction and assembly is straightforward, using methods already given. It is suggested that work on the base

Figure 220

is carried out first, in line with the methods given in Chapter 8, and that, if possible, the base is then mounted on a metal hot-melt pallet to complete the turning. It will be necessary to insert a small axial-grain plug in the base, to complete the unbroken inner profile.

The outer facets may be left flat, or may be lightly sanded to a curve, as illustrated. It is not at all easy to fabricate a suitable jig for this purpose, particularly for constructions employing odd numbers of staves, but the operation is not too difficult to carry out freehand on a disc sander. Even so, the operation requires care, to ensure that all facets match reasonably well.

Figure 221

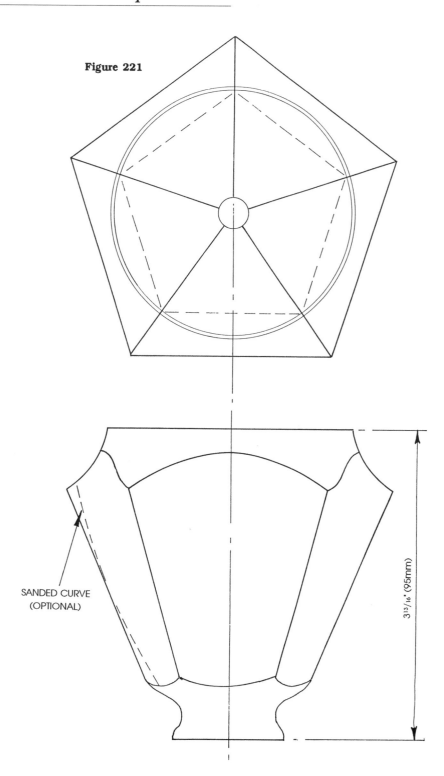

SANDED CURVE
(OPTIONAL)

$3^{13}/_{16}$" (95mm)

TABLE 4
Dimensions: Inches, Degrees

Parameter	Value
N	5
B	54
S	72
A	71
O_1	$4^1/_8$
O_2	$1^9/_{32}$
l_1	3
l_2	$15/_{16}$
q_1	3
i_1	$2^7/_{16}$
w	$7/_8$
h	$4^1/_8$
k	$1^7/_{16}$
D	66.9
C	56.2
v	$4^3/_8$

PROJECT 3. CURVED-SEGMENT WORK
(Platters, bowls)

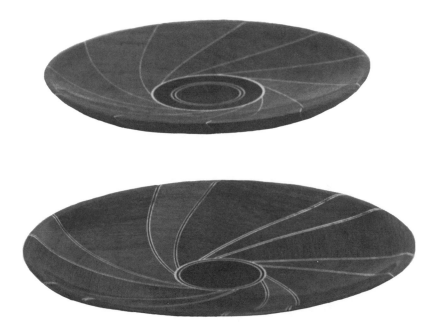

Figure 222

The preparation of segments for curved-segment work is not exactly the easiest of tasks. On the other hand it does offer considerable scope for decorative turnery and is, it is suggested, well worth the effort. The sawing, sanding and assembly of curved segments has been extensively covered in previous chapters, and it is on the basis of this information that the following designs are offered.

Fig.222 gives two examples of platter design, one employing two sets of six segments of different centre-angle, the other an apparently 'standard' form, but one which, on close inspection shows that it is comprised of eleven segments. Both designs are, in their original form, constructed from

teak offcuts of 4" (100mm) width and 1" (25mm) thickness; both are based upon a radius of curvature of 4" (100mm). Figs.223(a) and (b) give full design details for both arrangements, including the fence position 't' for the turntable jig necessary to cut the segments. Design procedure is that given in Chapter 2; the reader is invited to check the figures given in Fig.223 with reference to this chapter. Note that the only information required to give a full solution for any segment is that of stock width 'w', centre-angle 'S' (from which mitre-angle 'B' is easily derived), and the desired angular offset between segments 'P'. Note also that the width of the segments (4" (100mm) in this case) has no effect on the value of offset 'y' for any given angular

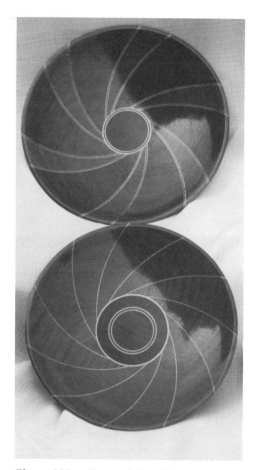

Figure 222a Upper platter show two sets of six
segments; lower platter shows eleven segments.

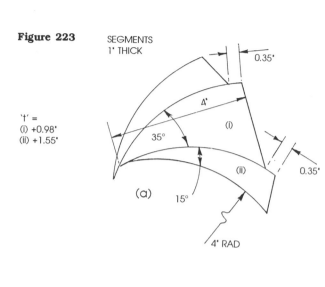

Figure 223

SEGMENTS
1" THICK

't' =
(i) +0.98"
(ii) +1.55"

(a)

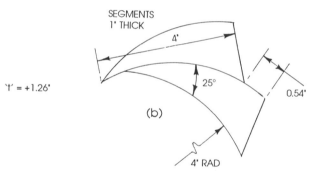

SEGMENTS
1" THICK

't' = +1.26"

(b)

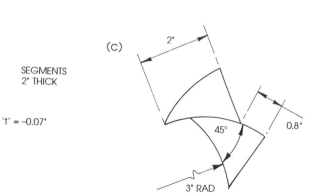

(c)

SEGMENTS
2" THICK

't' = –0.07"

relationship, but *does* affect the position 't' of the
sawing turntable fence. Assembly techniques are
given in Chapter 7. The inevitable central hole in
the assembly may be dealt with as described in
Project 1, by the insertion of either a single plug or
a series of plugs forming concentric rings. Work of
this kind benefits from the inclusion of veneer slips
between segments. Segments cut from 4" (100mm)
wide material will yield platters of about 6½" to 7"
(165 to 180mm) diameter. The assembly should of
course include a plywood shrinkage-protection disc.
Turning is straightforward.

Figure 225

Figure 226

The three designs offered in Fig.224 are all based upon the same construction; this particular set-up is very useful indeed for using up small offcuts. Full design details are given in Fig.223(c). In this case, the turnery can be quite interesting, because the relatively large offset 'y' and the small number of segments invites the use of the serrated outer edge of the construction as part of the design. In this case, some care must be given to the finish of the outer edges of the segments before assembly, since they are very difficult to deal with afterwards. By the same token, excess adhesive should be very carefully cleaned-off as soon as possible (certainly before it is fully set). Fig.225 shows one of the pieces being turned, and Fig.226 a rather fully-turned assembly. In this latter case, although the turning is not unduly difficult, the finished piece does look a trifle overdone, and is certainly of rather limited use as a receptacle. All designs require a central plug, and the use of shrinkage-protection discs is strongly advised, even for small pieces of this kind. The design as it stands will yield a bowl of about 4³/₄" (120mm) across the outer points.

Figure 224

PROJECT 4.   LAMINATED TURNERY
(Eggs, fruit, goblets etc.)

Figure 227

The assembly method comprising laminated triangles, described in Chapter 8. is essentially one of providing blanks for further turning and, in this sense, the finished blanks may be regarded in much the same light as solid pieces of timber with a distinctive and well-defined 'figure'. Although it pays to examine the figure of *any* turnery blank prior to commencing work on it, there is often considerable difficulty in visualising the final result. The laminated construction described, offers a particular advantage in this respect in that it will produce a result which is entirely predictable, since its design is regular. The effects of the juxtaposition of different timbers in successive layers of lamination is a rather different matter; this kind of knowledge (which applies to any form of segmentation or lamination), is only acquired by experience arising from previous successes and failures; it is also a very personal matter anyway, and it is therefore not possible to lay down hard-and-fast rules. It is however, possible to point out one or two essential characteristics of this particular form of construction, and to leave the reader to decide how best to apply them. Fig.227 shows a number of objects which feature the arrangement. Some of them have been produced entirely for photographic purposes, in order to demonstrate the effects obtainable. They are for this reason, somewhat overdone in terms of timber contrast; generally speaking, it is better to adopt a rather more restrained approach. Fig.228 shows the effect obtained by using the same timber type throughout, with contrasting veneer slips. No specific designs are offered; one can scarcely 'design' an apple or an egg; the final usage is therefore left to the reader.

Clearly, any finished 'blank' will, in its final assembled form, prior to turning, look like a solid piece of timber of whatever type comprises the outer layer; it is only by examining the end of the blank that one is able to perceive the nature of the construction (Fig.229). Further, if the blank is turned to a plain cylinder of precisely the maximum diameter allowed by the blank, it will still look like a solid piece. If it is turned down a little further, retaining the cylindrical profile, it will simply reveal plain stripes along its length as the second layer is revealed — a result which isn't particularly interesting. All this is perhaps obvious enough, but it is quite easy to fall into the trap of using such stock for a fairly plain piece of spindle-work, for example, which does not incorporate much in the way of diametral change; in this case, one may well end up with a result which doesn't do justice to the work involved in assembly of the blank. For example, the stem of a goblet will, in all probability, utilise only the centre-square of such an assembly. It is suggested therefore, that the best use of the construction is obtained from designs which feature significant diametral changes; in this way, the patterning available from the internal construction is revealed. Given smooth unbroken turned curves, the resultant pattern is that of a series of overlapping ellipses, or partial ellipses, with the semi-hidden layers appearing as 'mushrooms', or triangles with curved sides. Given the incorporation of discontinuities in the form of beads and coves, the shapes become rather more complex, but retain their basic characteristics. A hollow vessel such as a bowl or goblet will very rapidly reveal the essen-

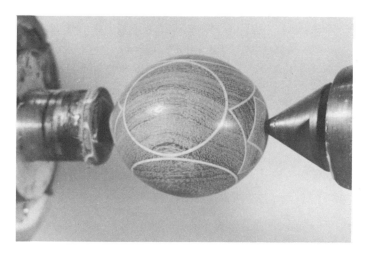

Figures 228 & 229

tial 'square-format' of the construction, as will a relatively flat base for, say, an eggcup.

To return to the goblet stem for a moment: aside from the fact that it makes no use whatsoever of the laminations, there seems to be little point in going to the trouble of assembling such a construction, only to turn most of it away. For this reason alone, there can be a fairly strong case for turning goblets in three parts, ie. a bowl, a base, and a stem, with the last-named in any suitable single piece of timber. Many workers have found ebony, in particular, to be highly suitable for applications of this kind, since it seems to combine well with most other timbers.

This type of lamination follows a 'power-series' (as mathematicians would term it). To the woodturner this simply means that the addition of any single layer is not simply like adding another layer to an onion; rather, each layer will make a significant increase in the overall size; constructions of this kind can get very big very quickly, and will be found to take the required timber well out of the realm of 'offcuts' after only four or five layers. The effect may be readily determined by freehand sketching on squared paper. It is therefore as well, before commencing a project, to be aware of the final required cross-sectional size, and to work from this backwards towards the centre (at least as an initial sketch), to determine the remaining sizes.

This may or may not result in a selection of dimensions which matches the available stock, but one will at least be aware of the likely result. If determination of sizes is made on an initial 'ad-hoc' choice of centre square, there could be two possible unpleasant consequences if the final piece is required to be of a specific diameter: first, a quite unnecessary loss of timber may result (Fig.230(a)); secondly, as a related effect, there will arise a rather poor 'pea-on-a-plate' pattern in the finished turning (b). There is, in fact, a strong case for determining lamination sizes on the basis of the final required pattern.

Although the lamination technique is excellent in terms of utilisation of offcuts (particularly the long thin ones), the decorative possibilities inherent in the construction may well lead to the occasional decision to convert a length of square-section stock into a laminated blank incorporating contrasting veneer slips, for example. In either case, it is as well to appreciate at the outset that there is absolutely no need for the outer layer to be made from full triangles, since the resultant square will inevitably be largely turned away (Fig.231(a)). Rather, they may be made from incomplete (technically 'truncated') triangles, whose thickness need be only a quarter of their base-length (b). This is in fact a fairly generous allowance as can be seen, but it is a convenient round-figure and, in most cases, a bandsaw-kerf could be subtracted from it without undue risk. If one is fairly sure of the final required appearance of the piece, it is possible to take matters a little further. For example, given that, for an ellipsoidal piece, the outer ellipses are required to have a distinct gap between them, the outer layer could be further reduced in both width and thickness. Such matters are best determined by drawing, or by freehand sketching on squared paper.

Figure 230

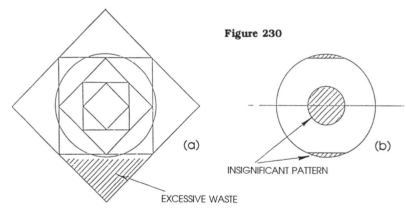

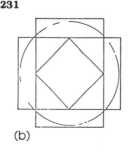

(a)

(b)

INSIGNIFICANT PATTERN

EXCESSIVE WASTE

Figure 231

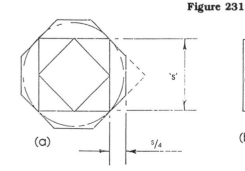

(a)

's'

$s/4$

(b)

PROJECT 5.   ELLIPSOID TURNING
(Cruets, small containers etc.)

The projects contained within this particular set are based upon a particular concept: that of turning spheres and 'ellipsoids of rotation' to a high degree of accuracy, albeit by essentially freehand methods. The first and most obvious question to be answered is 'why bother, if an effective result may be obtained purely by visual judgment?'. There are a number of possible answers, perhaps the most important being that many people simply cannot obtain an acceptable result by eye, in which case the method outlined here can be helpful. Moreover, it is one thing to turn a single piece, whatever its form; it is quite another to turn a pair or a set, which match in terms of dimensions and profile. Finally, a number of pieces to be described feature an ellipsoid which is seated in a matching recess; this is a very difficult operation to get away with by visual judgment alone.

As far as sphere (or ball) turning is concerned, some workers favour the 'swing-tool' principle, shown (in outline form only) in Fig.232. A jig of this nature is almost a 'must' for metalworkers desiring to turn a ball or a hemispherical recess, but for the woodworker, it is perhaps of somewhat limited value. In the first place, the attitude of the tool relative to the work is necessarily fixed, and unless extremely cunning methods of sharpening and mounting it are made, its action will be that of a scraper rather than a slicing tool. If this be the case, its action will be limited to fairly light cuts, which in turn demands at least some preliminary rough-turning by conventional methods. It is also necessary to provide some provision for feeding the tool into the work for successive cuts. This can be reasonably easily managed for recess-turning, since the entire assembly may be moved towards the headstock for successive cuts (b). It is less easy for the sphere since, in this case, some means of moving the cutter relative to the swing-tool jig itself must be provided; further, it is a fairly simple matter to position the pivot point of the device at a point laterally along the lathe axis such that it lies in a position which allows the cutter to embrace the blank; it is rather less easy to position the pivot precisely below the axis of the lathe, but this is the only position that will allow a perfect sphere to be turned. Any errors in this respect will tend to produce a final result tending towards either a Rugby football or a doughnut, dependent upon the nature of the error (shown in exaggeration in Fig.233). Finally, the degree of travel towards the headstock is limited to a greater or lesser extent, dependent upon design, since there will be a point at which some part of the device will come into contact with the headstock or the chuck, and this point may well occur before the profile is even reasonably complete. Given that accurate positioning over the lathe axis may be granted, the device does have distinct uses for the woodturner where hemispherical recesses are required, provided that these are rather less than a full hemisphere (ie. half a circle in profile), since the pivot cannot possibly

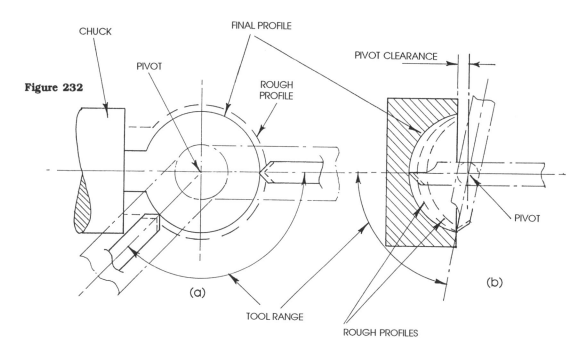

CHUCK

PIVOT

FINAL PROFILE

ROUGH PROFILE

PIVOT CLEARANCE

Figure 232

(a)

TOOL RANGE

(b)

PIVOT

ROUGH PROFILES

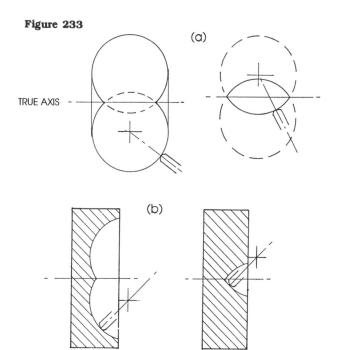

Figure 233

(a)

TRUE AXIS

(b)

lie inside the recess and must therefore be allowed some clearance (Fig.232(b)), at least for a simple swing-tool design, although rather exotic designs for 'imaginary' pivots do exist. Even so, the position of the tool relative to the pivot and the handle must be chosen with a fair degree of care, and the need to position the pivot precisely on the lathe axis remains pertinent.

At this point it might be as well to define an 'ellipsoid of rotation'. From the normal viewpoint of the turner, it is an object which presents an elliptical profile 'as seen' on the lathe, and a circular profile as viewed along the lathe axis. The ellipse itself has two axes, termed the 'major' and 'minor' axis respectively, and variation in the proportions of these two parameters can produce an infinite range of ellipses, all of which share the common property of being defined completely by a simple mathematical formula based upon the values of the two axes (the non-mathematical reader need not worry, since this particular problem will be taken care of). As can be seen from Fig.234, the range embraces two types of ellipsoid, of completely different character (from the turner's point of view), that shown in (c) being akin to an egg or a lemon, and that in (a) rather more like a tangerine or a slightly-flattened orange. At the changeover point between the two types of ellipsoid, the major and minor axes become equal (b); in this case, the resultant object is a sphere, (which is but a special case of the ellipsoid). Clearly, the swing-tool is quite useless for anything other than a sphere.

It is possible to turn both a full ellipsoid and a matching recess to a very high degree of accuracy, by entirely freehand methods. The trick lies in the provision of a series of precalculated guide 'steps' in the blank so that, when it is turned down such that these just disappear, an accurate profile is obtained. Fig.235 shows the general idea. In the case of the ellipsoid, the steps are formed with a parting tool or narrow chisel; for the recess, a square 'side-and-end' scraper must be used. In order to provide appropriate tool clearance in the case of the ellipsoidal solid, the smallest diameter is turned first, gradually working towards the larger. In the case of the recess, it is appropriate to very

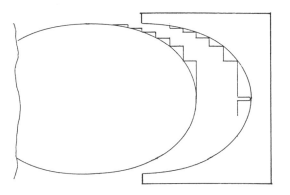

Figure 235

roughly hollow-out some of the waste (making quite sure not to overdo things), and then turn the steps down from the largest diameter to the smallest. Fig.235 shows that the same series of lateral and diametral steps may be used for both. It is of course necessary to calculate the diameters of the steps appropriate to the points on the blank at which they are turned. This is the function of Nomogram 10, which provides the required information for turned diameters between 1" and 10". Note that the Nomogram may be used to construct an 'ellipsoid of rotation' of any form, since is based upon an initial requirement to turn a cylinder of the required diameter and length, and then to divide the cylinder length into sixteen equal parts with

Figure 234

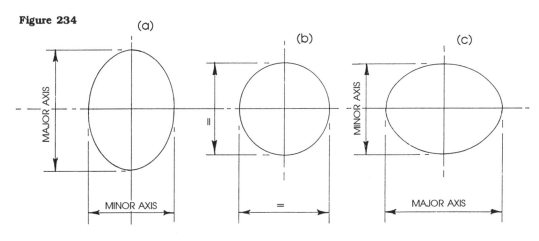

(a)   (b)   (c)

MAJOR AXIS

MINOR AXIS

MINOR AXIS

MAJOR AXIS

pencilled rings. In the case of the sphere, the length will equal the diameter; in the case of the ellipsoid it will be greater or less, dependent upon the type generated. These rings, which actually form the shoulders of the steps, may be mentally labelled 0, 1/8, 1/4, 3/8 etc., as shown in Fig.N10(a). The values are actually fractions of the overall length, whatever this may be. Note that, although the cylinder is divided into sixteen, only eight divisions bear corresponding diametral values, since the ellipsoid is obviously symmetrical about the half-way point.

Figure 236

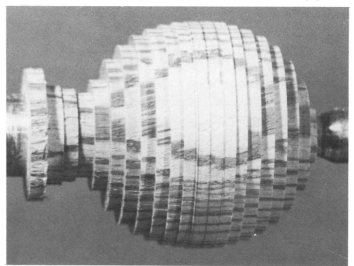

Figure 237

The Nomogram is used by selecting the required maximum diameter on the left-hand 'D' scale and, with this as a fixed reference point, using a straightedge against the values of 1/8, 1/4 etc on the right-hand 'N' scale to obtain the corresponding values of 'h' on the centre scale. These values provide the necessary caliper settings for the individual steps. It will be found convenient to work progressively from the smallest ('7/8') steps at both ends of the workpiece until the centre is reached. Note that, at this point, the two sectors at the centre remain untouched, since they both represent the full diameter of the piece.

It is now a fairly simple matter, if desired, to utilise the '1/16' divisions, and provide an even more finely-divided profile, by turning the outer half of each step down to the required diameter. If the ellipsoid is fairly small (say, less than 2" diameter) it will not be necessary to carry out this operation for all the steps; indeed it will rarely be necessary for those near the centre, regardless of the size of the piece. It will be found very useful at the extreme ends however, since the change in diameter between one step and the next increases quite rapidly as the ends are approached. There is one snag in this respect, as far as the Nomogram is concerned. It is not possible to include the '15/16' step on the Nomogram since for essentially mathamatical reasons, to do so would cause parts of the scales to become so cramped as to pose severe difficulties in using them accurately. One must therefore be prepared to carry out a small calculation for this one remaining value, which is simply to multiply the chosen maximum turned diameter by a factor of 0.35 to obtain the '15/16' step diameter. Thus, for a 1" max. turned diameter, the step diameter would actually be 0.35"; for a 2" diameter, the value would be 0.7", and so on. Fig.236 shows the appearance of a sphere turned in '1/8' steps. Fig.237 shows a similar sphere being turned to its final shape; in this case, a number of '¹/₁₆' steps have been included at the ends. It can be seen from Fig.238 that variation of the value of the lateral steps whilst retaining the same diametral values, can generate either an ellipse of any desired major/minor axis ratio, or a plain sphere. The drawing does not itself constitute rigorous proof, but this can be easily provided by mathematics.

When making the divisions of the cylinder, it may well be that these turn out as awkward values. For example, an ellipsoid required to be say, 2⁵/₈" long, will require each division to be 0.164" wide — not the easiest of measurements to make sixteen times along a cylinder. The matter is easily dealt with by adapting a very old schoolboy dodge for dividing an awkward length into any number of equal divisions. The idea is shown in Fig.239, where the width 'w' is required to be so divided (the actual value of 'w' being unimportant). A rule is laid across the workpiece such that the two extremities of the latter are exactly aligned with the required number of conveniently-read divisions on the rule. A line is drawn against the rule, and the divisions marked such that they just touch the line. The intersections of the marks with the line will thus divide the width 'w' into the required number of divisions. It is then a simple matter to use a mortise gauge, or

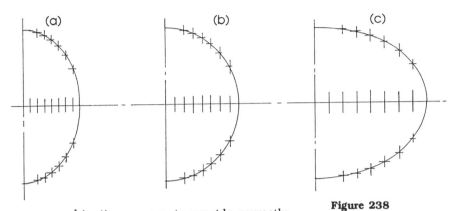

Figure 238

even a combination square, to provide correctly-spaced parallel lines along the length of the workpiece. The same idea may be transferred to the marking of the cylinder in the lathe as shown in (b) and Fig.240, by taking a strip of self-adhesive gummed label (the kind with a peel-off backing) and marking sixteen equal divisions at a convenient value, slightly larger than that required. The strip is wrapped around the cylinder such that its two extreme ends coincide exactly with the squared-off end-cheeks of the cylinder. The cylinder must, incidentally, be turned parallel along its entire length in order to permit the strip to seat properly and should also be provided with a short stub at each end to allow headstock and tailstock support. The marks on the paper may now be transferred to the cylinder. The paper strip is peeled off, and the

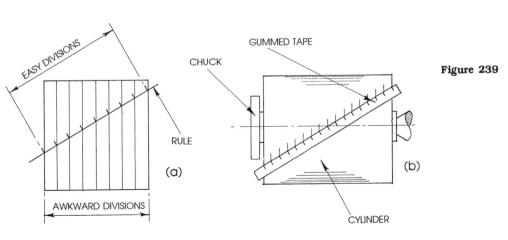

Figure 239

marks used to draw a series of pencilled rings around the cylinder. This particular operation is best made by turning the lathe over by hand, with the pencil firmly held against the toolrest in the appropriate position. It is not easily done with the lathe running, since the initial marks may not be readily observed with sufficient accuracy.

The steps are readily cut with a parting-tool, and there is some advantage in taking the last shaving or two one-handed, and allowing the calipers to drop over the work (Fig.241). This approach tends to minimise the risk of overcutting the steps, but is of course, dependent upon the skill of the turner. Turning is completed by removing all the corners, by whatever turning technique is preferred (Fig.237). It is assumed for the moment that the piece is to be turned as an unblemished display-piece, ie. with no holes or spigots, and is therefore required to have both ends accurately profiled and well finished. As a practical matter, it is advisable to support the workpiece with the tailstock for most of the procedure, removing the latter only to finish-off the outer end. Tailstock support may be provided by a normal cone live-centre, but there is much to be said for the use of a 'ring-centre' with the centre-point removed as shown in Fig.242(b); this will provide firm support without risk of indenting the workpiece at the axis.

This still leaves the problem of the chuck-end to be dealt with, and it is at this point that a further jig is required. A convenient device is the clamp-plate jig illustrated and described in Chapter 9. Given, however, that even a small hole in one end is not permitted, it may be necessary to shape the clamp-plates to suit the end-profiles of the workpiece. A second method, which works for the sphere only, but one which is capable of providing an excellent result, is illustrated in Figs.243 and 244. It comprises two hollow cone-centres, one in the headstock

Figure 240

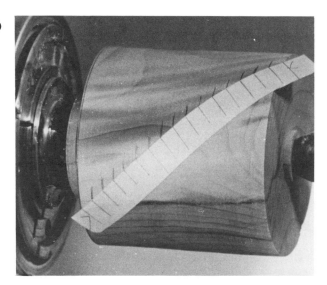

Figure 241

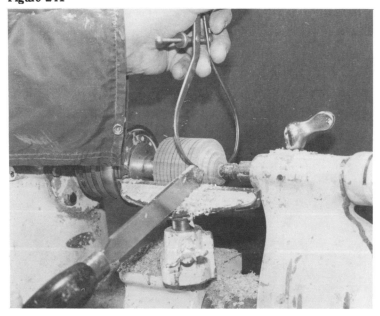

and one in a revolving tailstock. The workpiece is parted-off from the parent stock, and is mounted between the cone centres with the stub-end approximately in the centre. Given that the sphere has been accurately turned to begin with, it is now a relatively simple matter to turn away the stub-end, albeit with a little care, since the waste material will only be visible as a ghost-image on the revolving work. This particular operation must be regarded as the 'acid-test' of previous turning. In passing, it is possible to turn away two stub ends, from which it follows that the tailstock-end need not be finished-off as part of the first operation and indeed, if required, the initial turning may be performed between centres. There is some advantage in this process, since the extreme ends of the workpiece are the most difficult to handle, not so much from the actual turning point of view as from the difficulty in judging the true profile at these points. To begin with, there will necessarily be a fairly large flat area at the ends from which the required profile will need to be deduced; secondly, the presence of a mounting-stub (at either end) will render the judgment that much more difficult. Given that the sphere has been turned accurately it will, when repositioned in the cone-centres and the lathe started-up, still show a perfect spherical profile, against which the stub ends may be turned away with confidence. On no account should a 'between centres' set-up be used for supporting the hollow-cone centres for final turning, since the arrangement is only 'conditionally-stable'; that is, it will only run safely if all parts are in perfect alignment (fairly unlikely), but in any event, any pressure on the sphere will, in all probability, cause the whole assembly to fly apart. The cone centres must be fixed such that they run as integral parts of the headstock and tailstock respectively. Once the turning is complete, the sphere

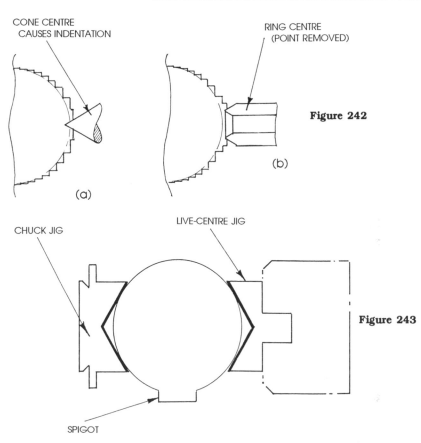

Figure 242

Figure 243

Figure 244

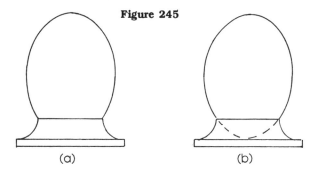

Figure 245

(a)   (b)

may be sanded with successively finer grades of abrasive, until the desired finish is obtained. It is of course possible to re-align the sphere by hand between the centres (with the lathe stopped) to present different surfaces to the work, thus ensuring even sanding all over, in several directions. The work may even be finished with friction and/or wax polish in this way. The final result should be as near-perfect a sphere as can reasonably be expected from essentially freehand work.

As previously noted, it is possible to mount such objects (whether they be cruets, bowls or whatever) on bases which reveal their shape. This particular line of thought demands a little further explanation: any plain-turned object, if mounted flat on a base of some kind, may be so positioned simply by

initially providing it with a flat face to suit the base. To the observer, it would make no difference whatsoever if this technique were employed or the rather more difficult one of turning a recess in the base to match the curvature of the object itself; the final result would appear the same in both cases (Fig.245). It is possible to use methods which do however, at least suggest that the base of the object is not itself flat, but is in fact a continuation of its profile. This particular idea will be developed in a little more detail later, but is shown in its simplest outline form in Fig.246. Such an approach requires the base to be turned with a recess which exactly matches the profile of the object, and this can only be done with some pre-knowledge of the required profile. One might argue that a template could be made to do the job in both cases, but it is quite difficult (in the absence of special equipment) to draw an ellipse of predetermined dimensions. Use of the Nomogram will, in general, dispense with the need for templates of this kind but, in the rare cases in which it may be found necessary or convenient, the Nomogram itself may be used to generate a card or acrylic sheet template. The method here is to mark a centre line and a series of parallel lines at right angles to it, their spacing being that of the lateral steps in the turned solid; this may be done as illustrated in Fig.238. A pair of dividers set to *half* the diametral values given by the Nomogram is located on the centre line and used to mark the profile limits on their respective lines. The points are joined, preferably with the aid of draughtsman's 'French curves', and the template cut, sawn or filed to the indicated profile.

The only snag with regard to non-spherical profiles is that the concave-cone chucks cannot be used to turn away any spigots left by the primary turning, since these require an essentially spherical profile at the point of contact between cone and

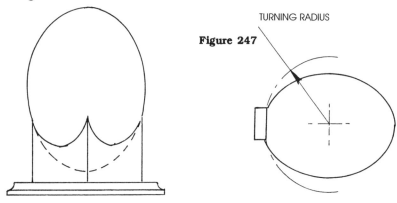

Figure 246

Figure 247

TURNING RADIUS

workpiece; moreover, even if this could be managed, the required ellipsoidal profile cannot be generated by normal hand turning methods (Fig.247). On the other hand, the clamp-plate jig described in Chapter 9 can be used. Both the 'lemon' and the 'tangerine' profiles may be dealt with in this way, albeit with the possible need to provide suitably profiled clamp-cheeks. Their shape will actually tend to resist any tendency for angular drift during turning, although the tangerine profile may be a little more difficult in this respect, and for complete safety, may require location with a central pin.

It is of course possible to finish off the free end of any ellipsoid during the primary turning process, in which case it might be sensible to delay turning the chuck-end down to the last step, in order to provide sufficient strength at this point to eliminate wobble. To begin with, the free end should have the tailstock spigot turned away exactly flush with the outer face of the last step, and a series of light pencilled rings, with a dot at the centre, made on the end face with the lathe running. These have no real dimensional value, but will provide some assistance with the formation of the correct profile; the final dot should still be visible on completion. The other end may be parted-off in the same way, exactly flush with the outer face of the last step; it may then be mounted in the cramping-plate jig for final finishing. There is one very important point to be observed during freehand sanding of the end of the workpiece. As one approaches the centre, the effect of the abrasive is markedly reduced, since the peripheral speed of the work relative to the abrasive is also necessarily reduced — in fact at the precise centre there is no relative movement at all. Even if the abrasive is moved to and fro across the end, the effect will tend to remain. The net effect of careless sanding therefore is to tend to produce a

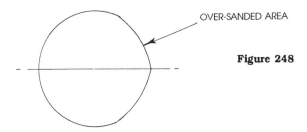

OVER-SANDED AREA

Figure 248

profile of the kind shown in Fig.248.

Having established a technique for turning ellipsoids, there remains the problem of what to do with them. In many cases the figure of the timber, or the nature of any segmentation or lamination technique employed on the base stock, will allow the pieces to stand in their own right as purely decorative non-functional objects. It is suggested however, that small pieces of the order of 2" diameter or so lend themselves particularly to cruets, since they are comfortable to handle. Any practical design of cruet must be carried out with reference to getting the appropriate condiment in at one end and out of the other, the former requirement tending to dictate the shape to some extent, due to the need to incorporate a bung of some kind. The designs offered are based upon a commercially available rubber bung, its essential dimensions being given in Fig.249. It is obviously necessary to commence proceedings with a hole at one end of the piece. Clearly this can be done from the tailstock prior to finishing and parting-off the piece in the

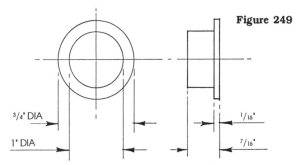

Figure 249

³/₄" DIA

1" DIA

¹/₁₆"

⁷/₁₆"

Figure 250

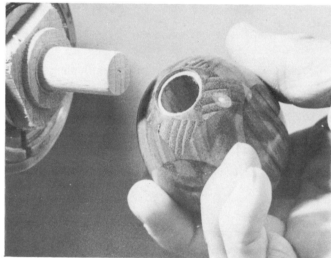

Figure 251

Figure 252

first place. Incidentally, this requirement is effectively implemented by drilling out most of the waste with twist-drills, and finally using a Forstner-style bit to bore out the hole to precisely the required diameter (Fig.250). All remaining work may be carried out with a home-made pin-chuck, as illustrated in Fig.251. If the pin-chuck is carefully turned, it may be possible to rely entirely on a friction-drive between pin-chuck and workpiece, a particular advantage conferred by using a Forstner bit to bore the hole. The free end may now be bored and shouldered to receive a turned insert for pouring purposes, or may simply be drilled with one or more small holes, dependent upon whether the cruet is to be used for salt or pepper.

Fig.252 illustrates an effective method of drilling a number of equally-spaced small holes in the end of a pepper cruet. The arrangement comprises a scrap wood block, cramped to a suitable toolrest, drilled with a small guide hole of suitable diameter; this is then used to drill the required holes in the workpiece. It is of course necessary for the lathe headstock to be fitted (or provided) with angular indexing. A common error when making cruets is to make the pouring-holes too large, resulting in the unfortunate diner swamping the food with condiments. The single hole for salt should be no greater than 2mm, and those for the six or so pepper-holes no greater than 1.5mm (even these are quite generous).

Regardless of the actual shape of the base, it is suggested that it is attached to the body of the cruet by means of a turned hardwood sleeve. This may be bored-out with a Forstner bit to suit the diameter of the rubber bung, and the outer diameter turned by hand to give an easy push-fit in the bored hole in the body. Fig.253 shows the arrangement which, for the projects offered, is used as a standard assembly method regardless of the pro-

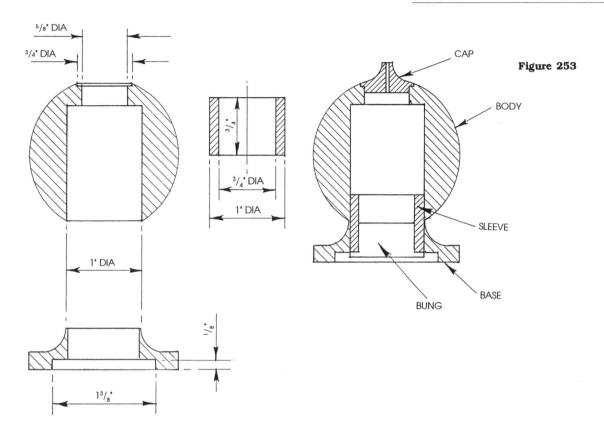

Figure 253

file of the body or the base. It allows a great deal of latitude with regard to the turned profiles, whilst providing a very robust joint. The wood for the sleeve should be chosen with some care, in that it is required to yield a good finish straight from the boring and subsequent parting-off operations, otherwise the base of the piece will tend to look a little rough when viewed from the underside. Yew is a particularly useful timber in this respect. When turning the base, the underside is prepared first, inclusive of a shallow recess to enable the lip of the bung to lie within the base profile, and also to provide the finger-gap essential to removal of the bung.

Three methods of reversal of the base on the lathe headstock (after boring and recessing) are offered. Perhaps the simplest is to mount the base on a hot-melt metal pallet in conjunction with a suitable home-made locating disc. Alternatively the base may be mounted on a stub pin-chuck. Finally, a rather more wasteful method is to use a larger blank, which is provided with a suitable combination-chuck spigot at the same time as the boring and recessing operations are carried out. This is then used to remount the work, and is eventually parted-off; the success of this particular method does however require the diameter of the internal recess to be appreciably smaller than that of the spigot. All three methods are shown in Fig.254.

The simplest form of base is that shown in Fig.253 but, with a little extra effort, a base can be made which shows the profile of the body to advantage. It comprises a matching recess which is cut

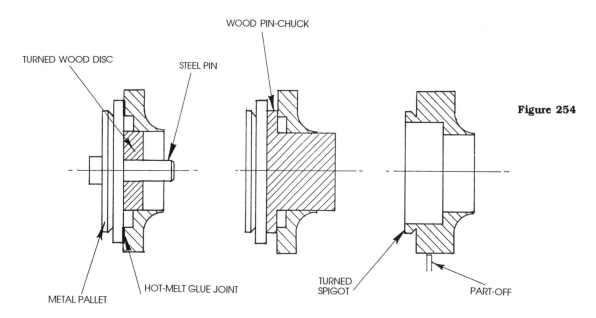

WOOD PIN-CHUCK

TURNED WOOD DISC

STEEL PIN

Figure 254

METAL PALLET

HOT-MELT GLUE JOINT

TURNED SPIGOT

PART-OFF

away on the outside to form a scalloped holder. That indicated in Fig.246 is of square planform, and is designed to match a four-sided laminated pattern on the body but in principle, it can comprise any convenient number of sides. The essential feature of the technique is to turn the recess in a solid piece of stock and to form the scallops and points in the base by sawing and sanding to a square external plan-profile afterwards. This particular exercise is a fairly simple one, but the general idea will be encountered again in a rather more difficult form, involving off-centre turnery, in another project series. An essential requirement is that the turner is prepared to trust the accuracy of his or her own work since, for best results, the profiles of body and recess must match closely, and there is no really effective method of making a direct comparison by trial-fits of the body, during the turning of the recess. A gap at the rim is readily detected; a gap on the inside will only be revealed after the outer profile has been formed, and will lead to a rather sub-standard result, since there is

no really safe way of correcting matters. However skilful the turner, the points are (or should be) so delicate that any further turning of the inner profile will almost certainly damage them; one must bear in mind that the nature of this particular error (which is essentially that of overcutting the lower part of the profile) *will* demand modification of the points. Herein lies a significant part of the usefulness of the Nomogram method. Provided that the Nomogram steps are turned accurately in both body and recess, and the subsequent turnery removes the waste only to the point where the 'corners' disappear, and no further, the two halves will match. It is also quite helpful that the same set of Nomogram values may be used for both the body and the recess. The stepped profile of the body may be dealt with by calipers, but that of the recess demands a little extra thought. It is of course, not practicable to mark the inside of the recess with a series of pencilled rings to indicate the depth of the steps, and some form of depth-gauge is thus called for. This can be a very simple affair comprising a straight rectangular section bar of any suitable material, including wood, plus a length of $^1/_8"$ diameter mild steel rod (Fig.255). Some form of locking device is useful; in its simplest form this could be a wood screw with the point ground away to give a rounded end. If the rod is arranged to be a moderately tight fit in the bar however, the locking device may be dispensed with. Setting the rod to the required depth-steps can be difficult if awkward dimensions are involved (and they invariably will be), but it is perfectly feasible to utilise the method of generating a number of equal divisions described earlier and construct a series of pencilled lines on a sheet of card, or better still, a series of fine scribed lines on a sheet of acrylic, against which the depth-gauge may be set. Given that it is intended at the outset to provide a matching body and recess, there is some advantage to be gained from making a set of diametral-step templates in acrylic sheet, at least for the '$^1/_8$' steps. This particular dodge has the advantage of embodying any minor diametral errors in *both* matching halves, since the templates may be used to check the recess diameters directly, and may also be used to set the calipers for turning the body.

Three typical projects are now offered, together with all necessary dimensions. The reader is invited to check the figures in the tables against the Nomogram, in order to acquire practice in reading the latter. The ellipsoid profile of Fig.256 and Table 5 may be used either with a simple flat base, or the rather more difficult scalloped base of Fig.257, both designs being illustrated in Fig.258. The dimensions given in both drawings will match those of the ellipsoid. Note that Fig.257 shows the two initial turned step-diameters missing, since it is not necessary to bring the scalloped points too far up the profile of the body; to do so would render them rather vulnerable to damage. Note also that

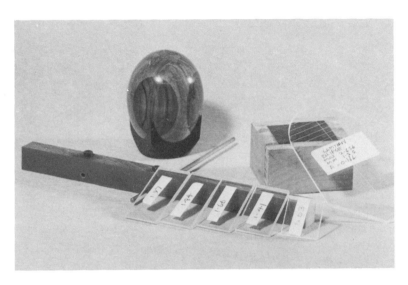

Figure 255

the diameter of the 'second-step' is not actually cut into the base but rather, is indicated by a scribed line, thereby providing a line at the outer rim which indicates the maximum turned diameter. In this particular design, the remaining six steps of 0.166" each add up to almost exactly one inch (0.996"), thereby fixing the depth of the recessed part of the base. In view of the fact that small turned items of this nature are frequently made in expensive timbers, the turning of a recess followed by removal of much of the timber to form the outer profile will result in unwanted waste of material. The problem is easily dealt with by initially preparing the base stock exactly to size, and then gluing a number of slips of equal thickness (in less-expensive timber) to the outer edges. Upon completion of the turning, the slips may be sawn and sanded away to return to the parent stock. The appearance of the base may be further modified in either or both of two ways: the flanks may be sanded at an angle as shown in Fig.257, and/or the corners part-turned away using a normal 'square-to-round' turning technique. The idea of glued-on slips of this kind

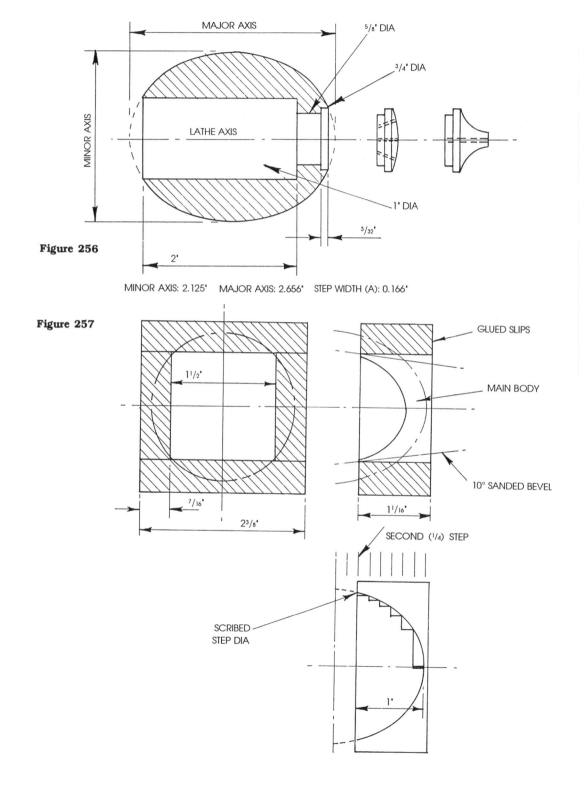

Figure 256

MAJOR AXIS

MINOR AXIS

LATHE AXIS

5/8" DIA

3/4" DIA

1" DIA

3/32"

2"

MINOR AXIS: 2.125"   MAJOR AXIS: 2.656"   STEP WIDTH (A): 0.166"

Figure 257

1 1/2"

7/16"

2 3/8"

GLUED SLIPS

MAIN BODY

10° SANDED BEVEL

1 1/16"

SECOND (1/4) STEP

SCRIBED
STEP DIA

1"

1/8 STEPS	1/16 STEPS	DIA
	1	2.121
1		2.108
	2	2.087
2		2.058
	3	2.019
3		1.970
	4	1.911
4		1.840
	5	1.757
5		1.659
	6	1.543
6		1.406
	7	1.239
7		1.029
	8	0.739
8		0

TABLE 5

Figure 258

does bring with it one or two further distinct advantages. First, if the outer slips are provided in a timber of fairly sharply contrasting colour, the shape of the scallops may be observed directly as the recess is turned (Figs.259 and 260). Rather more importantly, they provide a ready means of identifying the sawing and sanding lines for the final outer profile. In general, it is far easier to mark out and cut a planform, whether it be square, hexagonal or whatever, in a solid block of wood, than to attempt to do the same thing after finishing the recess. The latter operation will necessarily form the points as the sides are sawn, rendering them rather vulnerable, but in any case it is simply not possible to mark out the planform on the top face, since there is, by definition, no timber available to mark it on; this means that the marking out must be made on the underside, and the sawing carried out with only the points left in contact with the machine-table as they are produced — a somewhat risky operation. All things considered, the method offered is perhaps the safest.

Figures 259 & 260

TABLE 6

¹/₈ STEPS	¹/₁₆ STEPS	DIA
	1	2.246
1		2.232
	2	2.210
2		2.179
	3	2.137
3		2.086
	4	2.023
4		1.949
	5	1.860
5		1.756
	6	1.634
6		1.488
	7	1.312
7		1.089
	8	0.783
8		0

Figure 261

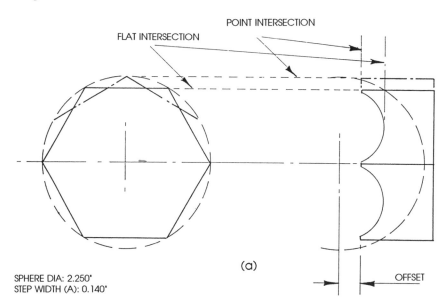

POINT INTERSECTION

FLAT INTERSECTION

(a)

SPHERE DIA: 2.250"
STEP WIDTH (A): 0.140"

OFFSET

A second project of similar nature, but featuring a plain sphere in a hexagonal 'coronet' base is given in Fig.261. Nomogram steps for the spherical body are given in Table 6. The sphere is provided with a standard sleeve-fitting and a suitable pouring cap as previously described. As a slight digression, it must be pointed out that it is somewhat risky to guess the depth of the scallops, since the result may turn out somewhat different from that intended. It is a very simple matter to make a construction of the form shown in (a). This essentially comprises a plan drawing of the full sphere diameter, with a hexagon (or other desired profile) inscribed within it. The top of the drawing shows one of the 'flats', but superimposed upon this is a further part-drawing, showing one of the 'points'. The side-elevation also comprises a circle drawn to the full sphere diameter, and the planned amount of 'offset' (ie. the amount by which the base recess falls short of a full hemisphere). Horizontal lines

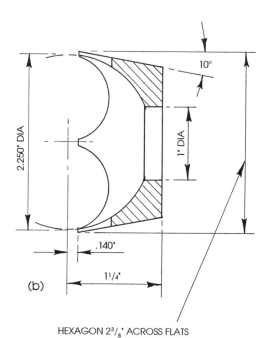

10°

2.250" DIA

1" DIA

.140"

1¹/₄"

(b)

HEXAGON 2³/₈" ACROSS FLATS

Figure 262

are now drawn from the plan, at the 'flat' and the 'point' of the hexagon. The intersection of these with the circle on the elevation indicates the upper and lower limits of the scallops. The depth of the scallops will actually be increased somewhat if the flanks are subsequently sanded to an angle, but this can be disregarded if only a fair idea of the scallop depth is wanted. Full dimensions for the base are given in (b), and Fig.262 shows the completed piece.

The 'tangerine' type of ellipsoid does not lend itself particularly to the scalloped-base technique, partly because the profile leads to rather unimpressive 'points', and also because the flattened shape of the body doesn't really allow them to be seen anyway; it follows that the work involved in providing a scalloped base is perhaps worthy of a better cause. Pieces of this kind tend to look a little better with a pedestal base. It might also be said that this particular ellipsoid style is better suited to small containers rather than cruets although, given a suitable protective finish, a mustard-pot might be a possibility. A design for a small container using a relatively slender stem base, together with a twelve-stave body construction, is given in Fig.263 and Table 7, and illustrated in Figs.258 and 264. The coopered stock is made in one piece, and sawn in two to provide the two half-shells; in this way, the segmented design will match when they are re-fitted. The inside profile does not in this case have to be particularly exact; the Nomogram steps may therefore be used to generate a template, from which the inside profile may be turned. There is a small trap inherent in the type of jointed lid/base construction shown: the depths of the two halves are unequal, by an amount equal to the depth of the stepped joint; this must be duly noted when preparing the blanks. The two halves are mounted on separate lathe mandrels (preferably of the metal hot-melt variety), and the insides turned-out and the joint made such that the two halves fit without play between them whilst being turned. Small holes (about ¼" diameter) are also drilled in the ends at this time. One of the pair is then divested of its mandrel, and the other mounted in the lathe chuck. The pair are held together whilst turning the outside by pressure from a live-centre in the tailstock. The base and knob are merely indicative of the type which may be provided, and may be made to choice.

Figure 263

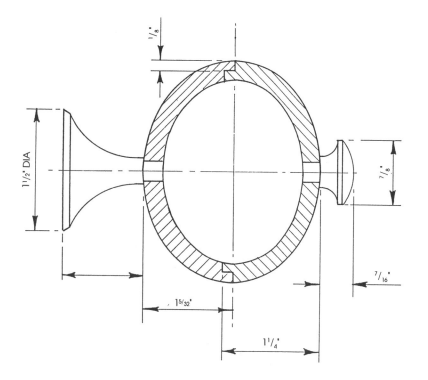

TABLE 7

1/8 STEPS	1/16 STEPS	INNER DIA	OUTER DIA
	1	2.246	2.745
1		2.232	2.728
	2	2.210	2.701
2		2.179	2.663
	3	2.137	2.612
3		2.086	2.549
	4	2.023	2.473
4		1.949	2.382
	5	1.860	2.274
5		1.756	2.147
	6	1.634	1.997
6		1.488	1.819
	7	1.312	1.603
7		1.089	1.331
	8	0.783	0.957
8		0	0

OUTER MAJOR AXIS: 2.750"
MINOR AXIS: 2.312"
INNER MAJOR AXIS: 2.250"
MINOR AXIS: 1.875"
OUTER STEP WIDTH: 0.145"
INNER STEP WIDTH: 0.117"

Figure 264

PROJECT 6.   THREE-AXIS TURNING
(Twelve-facet containers with lids)

An interesting way of driving oneself slightly crazy is to attempt to visualise the following problem: take a perfect cube, and bore three holes, one on each of the mutually perpendicular axes, such that all three intersect at the exact centre of the cube, one face of which is shown in Fig.265. What is the shape of the resultant 'hole-in-the-middle' (ie. the central void formed by, and common to, all three holes? Only marginally less difficult is the problem of taking a cube, and turning it to a 'cylinder' of the same diameter as the side-length of the cube, again on each of the three mutually perpendicular axes (as far as this can be managed). The resultant shape is the same in both cases, but in the second

it is at least possible to make an artefact of this shape and stick it on the mantelpiece. Equally puzzling perhaps is the depiction of the piece as a standard 'plan and two elevations', as shown in Fig.266, which shows, in an admittedly somewhat contrived arrangement, all three views as being identical. Whilst these are of no great help in visualising the piece, they do, somewhat surprisingly perhaps, contain all the necessary information; all that is necessary is to extract it by normal engineering drawing methods (albeit with some degree of head-scratching). The two auxiliary views shown in (d) and (e) were obtained this way. Even these two views, helpful though they are, convey a

Figure 265   **Figure 266**

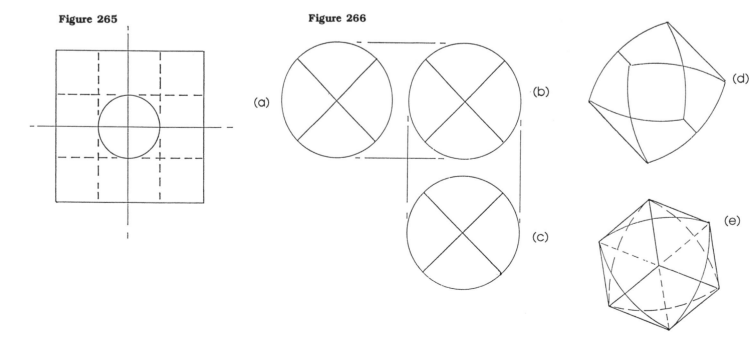

(a)   (b)   (c)   (d)   (e)

Figure 267

Figure 268

Figure 269

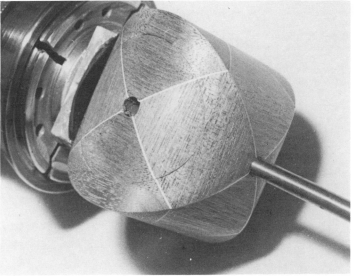

limited amount of visual information, and indeed perhaps the only really satisfactory way of appreciating the shape is to see it as a solid, although a photograph is a fair second-best (Fig.267).

It is not too difficult to make such a piece by normal freehand turning methods; in fact the actual turning process is quite easy, although it necessarily involves a degree of intermittent cutting. The real difficulty lies in making the headstock and tailstock chucks such that they drive and grip the workpiece with accuracy and safety. Initially, one makes a cylinder of length equal to its diameter. The cylinder is then re-mounted in the lathe such that its axis is at right angles to that of the lathe and turned again to a cylinder of the same diameter as the first. The workpiece is then re-mounted in the lathe such that both previously-used turning axes are at right angles to the lathe axis, and again turned to a cylinder, thereby producing the final shape. Figs.268 and 269 show the first two turning stages.

Individual turners will doubtless have their own preferences with regard to the tools used but, regardless of method, it is suggested that the length of the cutting-edge should be quite small. All things considered, a parting-tool of about $3/16$" width (*not* the kind with a hollow ground along one edge) does the job satisfactorily. Rough-turning is accomplished by pushing the tool into the work in a series of steps. As the final diameter is approached, the tool may be used to produce a slicing cut by angling it slightly and moving it sideways a little at a time (Fig.270). Even with a conventional slicing cut, the tool should be off-the-bevel, otherwise it will simply bump along the work. It is as well to bear in mind that much of the cutting will be against the grain in places, in addition to being intermittent, hence the need for a fairly cautious approach. Under no circumstances should a scraper be used since it will merely succeed in damaging the work. It is not easy to observe the progress of the tool directly against the workpiece and it is of course not possible to check

Figure 270

with calipers on the revolving work. In general it is better to observe the ghost-image at the back of the revolving workpiece and 'feel' the progress of the cutting-edge rather than watch it. The turning process should bring the work down to a little over the finished size. Abrasive sheet is required to determine the final size, as well as providing the necessary finish. Even the sanding process requires special attention; the abrasive must be used with a flexible backing, such as the very thin 3-ply used by model makers. This should be about 8" long and 3" wide with the grain running across its width, to offer sufficient flexibility to enable it to be curved around the workpiece.

The sanding process must be used to bring each of the three 'cylinders' to precisely matching diameters, since this is crucial to the appearance of the finished piece. If this stage of the work is done well, the natural edges between adjacent facets will meet at a blunt point at the centre (Fig.271(a)); any discrepancies will show up as a kind of 'tennis-ball' effect at the centre (b). There very little room for error in this respect. As an example, for a piece of $2^{1}/_{2}$" diameter, a discrepancy of $1/_{32}$" between any two diameters will produce a gap 'g' of over $1/_{4}$". A similar effect occurs if the work is mounted off-centre at any point during the exercise. Since it is necessary to produce a good result on six faces, it

Figure 271

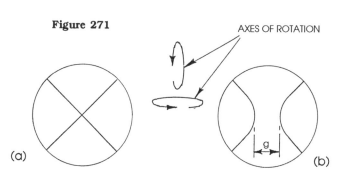

(a)   (b)

is clear that some care is required. It is, however, possible, given the rather blunt nature of the point, to cheat a little after the work is removed from the lathe, by a little preferential hand-sanding.

The real difficulty lies in the mounting of the work in the lathe. A plain cylinder is simple enough; after that, matters get a little tricky. Fig.272 is included for one very good reason; it appears to be an apparently sound mounting-method for second and third-stage turning, but this is positively *not* the case. The arrangement comprises a pair of 'vee' blocks one at each end (tailstock end not shown, for clarity), and was indeed used for 'first attempts'. However, there are a number of problems with the arrangement: first, it is necessary to mount the workpiece in the blocks such that it is accurately-centred with respect to the length of the 'vee' (c). For the second-stage turning of a cylinder, this is in fact sufficient, provided that the workpiece can be persuaded to remain in this condition throughout the turning process (by no means guaranteed). For the third-stage turning however, it is also necessary to ensure that the workpiece is set up in the correct orientation with respect to the lathe axis, so that the final facets are produced in exactly the right place. This is a rotational adjustment, and is fairly difficult to visualise, but if the workpiece shown in Fig.267 were imagined to be rotated slightly prior to turning, the job would clearly be ruined. The requirement thus imposed is that of making two simultaneous adjustments. This is difficult enough in all conscience, but if one adds to it the possibility that, during turning, the workpiece can 'walk' in the vee-blocks in either of these two modes, sufficiently perhaps to fly out of the lathe altogether, one has a real problem. Matters aren't exactly helped by the fact that the turning process makes it necessary to turn-down the vee-blocks to the same diameter as the workpiece simply in

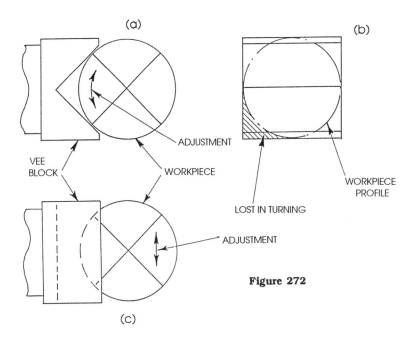

Figure 272

order to complete the turning on the latter, one such area being shown shaded in (b). This makes the actual area of contact between vee-blocks and workpiece unacceptably small.

It is therefore imperative that a more definitive, and above all safe, method of mounting is employed. The problem is to mount the workpiece in precisely the correct position at the second and third turning stages, and persuade it to stay there. This can only be done with any real degree of safety by drilling a small hole at the precise centre of each face of the original cube, and using a corresponding locating-pin in both the headstock and tailstock chucks. Admittedly this leaves six holes in the workpiece to be plugged eventually, an operation which can rarely be performed with total 'invisible-mending' quality, largely on account of the effect of incident light upon the surface of polished timber. It is however, possible to make a virtue of necessity and plug the work with contrasting timber as a decorative feature, to give the impression that things were meant to be that way all along.

In view of the somewhat limited contact area between chuck and workpiece, particularly at the third stage, it also helps a great deal if the driving-end, at least, is made to fit the workpiece. Note from the appearance of the fully-turned piece in Fig.267 that a concave cone or hemisphere is not entirely satisfactory, due to the angular junctions of the facets. The only really effective form of drive is that shown in Fig.273, from which it can also be seen that even this arrangement provides a relatively limited contact area (shown shaded) on the third turning stage. Note incidentally that, although there is some latitude with regard to the dimension 'w', it must be such that the length of the diagonal of the chuck is less than the diameter of the workpiece, otherwise the chuck will be partly turned away at the corners. The driving chuck shown in the photographs is actually made of metal, essentially due to the fact that initial efforts proved to be popular, and

it became necessary to provide a chuck which retained perfect dimensional stability indefinitely, and which could be re-mounted in the lathe at any time with complete confidence in its concentricity. The initial wood prototype was, however, completely successful, but required a little pondering before making it. The method involves gluing a number of stacked squares of birch plywood together, to obtain a block of the necessary thickness. MDF would doubtless be equally satisfactory, but it is a very dusty material to turn. Initially, the squares need only to be rough-sawn to slightly oversize dimensions. The block is used to make a jig of the form shown in Fig.274, the dimensions of which suit work of 2½" diameter, but the general idea can readily be adapted to suit any diameter within reason. The most important feature of the jig is that the small hole for the locating pin is placed in the centre of the finished chuck very accurately. The fact that the basic blank is assembled from a

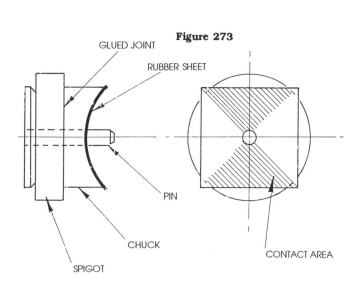

Figure 273

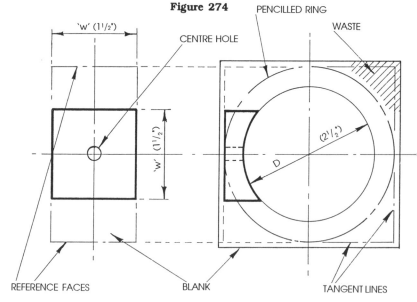

Figure 274

dimensionally-accurate material will fix the thickness of the blank, and also ensure that its faces are parallel, thus allowing the centre-point between these two faces to be easily found. Fixing of the centre with respect to the longer side must wait until a little further work has been done. Note that dimension 'w' is shown nominally but it will in fact be determined by the resultant stack of plywood squares.

The blank is mounted in the lathe, centred as accurately as possible on a faceplate, with a thin plywood backing sheet (not glued) to enable the turning tool to penetrate right through the workpiece without damage to tool or chuck. The four corners (one shown shaded) may be used for screw fixing, since these will eventually become waste. The face of the workpiece is lightly sanded off with the lathe running, using a flat block behind the abrasive, to provide a flat, smooth surface for marking. The required inner diameter 'D' is now pencilled in with the lathe running, plus a further ring which will indicate the final dimensions of the square blank. Both rings should be marked accurately with a finely pointed pencil. The internal diameter may now be bored, ensuring that the flanks of the hole are dead square with the face. The blank is removed from the lathe, and a fine line marked with pencil and knife, exactly tangential with the outer ring, and more or less parallel with one of the original sides of the blank. This side is now sanded down to the tangent-line on a disc-sander, ensuring first that the table is set dead square to the disc, thereby giving the first side of the final square. The two adjacent sides of the square are similarly marked with a steel try-square, the marked lines being exactly tangential to the outer circle. The blank may now be sanded down to these lines. The final side of the square is marked and sanded in the same way. The centre of the small locating pin may now be accurately marked using the sanded edges as a reference. It may be noted that at this point that four driving chucks may be made from the finished blank, one on each side of the square. Since only one is needed, the remainder may be held as spares. Drilling of the locating-pin holes should be carried out on a pillar drill (definitely not by hand) since the holes need to be precisely located and dead-square to the flat face. It is actually quite difficult to mark and drill a hole accurately on the edge-laminations of plywood, so particular care (or better still, a drilling-jig) is required for this operation. The chucks may now be sawn from the blank. Accuracy here is of less importance; it is merely necessary to ensure that they are 'about right'.

Mounting of the chucks in the lathe will depend upon equipment. On the assumption that a good combination chuck is available, a sound method is to turn a dummy spigot, which is then fitted in the chuck, faced dead-flat and bored with a centre locating-pin hole at a single setting. The spigot is fitted with a length of steel rod to provide the locating pin, which may be permanently held with cyanoacrylate adhesive. The special chuck is now glued on its flat face, pushed on to the spigot and held in place by light pressure from the tailstock until the glue sets. Finally, a sheet of thin rubber is glued to the chuck, to protect the workpiece. The final arrangement should appear as in Fig.273.

The tailstock fitting is much simpler. Since it is necessary to use a 'live' or revolving tailstock centre, it is also possible to use the plain cone-centre direct on the locating hole in the workpiece. The latter idea cannot however, be fully-recommended, since undue pressure will tend to 'dub-over' the locating-hole in the workpiece, making subsequent plugging and finishing a rather difficult job to do cleanly. It is possible to provide an excellent little

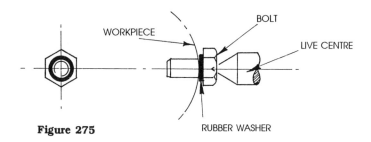

WORKPIECE   BOLT   LIVE CENTRE

RUBBER WASHER

Figure 275

locating-pin from a ¼" diameter bolt, which must have at least ½" of unthreaded length adjacent to the head. The threaded portion is sawn off, and the cut end dressed on a grinder to remove sharp edges. The bolt is now mounted in a drill-chuck in the lathe headstock, and the head drilled with a No.BS.3 centre-drill. The resultant device (Fig.275) is a plug which fits the workpiece and which may also be located accurately on the cone of the tailstock live-centre. Admittedly this operation requires two drill chucks, both of which fit the lathe. It is possible to dispense with one of them by making a dummy spigot to suit the combination-chuck and boring it with a ¼" diameter hole. The bolt may now be held in the hole, with a dab of adhesive. If epoxy adhesive is used for this purpose, subsequent removal may be effected by heating the head of the bolt. This will 'denature' the adhesive and persuade it to realease its grip. Alternatively the spigot may simply be broken away from the bolt. In use, the bolt is fitted with a thin washer cut from sheet rubber, to protect the workpiece. The arrangement described takes care of the second and third-stage turning processes. The first, that of turning the basic cube to a cylinder, may be carried out in much the same way, but to ensure total accuracy, the tailstock pin should be used, and the driving arrangement should also feature a locating-pin, which may be used in conjunction with a dummy spigot. This is glued to the workpiece with the spigot in its original

'as-turned' position in the lathe. The bulk of the spigot may be band-sawn off fairly close to the workpiece after turning the cylinder; the second-stage turning will remove whatever remains.

An interesting variant of the idea is to build the original cube from segments which feature veneer slips running diagonally across the cube faces. The cutting and assembly arrangements for this particular construction have already been described in detail in Chapter 7, and a typical finished cube is shown in Fig.276. This arrangement will place the veneer slips on the angular junctions between facets (Fig.267), a cunning plan which is very rewarding to its maker if noticed by the observer, and distinctly annoying if it isn't. The one snag is that the assembly of the sides of the cube and that of the whole cube, plus the placement of the locating-pin holes in the centres of the faces, must be carried out with the greatest possible care. If one is at all lax in this respect, the veneer strips will tend to miss the junctions slightly — and it doesn't need

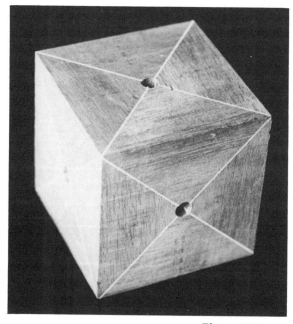

Figure 276

very much of an error in this respect to produce a very obvious mismatch. If well-made, the piece is one which its maker can well be proud of; it is a sad fact however, that only the maker will really appreciate all the hard work involved.

As it stands, the finished piece is merely an ornament, with no practical application. It can however, be made into an attractive cruet, given a little preparation at the first turning stage. At the time of turning the initial cylinder, the piece is also bored with a shouldered hole as shown in Fig.277(a). Prior to mounting however, the cube is slightly countersunk at the mounting end, to receive the head of a No.8 wood screw. The countersink should

Figure 277   WORKPIECE

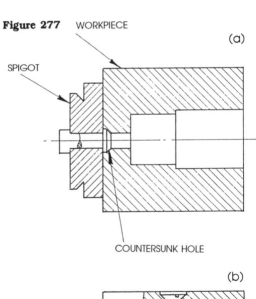

(a)

SPIGOT

COUNTERSUNK HOLE

(b)

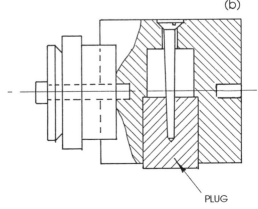

PLUG

be just sufficient to allow the head of the screw to lie inside the final turned profile (b). On no account must it be so deep as to impair the function of the locating-pin. It is necessary also to turn a plug to be a fairly tight push-fit in the larger diameter of the counterbored hole (but it must be removed eventually). The function of the plug is to protect the edges of the hole during subsequent turning stages. The cylinder is now mounted for second-stage turning with the plug fitted and held firmly in place with the wood screw. In passing, the parallel-shank double-start Nettlefold 'superscrew', or similar pattern, is perhaps best suited to this type of work, since it will grip end-grain firmly without expanding or splitting the plug, provided that a pilot hole of the correct diameter is drilled in the plug to receive it. Turning of the second and third stages may now proceed as before.

The completed piece must of course be mounted on a suitable base; it must also be appreciated that the top end of the cruet, whether it be required for salt or pepper, has yet to be dealt with. The shape of the body thus formed is such that it cannot be fitted flush on to a plain-turned base, neither can a recess be turned in the base to receive it accurately. Even if the body is sanded flat at the mounting end, the resultant mating-face will not be a true circle; in fact any form of direct-mounting will betray an inadequacy of one kind or another. The only really satisfactory solution is to turn a hollow cylinder (perhaps in a contrasting timber) which fits the bored hole exactly (and is stopped at the internal shoulder). Methods of dealing with this particular problem, together with those presented by the pouring-end, have already been dealt with in Project 5; it is not, therefore, proposed to repeat them here. There is however, one small feature peculiar to this body shape, in that parts of the joining-cylinder will be visible. It is possible to make an attractive design feature of this property, by allowing the body to sit slightly above the base, thus showing a little more of the cylinder.

It is possible to develop the potential of the body shape a little further by making it in the form of a hollow lidded box, with the lid being a continuation of the faceted profile. In this case one needs to prepare seven segmented assemblies, six for the basic piece and one for the lid; the last-named can however, be rather smaller than the others. The cylinder is mounted on a dummy spigot, the free end bored to a suitable diameter, and hollowed-out to an approximately spherical profile, leaving a shoulder at the free end to allow the lid to seat firmly. The lid blank is pre-drilled with a central hole, mounted on a dummy spigot complete with locating-pin, and turned to be a fairly easy fit in the body recess. In this particular construction, the fact that the inner face of the lid must pass inspection calls for some modification of the mechanism which holds it in place. The best method is undoubtedly a light-alloy collar which is tapped to receive a suitable (say 2BA) machine screw, (Fig.278) but in view of the fact that facilities for making such an item may not be available, a serviceable alternative may be fashioned from a 2BA nut, soft-soldered to a steel or brass plate drilled with a ³/₁₆" (5mm) diameter central hole. The outer shape of the plate may be of more or less any convenient shape, ie. square, circular etc. The plate is attached to the lid by heating it on a hotplate and coating it with a film of hot-melt glue (or a small piece of 'glue-film'). It is fixed to the lid whilst still hot and moved into position, ensuring that the holes in both plate and lid are in reasonable alignment. This is easily effected by rapidly screwing in the 2BA screw such that it projects into the hole in the lid. The screw is unscrewed when the assembly has cooled. The lid may now be assembled to the box as shown, but in view of the fact that it is an easy fit, it must be made temporarily tight by wrapping Sellotape around the rim until it can be fitted without any lateral movement whatsoever; excess tape is then trimmed away. The procedure will protect the inevitable sharp edges which will be formed on the box during subsequent turning. The arrangement is quite clearly seen in Fig.268.

The fitting of the lid requires observance of two very important points. Firstly, the depth of the shouldered recess (and that of the lid itself) must be sufficient to allow the inner face of the lid to sit well inside the turned profile of the box. If this is not done, both the lid and the top of the box will assume a somewhat unattractive appearance and will moreover, generate rather sharp edges on the lid (Fig.279(b)); these will be prone to accidental damage. The dimensions given in Fig.278 will deal with the problem for the particular design offered, but in the case of any desired dimensional variation, the simple construction and formula given in

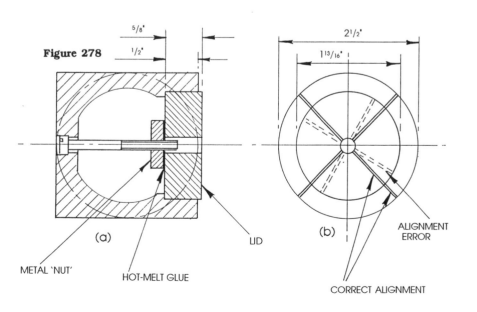

Figure 278

⁵/₈"   ¹/₂"   2¹/₂"   1¹³/₁₆"

(a)

METAL 'NUT'   HOT-MELT GLUE   LID

(b)   ALIGNMENT ERROR   CORRECT ALIGNMENT

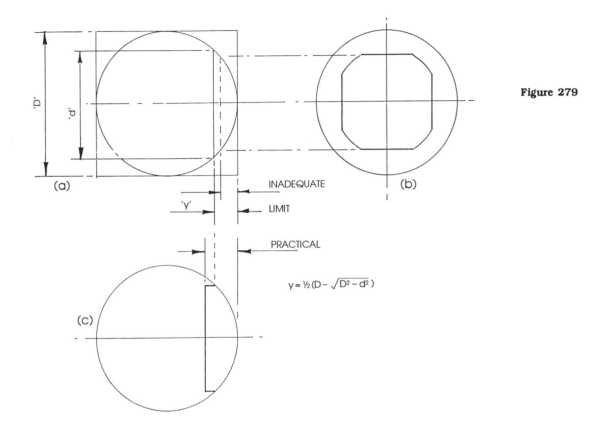

Figure 279

$$y = \tfrac{1}{2}(D - \sqrt{D^2 - d^2})$$

Fig.279 will be found of assistance. The second problem involves the possibility of a very silly mistake, easily made nevertheless, which is capable of ruining the appearance of the entire piece. It is simply that of making sure that the veneer strips in the lid and the box are in perfect alignment before turning. Fig.278 shows the correct alignment and the possible error. At the risk of labouring the point, if the error is made, there is no recovery from it, short of re-making the lid, and even this will be impossible if the locating-pin holes are plugged before the error is spotted. Re-making of the lid, given that the locating-pin system remains available, is possible in principle, but does involve re-turning the piece such that only the lid is touched

by the turning tool, a very difficult business indeed. Even subsequent sanding must be done with very great care. It really is far better not to make the mistake in the first place.

Fitting a suitable base to the completed box poses much the same problems as previously, but matters are perhaps just a little easier in that the absence of a cruet 'filling hole' of respectable diameter in the base does at least admit the possibility of a fairly small diameter junction between body and base. The base and the box may be firmly held together by making the top end of the base into a dowel which fits the body exactly, leaving just a little projecting inside the body (Fig.280). If the two are glued together whilst the base remains in the

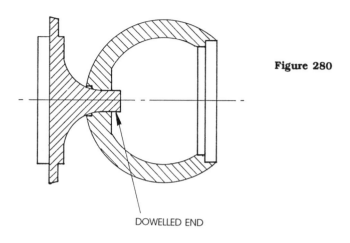

Figure 280

DOWELLED END

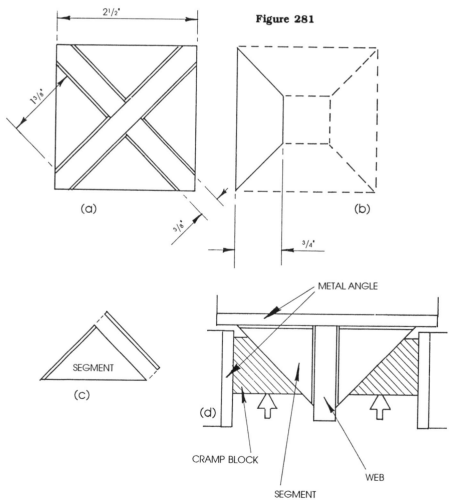

Figure 281

2¹/₂˝

1³/₈˝

³/₈˝

³/₄˝

(a)

(b)

SEGMENT

(c)

(d)

METAL ANGLE

CRAMP BLOCK

SEGMENT

WEB

chuck, the excess dowel may then be carefully turned away. The remaining holes must be plugged by hand. In general, both the veneer slips and the plugged holes should be made in a timber which sharply contrasts with the main body of the piece. Further, it is suggested that the best appearance is achieved by making the veneer and plugs in a very light-coloured timber such as sycamore. Whatever the timber employed, it is well-known that, after finishing, side grain invariably appears appreciably lighter in colour than end-grain. Thus the dowel plugs, if turned in the normal axial-grain fashion, will show end-grain on the finished piece and will appear darker than the veneer slips - not a particularly desirable result. The plugs are therefore best turned cross-grained. Turning a length of cross-grained dowel is not exactly the easiest of tasks, but is made easier by working in fairly short lengths, turning down almost to the finished size with a chisel and then finally finishing with a steel bar, pre-drilled with a hole of the required size. This can, given due care, produce a highly-acceptable result, but any attempt to remove more than the merest shaving by this means can result in a form of 'wandering' of the steel bar which causes the dowel to end-up a good deal smaller than expected. Some prior experimentation is worth the effort. The dowel is cut such that it projects a little on both sides of the box; it is glued in position, and excess carefully pared-off with a normal cabinet-making chisel on the outside, and a suitable carver's gouge on the inside. To gild the lily somewhat, the inside of the lid may be similarly plugged, but only part-way. This allows a knob for the lid, turned to individual choice, to be fitted from the outside.

It is possible to make the initial cube assembly a little more complex by using the form shown in Fig.281, and demonstrated in the photograph of the salt cruet (Fig.282). Note that the method of assembly of the veneers is somewhat different in this case, but the general principles follow those outlined in Chapter 7. In view of the three stages of turning necessary to complete the body-shape, it is possible to make a kind of 'matching-set' of pieces, starting with the plain cylinder, two forms of the second-stage turning (with the lid in different positions), the third stage arrangement, and finally a plain ball. These are shown in Figs.283 and 284.

Figure 282

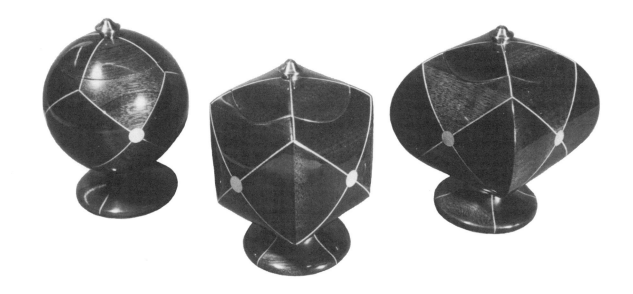

Figures 283 & 284

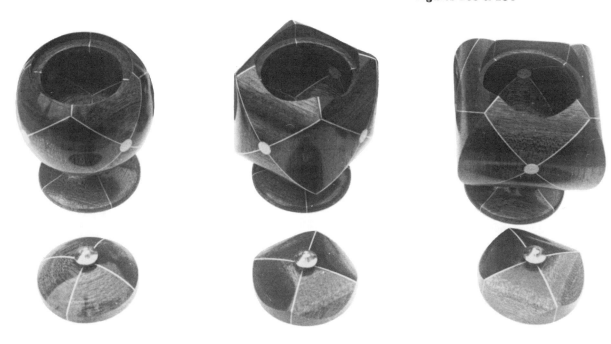

PROJECT 7. THE PLATONIC SOLIDS
(Ball and bowl turning)

When trying to dream up new ideas for woodturning projects, it is a very rare occurrence indeed to have an idea 'presented on a plate' in more or less finished form. It is even more rare for the idea to be over two thousand years old. Nevertheless, such an idea is embodied in the picture of two solids illustrated in Fig.285 and shown as line-drawings in Fig.286. They are familiar objects to individuals interested in mathematics and geometry, unsurprisingly perhaps in view of the fact that they were known in this connection at the time of Plato (427–347BC), and it is for the latter reason that they are generally referred to as the 'Platonic Solids'. They follow strict geometrical rules, in that for any given solid, all facets must be flat, and of identical shape and size; moreover any face must

Figure 285

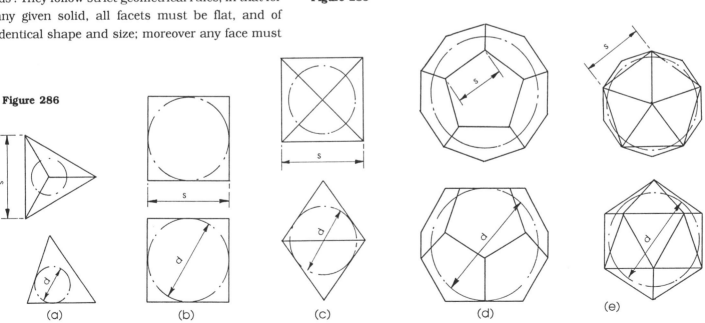

Figure 286

(a)   (b)   (c)   (d)   (e)

itself be 'regular' in that all side-lengths and contained angles are equal. Such shapes are known as 'regular polygons'. Each of the solids may be referred to as a 'regular polyhedron' for the reasons given, and there are only five possible configurations, these being:

Tetrahedron	Four equilateral triangles
Hexahedron	Six squares (better known as the cube)
Octahedron	Eight equilateral triangles
Dodecahedron	Twelve pentagons
Icosahedron	Twenty equilateral triangles

There are eight further 'semi-regular' solids which essentially involve mixtures of regular polygons, perhaps the best-known being the 'soccer-ball' configuration, which comprises a combination of hexagons and pentagons, and bears the rather fearsome appellation of 'truncated icosahedron'. These are not featured in this series however, since they are rather difficult to fabricate accurately, particularly in small sizes.

Figure 287

To return to the Platonic Solids: the original thought, in woodturning terms, was simply that of making one of each and turning a ball from it (Fig.287). The idea was pursued a little further, and a number of small bowls were also made; one of these is illustrated in Fig.288. The idea of using a tetrahedron for ball-turning was, however, rapidly abandoned in view of the fact that the wastage of timber scarcely justifies the exercise. The remaining four behave extremely well in this respect with perhaps the dodecahedron and the isocahedron taking the top prizes, both in terms of timber utilisation and general appearance. All five solids may be regarded as having a certain appeal in their own right however, and although the woodturning content is non-existent, it is suggested that the exercise of making a complete set as a display is worth carrying out, particularly if they are mounted with care and imagination. There is also the possibility of making them as boxes (lidded or otherwise), by leaving the outer shape as it is, and turning out the inside to an approximately spherical shape.

The project is a fairly difficult one, in that it presents a stiff examination of the skill of the worker in terms of cutting and assembling the segments such that good clean hairline joints are maintained throughout. Some idea of the difficulty may be gained from the number of mating faces which need to be cut and glued. Starting with the tetrahedron, these are 12, 24, 24, 60 and 60 respectively; halving these values gives the number of joints to be assembled per solid. For this reason, the concept is very unforgiving of the slightest inaccuracy, and it pays to be fussy. With plain ring-segmented work, such as is used for bowls, platters and the like, where all joints lie in the same plane, it is at least possible to examine the dry assembly, and make corrections to the joint mitre-

Figure 288

drawings except (a) may be explained at this point. These edges, when placed in contact, will form a closed ring involving most of the individual segments. The remaining segments may be regarded as top and bottom lids which are effectively hinged as-drawn, and may be closed after the joint 'X-X' has been taped-up These are bent along the joint lines and finally held in place with transparent adhesive tape. The assembled planforms are of great help, not only in giving an appreciation of the actual shape of the solids (very difficult to do by drawing, and practically impossible for most people by mental gymnastics), but also in planning the grain direction and timber species of individual segments in order to produce an attractive overall design. The construction of squares and triangles requires no more than a draughtsman's square giving angles of 30°, 60° and 90°. The pentagon requires a construction to be built up with the aid

Figure 289

angle if necessary. There is no such luxury with the Platonic Solids, since the insides of the joints tend to disappear from view as the assembly is built-up (Fig.289), and in any case, fiddling about with several pieces in three dimensions with the intention of correcting bad joints is something of a lost cause; moreover, any attempt at local adjustment of any one joint during assembly may well give rise to a cumulative error which eventually spoils the entire workpiece.

So much for the lecture; of more interest perhaps is the practical matter of actually making the solids. To begin with, it is quite easy to construct cardboard models using planforms as shown in Fig.290. The joints between segments should be creased to allow easy formation of the closed solid. The purpose of the symbols in (d) will be explained later, but the pairs of edges marked 'X' in all the

TABLE 9

FACE	EDGE	VENEER	MATING EDGE
1	A	+	12A
	B	–	2E
	C	–	4C
	D	+	3A
	E	+	11A
2	A	–	12E
	B	+	10E
	C	+	5A
	D	+	4D
	E	+	1B
3	A	–	1D
	B	+	4B
	C	+	6E
	D	+	8B
	E	–	11B
4	A	+	6A
	B	–	3B
	C	+	1C
	D	–	2D
	E	+	5E
5	A	–	2C
	B	+	10D
	C	+	7D
	D	+	6B
	E	–	4E
6	A	–	4A
	B	–	5D
	C	–	7C
	D	+	8C
	E	–	3C
7	A	+	9A
	B	+	8D
	C	+	6C
	D	–	5C
	E	–	10C
8	A	–	11C
	B	–	3D
	C	–	6D
	D	–	7B
	E	+	9E
9	A	–	7A
	B	–	10B
	C	–	12C
	D	–	11D
	E	–	8E
10	A	+	12D
	B	+	9B
	C	+	7E
	D	–	5B
	E	–	2B
11	A	–	1E
	B	+	3E
	C	+	8A
	D	+	9D
	E	–	12B
12	A	–	1A
	B	+	11E
	C	+	9C
	D	–	10A
	E	+	2A

Figure 290

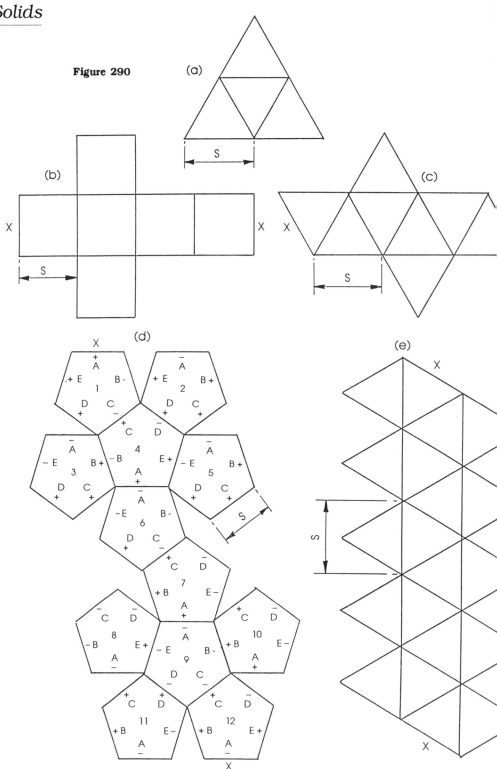

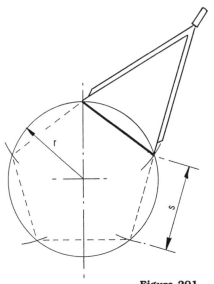

Figure 291

	MITRE ANGLE (B)	FACE SUPPORT ANGLE (2B)	VERTEX SUPPORT ANGLE (A)	MAX BALL DIAMETER (FACTOR) (d)	MIN THICKNESS (FACTOR) (t)
SOLID					
Tetrahedron	35.264	70.529	70.529	.408	.136
Hexahedron	45.000	90.000	109.472	1.000	.211
Octahedron	54.736	109.472	90.000	.816	.173
Dodecahedron	58.283	116.565	138.190	2.228	.228
Icosahedron	69.095	138.190	116.565	1.512	.155

TABLE 8

of compasses as shown in Fig.291. This can be done by trial-and-error, but a good starting point is to use Nomogram 8 to determine the side length 's', corresponding to the chosen value of 'r'. Note however, that this is a 'secondary' use of the Nomogram, for which reason the symbols need to be mentally changed: the side length is given as 'y' and the centre angle (which must be found by simple arithmetic), as 'S' in Fig.N8(a). If the value of 's' is chosen first, the Nomogram may be used in reverse to obtain 'r' for initial compass-setting. Once a single pentagon has been drawn accurately on card, it may be cut out with a knife and steel rule and used as a template for the planform.

It is important to know a few facts about the solids before attemping to construct them. These are presented in Table 8, and the use of each variable will be explained as required. The angles involved are constant for each type of solid, and will remain as given regardless of the size of solid constructed, but the sizes of the solids themselves will necessarily depend upon the sizes chosen for the individual segments comprising them. For this reason, the linear dimensions involved are presented as multiplying factors in terms of the segment side length 's'; in other words, the values given in Table 8 for ball diameter 'd' and segment thickness 't' should be multiplied by the chosen value of 's' to produce the required result. For example, in the construction of a dodecahedron, a pentagon of side length 's' of 1", will produce an 'across-flats' diameter of just under 2¼" in the finished dodecahedron; this value represents the maximum diameter of a ball which may be turned from it. Perhaps the two most important constructional parameters are the side length 's' and the mitre-angle 'B'. Both must be produced to a very high order of accuracy to produce an acceptable result. Fig.292 gives a line drawing representation of each segment type, and Fig.293 shows a typical partial assembly.

At the risk of labouring the point, it is stressed

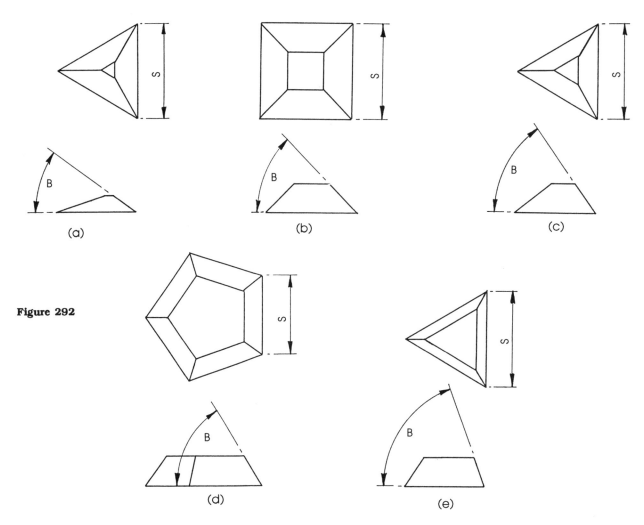

Figure 292

that there is simply no future in cutting segments to only a fair degree of accuracy, and then trying to make on-the-spot adjustments as assembly proceeds. It is vitally important to machine each segment as accurately as possible, and then to trust one's own work implicitly during assembly.

Segment thickness is of no particular importance if the solids are to be left as geometric forms, but if they are to be subsequently turned to spherical form, then it is necessary to allow sufficient thickness to ensure that the turning tool does not

break through into the hollow centre. Values for minimum thickness 't' for each solid are given in Table 8. Note that the values given are those which *just* allow the tool to break through. This will occur first at the 'vertices' (or points) of the solid. The values given thus represent a non-practical limit, and it is necessary to increase them somewhat (the amount being determined by individual judgment), to give a sensible joint-area, and also to cater for any errors in centring the work in the lathe. In passing it may be noted that it is quite possible to

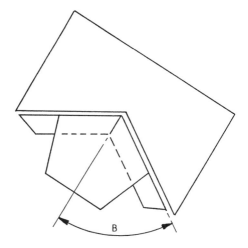

Figure 293

turn a non-spherical shape from the solids; this will vary the sizes and shapes of the resultant curved 'facets' after turning, and can lead to quite interesting results; it must be borne in mind however, that it is no longer possible to predict the required segment thickness, and very great care must be exercised in order to avoid breakthrough. Perhaps the best approach in such cases is to make the segments as thick as conveniently possible. From a turning viewpoint it is also important to know the diameter of the ball which can be obtained from a given solid; this is given as 'd' in Table 8. The chain-dotted circles in Fig.286 show the sizes of ball which can be obtained relative to their parent solid, together with their position within the solid. It can be seen from (a) that the size of ball which can be obtained from its parent tetrahedron renders the attempt to produce it rather pointless.

Individual wood segments are best marked from an accurate master template, constructed in something rather more robust than card. It is possible to make such a template in brass sheet for example, but this approach does require metal-working facilities. A good compromise may be achieved by using 1/8" thick acrylic (eg. Perspex) sheet, since the edges may be sanded very accurately on a disc sander fitted with a fine grade disc. This technique has been discussed in Chapter 7 but, in view of the special demands on accuracy, it is expanded a little here. The template may be checked after it is made by first sanding a piece of scrap timber dead smooth on one surface, and then marking around the template with a fine-pointed hard pencil (at least 3H grade); the template is then rotated one step at a time and checked against the marking. It is then turned upside-down and checked again in the same way (this last exercise ensuring that the edges of the template are dead square to the faces). The procedure may appear to be overdoing things a little but, from experience, it is not; the errors discovered will invariably be tiny, but if applied via the template to every segment, they are likely to produce unacceptable cumulative errors. Note that the marking-out of the final segments against the template must be carried out by sanding dead smooth on the outer face and using a razor blade or craft knife; a pencil or ordinary marking knife does not provide sufficient accuracy for sanding, although a pencil may be used (in addition to the knifed line) to give a stronger visual indication of the required sanding line. The method of using templates to mark out segments of this type is given in detail in Chapter 7.

An effective way of cutting the mitres on the segments is to first saw them fairly close to the line on a bandsaw or power fretsaw with the table set to the required angle, followed by a finishing process on a disc sander, using the finest grit size available. In fact the extremely acute angle of the tetrahedron is perhaps beyond the table-setting capacity of most home-owned equipment, and machining of this particular angle can be quite difficult; for this reason it will be discussed separately later. Sanding of individual segments may be carried out in the manner described in Chapter 6, using a home-made card template to set the table-angle accurately. This is one of the cases where sanding must be carried out with reference to the outer face of the segments; the operation thus requires a sub-table. As previously noted, the tetrahedron poses special problems, due to the acuteness of the mitre angle. It is likely that few machine table settings go much beyond 45°, and even if they did, the sub-table described in Chapter 6 would not be of much use. It is better therefore, to set the table at right angles to the sander, and fit a home-made fence to the table, set to the required mitre angle (Fig.294). The edge to be sanded is held at right angles to the table and may be observed fairly readily by leaving a gap

between the fence and the sanding disc. Given that the abrasive face of the sanding-disc is dead flat, it is thus possible to apply selective pressure to the upper or lower portions of the segment to ensure that the entire length of the sanding line meets the disc at the same instant. Even this arrangement is u satisfactory on its own however, due to the diffic lty in holding the workpiece in the required p sition, but the matter can be resolved with the aid of a support stick attached to the workpiece wit hot-melt glue (b).

Assembly of the complete solids varies in difficulty more or less directly in proportion to the number of segments involved, but the cube, although not the easiest, does at least possess the advantage of familiarity of shape. Further, the mitre angle of 45° *is*, perhaps, the easiest to establish and, above all, the component parts are assembled mutually at right angles. This is not to say that one can take liberties with either the side length or the mitre angle, but at least it is easy to observe whether errors are present or not. One could use normal right-angled cramping methods to assemble this particular solid, but this is not altogether necessary, and in any case the technique is of no help at all with the remaining solids, so one might as well evolve a more generally useful approach. A method which has been repeatedly used with success involves the use of electrician's adhesive tape and is described in detail in Chapter 8. The tetrahedron, although the most difficult to machine, is the easiest to assemble in this way, and the octahedron will also be found quite easy. The dodecahedron and icosahedron can be decidedly tricky, on account of the number of joints to be glued and handled, and it is necessary to examine the closed-up dry assembly very carefully to ensure that all joints are good (although obviously this can only be done with certainty for the out-

Figure 294

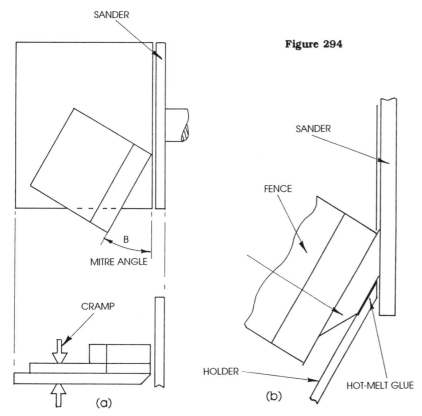

SANDER

B

MITRE ANGLE

CRAMP

(a)

SANDER

FENCE

HOLDER

HOT-MELT GLUE

(b)

side). Some difficulty may be found in closing the top and bottom groups of segments after closing the open ring, dependent upon the thickness of the segments; this is because some interference on the inner edges of the segments may be experienced with a hinged assembly, as distinct from a plain 'drop-in' assembly. The elasticity of the adhesive tape will normally permit final closure however. Getting the solid open again after a 'dry' inspection is another matter, and it will almost certainly be necessary to cut the tape at the 'X-X' joint and open out the ring to do so. When applying glue, particularly with the larger assemblies, it is all too easy to miss joints altogether, so a careful inspection before final closure is advised. When closing up a glued assembly, pressure should be applied slowly, to allow excess glue to escape in its own time, and thereby avoiding undue stress on the adhesive tape. One further small point will bear watching: the timber faces must be clean and, above all, free from dust, since the latter will seriously impair adhesion of the tape.

However careful the work to this point, it may still be found after the glue has set (particularly on 'first efforts'), that one or two joints are not quite as they should be. Such joints should never be ignored in the hope that they will get by unnoticed; the chances are that they won't. It is possible however, with care, to snatch victory from the jaws of defeat by filling any gapped joints with a thin sliver of the appropriate timber, prepared by sanding down a suitable length of timber at one end to produce a small tapered sliver. This may then be inserted into the gap, and manipulated to fill it, regardless of whether the gap is straight or tapered. The gap itself may need to be prepared by inserting a razor blade to cut away any small 'nibs' of glue inside it, which may impede insertion of the wedge. Sometimes a better approach is to lightly saw along the joint with the aid of a piercing-saw blade (these are the metalworking equivalent of fretsaw blades). The joint is then filled with adhesive, the wedge inserted, and excess trimmed away with a razor blade. With care, partly or even fully cross-grained slivers may be handled in this way. A quick tip with regard to the insertion of adhesive into a narrow joint: this is readily done with the aid of a small piece of the backing-sheet supplied with 'glue-film'. The material posseses the twin advantages of being very thin and surprisingly rigid. If the piece is to be turned into a ball, it should be turned to a close approximation to its final shape before dealing with the joints, since a joint which looks good on the parent solid may be rather less so after turning.

There remains the question of choice of timber. Quite satisfactory results may be obtained by using one timber type only, and organising the grain direction such that the normal changes in the reflectivity and appearance of polished wood when viewed or illuminated from different angles serves to outline the segment shapes. Alternatively, one may use different timbers, ensuring that no two adjacent faces show the same type. This can be done with a maximum of five types, but it is suggested that an arrangement which shows the same timber on opposing faces is better. This cannot be done with the tetrahedron, since there are no opposing faces, but the remainder require three, four, six and ten timber types respectively. It is quite easy to become confused and get the timbers mixed up during assembly on the two largest pieces. This may be avoided by preparing a list of the chosen timbers against numbers, arranging the assembly patterns on the appropriate card planform, and finally transferring the numbers to the segments for ease of identification during assembly.

An effective presentation is achieved by using the same timber type throughout, but separating the segments with a veneer slip of contrasting timber on every joint; this method is particularly effective if the solid is subsequently turned, but it is also somewhat difficult. On the face of it, the safest method would appear to be that of gluing a slip of veneer to every face of every segment, thereby presenting a double thicknesss of veneer at every joint. This method does however, tend to make the joints look rather heavy and clumsy and also, surprisingly perhaps, leads to loss of joint accuracy. In view of the fact that modern veneers are sliced with a great deal of precision, the most likely

culprit in this instance would appear to be the gluing and cramping of the veneers to the segments. Be that as it may, the single-thickness approach seems to offer the better result in terms of appearance and accuracy. The method does however, bring a few planning problems with it, due to the fact that it is necessary to glue veneer slips to selected faces only; moreover, these faces must be identified and each segment must be placed in correct relationship to those around it. Fig.295 shows the nature of the problem, applied to a small detail comprising four segments. Clearly the application of the same idea to a complete assembly demands some thought; it involves the use of the card planform once again, together with the preparation of a table identifying each segment, and showing which edges are to be pre-veneered. A complete construction is shown in Fig.290(d), the 'plus' and 'minus' signs indicating the presence or absence of veneer respectively. Table 9 (to be used in conjunction with the identifying letters in Fig.290(d) shows one of many possible arrangements for the dodecahedron, which is by far the most difficult to deal with. Note that the basic segments are prepared in the normal way, as though they were not to be veneered at all; there is no need to make dimensional allowance on any of the faces for the thickness of veneer, since it will be found that things 'sort themselves out' automatically.

Attachment of the veneer to the mitred segment faces can be unexpectedly tricky. It must be remembered that any variation in thickness of glueline between segment and veneer slip is likely to show up ultimately as an error in mitre angle. In view of the fact that the area available for cramping on the inside face of a segment can be quite small, cramping arrangements must be made with particular care. It is also risky to attempt to cramp a

Figure 295

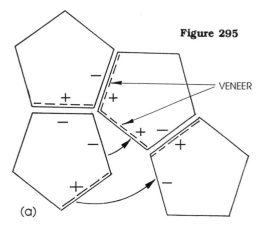

(a)

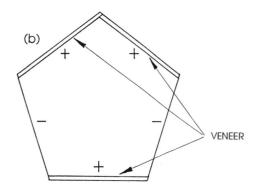

(b)

Figure 296

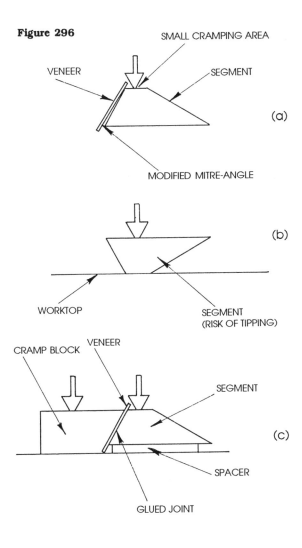

SMALL CRAMPING AREA

VENEER

SEGMENT

(a)

MODIFIED MITRE-ANGLE

(b)

WORKTOP

SEGMENT (RISK OF TIPPING)

CRAMP BLOCK

VENEER

SEGMENT

(c)

SPACER

GLUED JOINT

a *light* hand-sanding of the trimmed edges, with the abrasive sheet laid on a flat surface. It must be carried out with care, such that the edges of the veneer slip follow the profile of the segment precisely; any 'dubbing-over' at the corners, for example, will produce a small but noticeable hole in the final assembly. Note the spacer between the segments and baseboard in Fig.296(c). This permits the veneer to protrude below the face of the segment to provide an allowance for subsequent trimming.

Mounting of the finished pieces can be done in a number of ways, that shown in Fig.297(a) being perhaps the simplest. It is also possible to make small mounts which support the pieces on an intersection of two faces (b), the angle required being twice the mitre angle (ie.2B). The tetrahedron

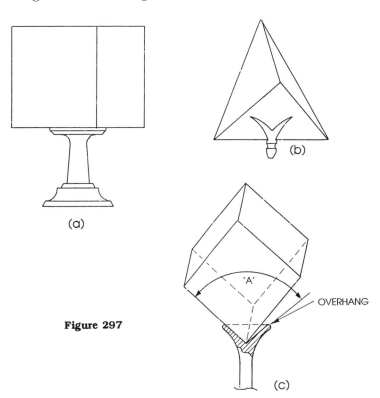

(a)

(b)

'A'

OVERHANG

(c)

Figure 297

segment to a worktop with the outer face uppermost, since it may tilt slightly and produce a poor joint. Fig.296. shows the possible problems, together with a simple arrangement for dealing with them. It is convenient to prepare a number of jig blocks at the same time as the segments themselves are prepared, since the same machine-table settings can be used. Trimming of the veneer after gluing can be done with a sharp chisel, followed by

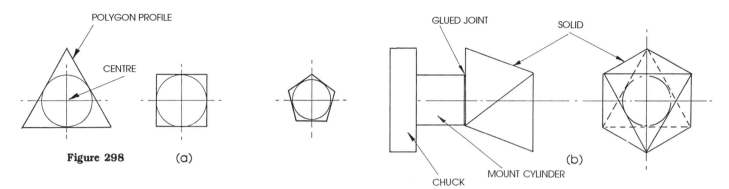

Figure 298   (a)   (b)

looks particularly attractive mounted in this way. Finally, it is possible to mount them on a vertex or 'point' by turning a pedestal which includes the necessary internal angle at the top (c). This angle is given as support-angle 'A' in Table 8. This particular method can in some circumstances look a trifle odd, due to the overhang of the support which occurs when viewed from some directions, and must be approached with care for this reason. It is a method which some individuals may not particularly care for, but is offered nevertheless as a possibility. The internal angle of the support, or the double mitre angle required by the arrangement shown in (b) may be checked against a card template, which may itself be constructed by the methods outlined in Chapter 2.

It is possible to provide bowls and goblets from the solids, as well as plain turned balls, the limitation perhaps being that the overall shape of the finished artefact will necessarily be all or part of a sphere, or some approximation thereto. As a result of personal experience, it is suggested that such pieces look better in dark timbers, with light veneer lines. To obtain the maximum available diameter from a given solid, it is necessary to mount the solid such that the lathe axis is on the exact centre of any flat face. One method of doing so is suggested here. A scrap block of hardwood is attached to the lathe chuck, faced off dead flat, and turned to a cylinder of a diameter that just sits nicely within the edges of one face of the solid (Fig.298(a). The end of the cylinder is then glued to the workpiece and the assembly left until the glue has set hard (b), after which the solid may be turned and subsequently parted off from the cylinder. It is perhaps as well to leave the cylinder attached to the chuck throughout the process, unless it can be remounted accurately. Ball-turning of the dodecahedron and icosahedron is fairly easy, since the relatively large number of faces allows plenty of 'witness points', and it is necessary only to turn the solid down until the flats just disappear. The cube is first turned to a cylinder of diameter equal to side-length, and then fashioned into a ball; at this point, Nomogram 10. may be invoked to complete the process. The octahedron is also first turned to a cylinder, but in this case it is not readily apparent by inspection when the required diameter has been reached. All that can be done here is to rely upon calculations by setting a pair of caliperss to the theoretical maximum ball diameter in relation to side length (Table 8) and using a parting-tool to establish the diameter prior to further turning. Note, however, that, for safety's sake, the use of calipers on a piece of this kind must be made only with the lathe stopped. The method will handle the tetrahedron also, but as previously mentioned, this particular exercise isn't worth doing.

PROJECT 8.   OFF-CENTRE CAGE TURNING
(Cutlery set from laminated blanks)

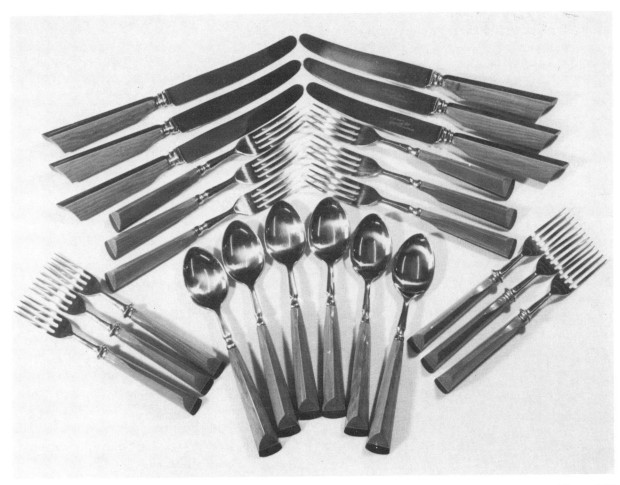

Figure 299

This project is offered as an introduction to off-centre turnery, since it represents an easy turning exercise, (to the extent that any form of intermittent turnery can be described as 'easy'). Perhaps the greatest difficulty in turnery of this type is that of observation of the turned profile since, as mentioned in Chapter 3, this may be seen only as a 'ghost-image'. The problem, of course, becomes increasingly acute as the gap between workpieces is increased. In this particular project however, six workpieces are turned simultaneously in a 'cage' formation, with the occasional introduction of a further six 'guide blocks' between them. This reduces the intermittency and ghost-image problems considerably. Moreover, the actual turned profile of the assembly as an entity is a plain straight shallow taper, with the upper and lower diametral limits defined by the diameters of the mandrels at the ends of the cage, thus providing an easy dimensional reference. In view of the fact that metal blanks for forks and spoons are supplied with a circular or slightly elliptical profile at the point where they join the tang, handles of equilateral cross-sectional profile are offered for these. Knives demand slightly different treatment, since the junction at the blade and the tang is generally of pronounced elliptical cross-section; moreover, the flat cross-sectional profile of knives would indicate something similar in terms of a handle. Accordingly, the handle profile offered for these is of isosceles cross-section. Design methods for both profiles have already been given in Chapter 3. Fig.299 shows the complete 24-piece set.

To deal with the equilateral shape first, a set of identical blanks, together with a set of guide blocks, is mounted around the periphery of two disc mandrels, and sandwiched between them (Figs.300

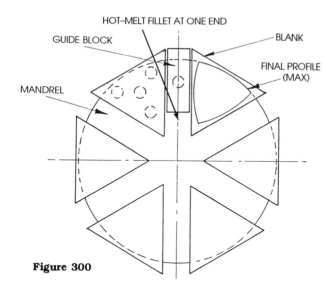

Figure 300

Figure 299(b)

and 301) and turned as a group; the blanks are then individually rotated on the mandrels by 120° and turned to the same longitudinal profile as the first, the process being repeated for the third face.

Turning is carried out in the normal way with gouge and chisel, with due reference to the precautions suggested in Chapter 10, and with particular reference to the fact that the effective turning diameter of the cage is of the order of 3" (Figs.302 and 303). Even so, the process is very much easier than it might appear; in fact, the bulk of the real work lies in the construction of the mandrels, which need to be marked out and drilled as accurately as possible.

The equilateral mandrel is shown in Fig.304. It is perhaps as well to mention at this point that *all* mandrels are made in MDF or birch ply stock. The six 'work-stations' are produced by drawing diametral lines to divide the basic disc into six equal segments, and then striking radii as shown in the 'detail' annotation, to give the centres for the twenty-four $3/16$" dia. holes. A further six $3/16$" dia. holes are

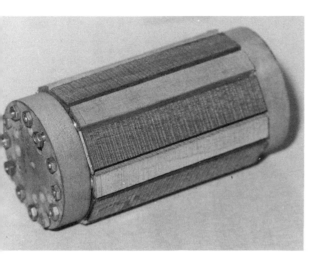

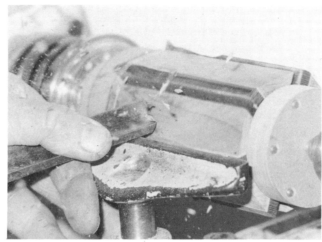

Figure 301 (above)

Figure 302 (top right)

Figure 303 (right)

Figure 304

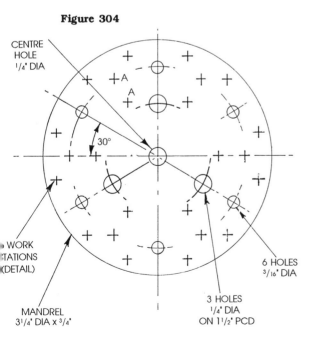

CENTRE
HOLE
1/4" DIA

+A

A

30°

WORK
STATIONS
(DETAIL)

MANDREL
3 1/4" DIA x 3/4"

3 HOLES
1/4" DIA
ON 1 1/2" PCD

6 HOLES
3/16" DIA

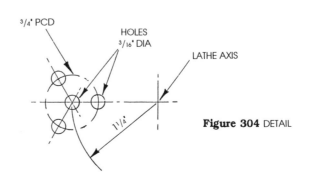

3/4" PCD

HOLES
3/16" DIA

LATHE AXIS

1 1/4"

Figure 304 DETAIL

required midway between the groups; these are required for the guide blocks. A further four ¹/₄" dia. holes are required to accommodate a driver for the mandrel. All hole centres are marked at the same time, and all are drilled right through the stock; it is important that they are drilled at right angles to the face of the disc, which may then be bandsawn somewhat oversize and left in this state for the moment. It is necessary to keep a fairly clear head when marking out and drilling this number of holes, in view of the fact that the completed disc does look rather like a piece of Gruyere cheese.

The tailstock mandrel (Fig.305) carries a set of twelve holes which must exactly match the corresponding holes in the headstock mandrel (ie. all those on a 2¹/₂" pitch-circle diameter). These may be 'spotted-through' from the headstock mandrel, using the centre-hole as a reference. In view of the possibility of minor inaccuracies, it is also as well to make a registration mark on both discs, so that they can be used in the same relative alignment at all times. Since lathe facilities will vary from one user to another, it is not possible to give hard-and-

fast guidance with regard to marking out, to achieve the all-important concentric running of the holes and the periphery of the discs, but a suggested method, making use of a 'driving-mandrel' will be given. In the meantime, it should be noted also that the tailstock mandrel includes twelve mild-steel pins, which must be a permanent fit; on no account must these be allowed to work loose, since this would render the set-up potentially dangerous.

The driving mandrel shown in Fig.306 is made such that it may be removed and accurately re-placed as needed in the lathe chuck; the 'chuck-face' of this particular item must of course be made to suit the particular chuck in use. It is strongly advised that a metal pallet of the type described in Chapter 9 is used if possible, since concentricity is of paramount importance. It is not advisable to treat the project as a 'between-centres' task in the sense of using a pronged driving centre, since concentricity may be impaired over a period of use, and the fact that the set-up is an assembly rather than a solid piece of wood may induce a little wobble. The driving mandrel permits the main mandrel (and indeed the whole cage) to be removed from the lathe without loss of concentricity. The arrangement is merely convenient with respect to the equilateral blanks but is essential in connec-tion with the iscosceles blanks, as will be seen. The reader is reminded however, that any 'between-centres' turning where the driven end of the workpiece is firmly attached to a combination chuck or faceplate requires the tailstock axis to be accu-rately aligned with that of the headstock. Note that the driving mandrel also requires three fixed steel pins. It is also necessary to bear in mind the 'delamination-strength' of MDF if this is made as a 'one-piece' item with an integral compression-mode spigot. With the driving mandrel available, the disc blank for the headstock may be prepared by first

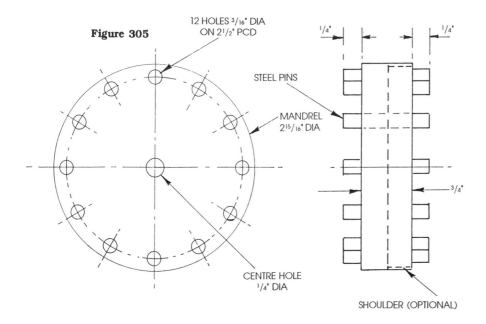

Figure 305

12 HOLES ³/₁₆" DIA ON 2¹/₂" PCD

STEEL PINS

MANDREL 2¹⁵/₁₆" DIA

CENTRE HOLE ¹/₄" DIA

¹/₄"   ¹/₄"

³/₄"

SHOULDER (OPTIONAL)

marking out and drilling the three driving holes, using the centre hole as a reference. If the lathe possesses indexing facilities, the task becomes that much easier, since the disc-blank may now be mounted on the driving mandrel, and the holes marked out. At this stage, the outer diameter of the mandrel may be turned also; it is of course necessary to give tailstock support. After spotting-through the holes, the tailstock mandrel may also be turned to its final diameter by mounting it on the main mandrel with a few well-fitting dowels in three or four of the peripheral holes, and the tailstock live centre holding the assembly together. A parting-tool used as a chisel is useful when turning the tailstock mandrel, since the headstock mandrel is of rather larger diameter and therefore presents a shoulder. It will be seen that Fig.305 features an 'optional shoulder' in side-elevation; this is merely a device for changing the end-dimensions of the completed cutlery blanks, since these may well be required to be different for, say, knives and forks (the same tailstock mandrel is required for both). Thus, since the mandrel is reversible on the tailstock, two dimensions may be accommodated. As previously noted, the cutlery blanks are turned with a plain, straight taper, using the outer diameters of the mandrels to 'size' the work. As drawn, the taper is 'downhill' from left to right. Readers who feel more comfortable moving the tool in the other direction might find it preferable to place the three driver holes in the tailstock mandrel rather than the headstock mandrel, and reverse the entire set-up; in any event, whichever mandrel is chosen for the tailstock should have its centre hole very lightly countersunk at 60° to suit a live-centre.

At the completion of each turning operation, the work should be sanded to the best possible finish (there should be absolutely no need to repeat the entire 'blank-rotation' process simply for sanding

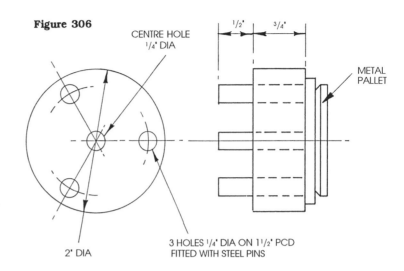

Figure 306

CENTRE HOLE ¹/₄" DIA

METAL PALLET

¹/₂"   ³/₄"

2" DIA

3 HOLES ¹/₄" DIA ON 1¹/₂" PCD FITTED WITH STEEL PINS

purposes). Apart from their primary function, the guide-blocks serve one further purpose: if they were absent, it would be found that the work is sanded to different depths on the leading and trailing edges of the workpieces, an effect very noticeable if they are made from contrasting laminations. The sanding abrasive should be used backed by a thin flexible material in order to ensure that the sanded faces are maintained true to the overall cage 'turning-circle' as far as possible. The abrasive sheet and its backing should, for safety, also be long enough to keep the leading and trailing edges (and hence the fingers) well away from the revolving work (Fig.307).

The equilateral blanks and their associated bridge-pieces are shown in Fig.312(a and c). Note that the holes which provide the centre of rotation of the blanks (one at each end) must be in the centre of the triangular blank; this may be found with the aid of a mortise gauge. It is strongly advised that initially, at least one set of 'practice blanks' is made in plain hardwood stock, such as beech, with no attempt at laminated construction.

Figure 307

Quite apart from the experience thus acquired, the blanks will serve a second purpose, in that they may be experimented with later, when dealing with the 'side profile' machining. It is essential that all blanks are prepared to exactly the same length, with both ends accurately squared-off, and the dowel holes precisely located, preferably by means of a drilling-jig. The blanks are fitted to the headstock mandrel with a pair of $3/16''$ dia. mild steel dowel pins which should be a firm 'push-fit' in the holes in the blanks and a rather easier fit in the mandrel; on no account must the fit be sloppy in either. The entire cage is supported by the tailstock live-centre.

The main mandrel for turning the two long sides of the isosceles knife blanks is shown in Fig.308, and its mating tailstock mandrel in Fig.309. Six 'work-stations' are produced as shown in the

Figure 308

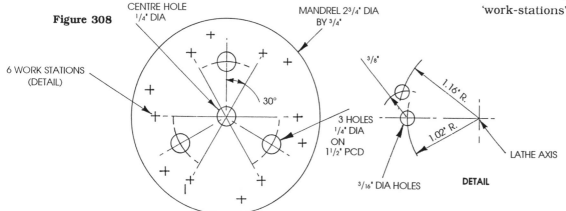

CENTRE HOLE
$1/4''$ DIA

MANDREL $2^{3}/4''$ DIA
BY $3/4''$

6 WORK STATIONS
(DETAIL)

30°

3 HOLES
$1/4''$ DIA
ON
$1^{1}/2''$ PCD

$3/8''$

1.16" R.

1.02" R.

$3/16''$ DIA HOLES

LATHE AXIS

DETAIL

Figure 309

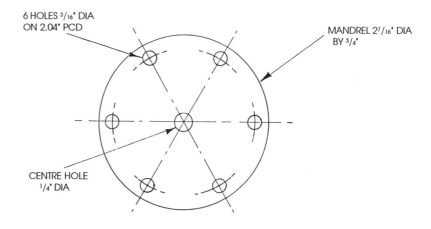

6 HOLES $3/16''$ DIA
ON 2.04" PCD

MANDREL $2^{7}/16''$ DIA
BY $3/4''$

CENTRE HOLE
$1/4''$ DIA

'detail' annotation, the positions of the holes being located entirely with compasses or dividers. The turning is once again a straight taper, using the outer diameters of the mandrels as a guide. The first cut is made with the blanks positioned relative to lathe rotation as in Fig.310(a). This allows the more acute edge to be turned as a 'leading-edge' on the second cut, thereby reducing the risk of a ragged finish on this particularly vulnerable edge. At this point, the primary purpose of the driving mandrel becomes apparent: to turn the second set of faces, the blanks are removed, the main mandrel reversed on the driving mandrel, and the blanks replaced facing in the opposite direction (b).

Turning the backs of the knife handles may be done by using the equilateral mandrel Fig.304, with only the pairs of holes marked 'A' being actually used to mount the blanks. The orientation of the part-turned blanks is shown in Fig.311(b). However, since the cage must be turned to a 'cylinder' of 3" diameter the mandrel presents a shoulder above the work, adding to turning difficulties. For this reason, readers may find it preferable to turn a separate mandrel of 3" outside diameter, drilling only those holes necessary (Fig.311(a)). Turning is done in conjunction with the 'equilateral' tailstock mandrel Fig.305. The dimensions of the blanks are given in Fig.312(b). Due to the rather large gap between blanks, guide blocks are essential for sanding.

Fig.313 shows a collection of blanks and mandrels, and Fig.314 shows the assembly complete with guide-blocks. Note however, that in these illustrations, the blanks are mounted with hot-melt glue on special pallets which allow the assembly to be screwed into the headstock mandrel. This particular set-up is useful if a fair quantity of pieces is to be made, but does require metalworking facilities.

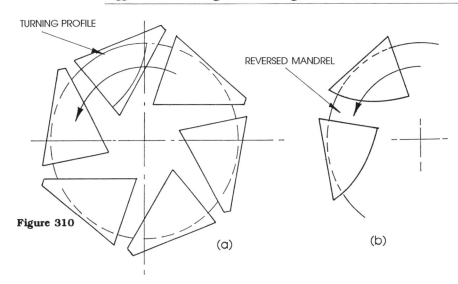

Figure 310

(a) (b)

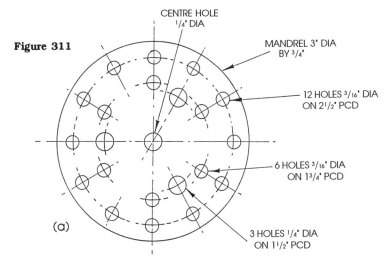

Figure 311

(a)

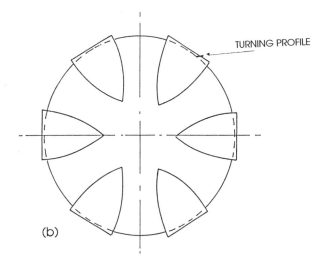

(b)

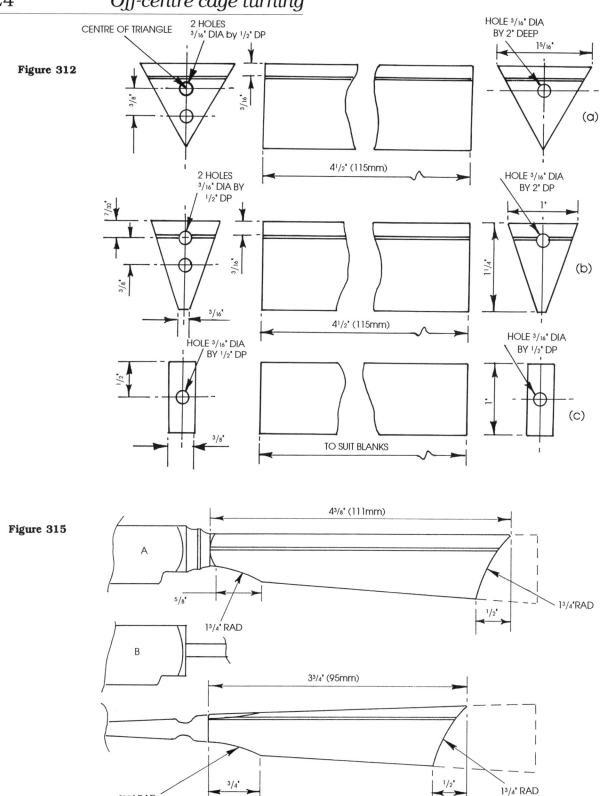

Figure 312

CENTRE OF TRIANGLE

2 HOLES
³/₁₆" DIA by ¹/₂" DP

HOLE ³/₁₆" DIA
BY 2" DEEP

³/₈"

³/₁₆"

1⁵/₁₆"

(a)

2 HOLES
³/₁₆" DIA BY
¹/₂" DP

HOLE ³/₁₆" DIA
BY 2" DP

⁷/₃₂"

³/₈"

³/₁₆"

³/₁₆"

4¹/₂" (115mm)

1"

1¹/₄"

(b)

HOLE ³/₁₆" DIA
BY ¹/₂" DP

HOLE ³/₁₆" DIA
BY ¹/₂" DP

¹/₂"

³/₈"

1"

(c)

4¹/₂" (115mm)

TO SUIT BLANKS

Figure 315

4³/₈" (111mm)

A

5/8"

1³/₄" RAD

¹/₂"

1³/₄" RAD

B

3³/₄" (95mm)

1³/₄" RAD

³/₄"

¹/₂"

1³/₄" RAD

Figure 313

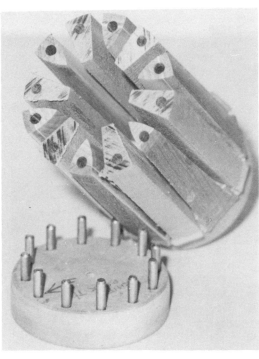

Figure 314

The side profiles (Fig.315) may be cut with a home-made drum-sander of 3½" diameter, after first sawing away the waste (at the larger end). Matters are greatly helped with a jig as described and illustrated in Chapter 6 to hold the blanks. The deep hole in each handle, required for the 'tang' of the cutlery, is very useful for mounting and aligning the work for sanding. The 'tang-ends' of the handles are shaped by the same means (see photographs, Chapter 6) to match the cutlery blanks which, for this reason alone, must be purchased before work is started. In this connection it is advised that knife blanks are available in at least two styles, that marked 'A' being preferable, since the 'B' style forces the handle to look rather heavy. The previously-turned turned practice-pieces may be used experimentally with the drum-sander, to ensure a good match with the metalwork, and to arrive at an individually-preferred profile, before committing more exotic timber or lamination work.

It is suggested that, although not essential, the appearance of the handles is enhanced by a laminated construction using woods which give contrast of shade but harmony of colour, suggested dimensions being given as part of Fig.312. Those illustrated have the main body of yew heartwood, with cocobolo backs, separated by sycamore veneer. Readers contemplating using cocobolo are advised that it is very difficult to glue and an epoxy adhesive (eg. Araldite) is recommended here. Finally, the metal cutlery blanks will almost certainly have a 'flash' or bump, caused by the manufacturing process, at the point where the tang meets the main body; this should be filed away to ensure a flush fit with the handles.

PROJECT 9. OFF-CENTRE — 3 and 4 FACETS
(Cruets, containers, etc.)

The cutlery handles discussed in Project 8 represent a fairly easy intermittent-turning exercise, in view of the fact that the cage arrangement comprising a number of fairly closely spaced workpieces permits a moderately-continuous cutting action. The turning of larger pieces, as illustrated in Chapter 3, possibly with larger gaps between them, makes this class of work rather more difficult. In fact it must be stated at the outset that projects of this nature are *not* for the beginner. They demand fairly confident handling of tools, with well-developed instincts on the part of the turner for the correction of incipient digs or snatches before they get out of hand. They also require that the tools are presented to the work by feel rather than by observation. This is because the progress of the turned profile is usually best judged by watching the *back* of the work, since this is often the only place which conveys any real visual information. The question of balance must also be considered. Where at all possible this is best dealt with by turning two or more identical workpieces equally spaced around the periphery of a sub-faceplate or similar mounting arrangement. Even so, the repositioning of the workpieces to enable successive facets to be turned will necessarily give rise to a degree of imbalance, at least until preliminary turning is completed. In general therefore, the lathe must be run fairly slowly, regardless of any balancing arrangements which may be made. Fortunately, it is fairly natural to run the lathe slowly in any case, since the

effective diameter of the complete set-up will generally give rise to high peripheral speeds. Although it is theoretically possible to turn work of this kind with any number of facets, it pays to keep the number fairly low, since it is quite difficult to turn sets of facets which are well-matched, and the greater their number, the more formidable the task — exacerbated by the fact that, upon completion of the work, the fact that more than one facet may be seen in its entirety from a given viewpoint, renders any discrepancies between them that much more obvious. It will indeed be found that only one of the projects which follow has four facets; the remainder have three only.

One essential feature of multi-facet work is the provision of some means of mounting the work such that each workpiece may be rotated on its own axis, and locked in any of the desired number of positions, thereby allowing each individual facet to be turned. A method has already been described in Project 8, and the following projects also employ this technique. The idea of a number of spaced 'visual-aid' guide-blocks is used also. Fig.316 shows the general arrangement for work of this kind. It is not particularly easy (or indeed all that helpful) to provide overall dimensions for three-sided work; accordingly, a method is offered which makes use of the distance between the centre of the mounting mandrel (ie. the lathe axis) and the centre of the workpiece, together with the turning radii required to generate the shape. It will be found quite easy to reproduce such shapes (and generate new ones as required) on paper with basic drawing implements by this means. The reader is referred to Chapter 3. for more detailed information. It is highly important (and very easily overlooked) that the multi-station turning set-up is capable of accommodating the *blanks* from which the workpieces are turned. It will usually be found helpful to truncate triangular blanks for example, to avoid a clash at the centre. Figs.316 and 317 indicate the general nature of the problem. A further desirable feature is that permitting each individual piece to be mounted centrally on the normal lathe axis, after offset turnery has been completed, to permit boring axial holes or recesses, and also to turn-away part of the outer profile to provide compound curves generated by the interaction of the two forms of turnery. Fig.317 gives an indication of the effect that may thus be produced. Dimensions are given on this drawing, since it is a project in its own right, and will be referred to later. Note that the plan view of the drawing appears to show an outer profile-radius for the piece which is not the same as the

Figure 316

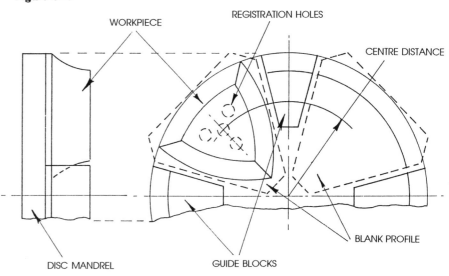

Figure 317

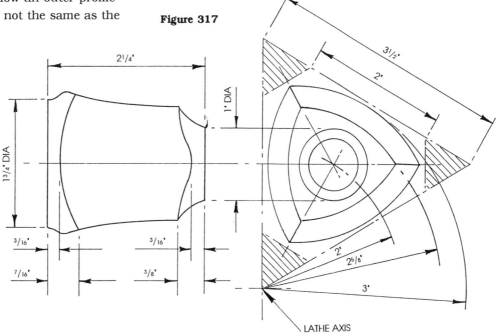

radius provided by the turning process. This is quite in order, since the subsequent modification of the base profile by 'on-axis' turning does in fact produce this effect; the point is mentioned only because the drawing might otherwise appear incorrect. It should be appreciated that the dimensions given in this and similar drawings of this type are intended only as a guide, and may quite easily be modified as desired.

Work which is long in relation to its cross-sectional dimensions positively demands the use of a tailstock mandrel, as arranged for the cutlery handles, since it would be virtually impossible to turn it in any other way. The reasons are fairly obvious: long slender work invariably requires such support, even when turned in the normal axial fashion; it requires it even more when mounted off-axis, particularly if the nature of the turning tends to give rise to an increased gap between workpieces. Fig.318 illustrates a typical set-up, and Fig.319 shows a complete set of pieces with the tailstock

mandrel removed. For work of a more 'stubby' nature, tailstock support may be dispensed with, but remains a perfectly viable method nevertheless, provided that the tailstock mandrel allows unimpeded tool-access to the work (this can usually be arranged). It possesses the advantages of simplicity and safety, but is not necessarily the most convenient in all cases.

The following method is therefore offered for the benefit of readers prepared to indulge in a little preliminary metalwork. Note that it is suitable only for work of equivalent cross-sectional 'diameter' of about two or three inches; moreover, the depth of the workpiece should be rather less than this. Each mount (or pallet) is fashioned from sheet light-alloy (which should never be less than about 1/8" thick, regardless of other dimensions) and a couple of 2BA or metric equivalent countersunk-head screws. The pallet is shaped to suit the proposed workpiece, and a couple of countersunk holes drilled in it, one at dead-centre, the other at

Figure 319

Figure 318

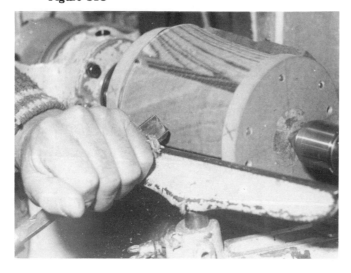

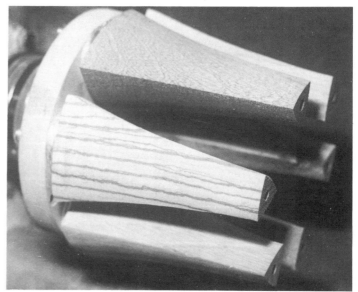

some convenient distance from it (Fig.320). The screws are inserted into the holes, and the parent sheet then peened over to lock the screws in place and to prevent subsequent rotation. An even better arrangement is to make the pallets from brass, which then allows the screws to be hard or soft-soldered in place. The workpiece may then be attached with glue-film as described in Chapter 9 (and actually used in Project 8). This type of hot-melt pallet does, however, require an additional light alloy 'heat-transfer' block (Fig.321(b)). The assembly is then mounted by means of the central screw on a disc mandrel comprising as many work-stations as desired, a typical assembly being shown in (a). A further advantage of the system lies in the fact that each individual item may be re-mounted on a turned hardwood spigot, designed to fit a combination chuck in compression mode (c). Further axial boring or turning may then be carried out as desired.

Given the possession of a number of pallets as described in Chapter 9, the whole procedure becomes very simple indeed, since the design embodies all that is needed for this type of mounting. Indeed, with one extra hole, the standard pallet may be used exclusively, although this may then become the limiting factor with regard to the number of work-stations available on a given set-up (Fig.322). One must, of course, be conscious of the possible limitations imposed by the combination chuck in use; for example, a chuck with an effectively 'solid-centre' may require the length of the

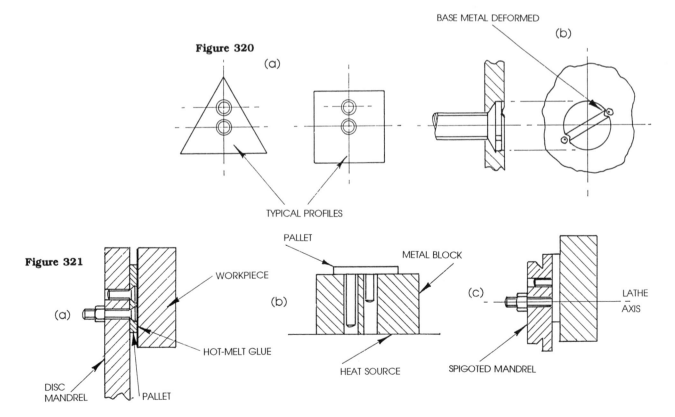

Figure 320

(a)

TYPICAL PROFILES

BASE METAL DEFORMED

(b)

Figure 321

(a)

WORKPIECE

PALLET

METAL BLOCK

(b)

(c)

LATHE AXIS

HOT-MELT GLUE

HEAT SOURCE

SPIGOTED MANDREL

DISC MANDREL

PALLET

central screw to be kept to an absolute minimum to avoid interference. Fig.323 shows such an arrangement in use; it comprises four workpieces and two guide-blocks.

So much for generalities. A number of projects are now offered as a basis for further experiment; they are presented in increasing order of difficulty.

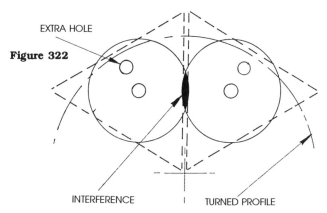

Figure 322

EXTRA HOLE

INTERFERENCE   TURNED PROFILE

Figure 323

SPECIMEN VASE

This is an example of the kind of work which requires a tailstock pressure-plate, since it is fairly slender and also results in a large gap between workpieces at the tailstock end. Six pieces may be turned at one session, given that the stock is suitably-prepared initially (Fig.319). One of the pieces may be a blank, which may be used as a profile-reference after the first turning operation. Alternatively it may be turned on one facet only and used as a reference to complete all facets on the remaining pieces; it may then itself be completed, using the remaining five pieces as a reference. Finally, each piece may be individually mounted for finishing off the end, and drilling or boring the central hole. In passing, it is to be noted that faceted work needs to be hand-finished. Some sanding is possible whilst the pieces are cage-mounted, but polishing is both unsatisfactory and potentially dangerous if carried out in this way. All necessary dimensions are given in Fig.324.

LARGE BARREL

These may be conveniently made two or three at a time, dependent upon required size relative to lathe centre-height. By way of explanation, the cage-diameter, and therefore the radius of curvature of each facet, will necessarily be governed by lathe centre-height, since this project must also be given tailstock support. This in turn governs, to some extent at least, the number of workpieces which may be accommodated at a single session, since the mutual interference between workpieces is a limiting factor. It is rarely possible to insert guide-blocks of any substance between workpieces; it follows that they must provide their own profile-references, as described for the specimen vase project. Fig.325 gives all necessary dimensions.

SMALL CONTAINER

This may be dealt with in the same way as the barrel, with the exception that it doesn't necessarily require tailstock support. Dimensions are given in Fig.326.

CRUET

This piece is shown in Fig.317. It may be turned without tailstock support. Preparation for the necessary top and bottom fittings requires a little extra work however. After competion of faceted turning, each individual piece may be axially mounted and the pouring-end bored. This operation is followed by removal from the original pallet, and reverse-mounting on a pin-chuck. The base end may now be bored and counterbored as required, together with any desired axial profiling. Finally, the pouring cap may be turned as a separate item and glued in place. This particular piece positively demands some form of axial profiling on the base if it is required as a practical cruet rather than an ornament, since it will otherwise be found very difficult to pick up.

PEPPER CRUET (Fig.327)

A number of earlier projects featured the use of an ellipsoidal recess in a base of faceted outer profile, thereby featuring a scalloped effect. In this particular instance, the outer profile was generated by sawing and sanding, but it is possible to achieve the same effect by off-centre turnery, the particular feature being that, in this case, it looks a rather more difficult exercise (which it is).

To deal with the main body first: This is a plain sphere, generated from a cube, which is itself of segmented construction. One side of the cube is shown in Fig.328, and it is of course necessary to

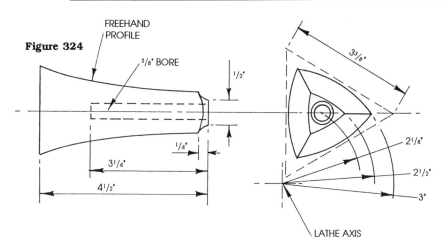

Figure 324

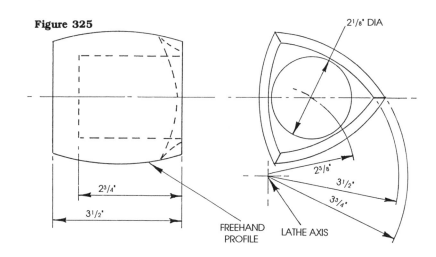

Figure 325

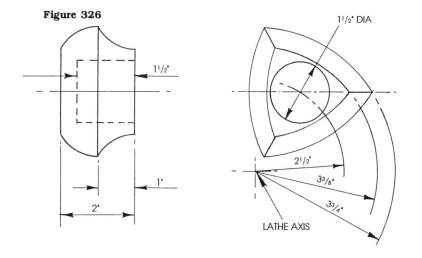

Figure 326

make six of them. The assembly of this type of segmented construction has already been described in Chapter 7, but there is one extra point to be watched in this particular case. The fitting of the trapezoidal pieces requires particular care, since they must fit precisely around the central square

Figure 327

Figure 328

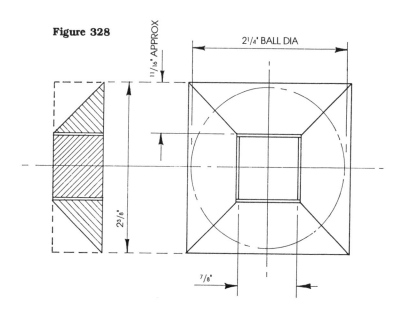

and invariably require work on at least two edges, a little at a time, to get the fit absolutely right. Remaining assembly of the cube itself follows the lines indicated for three-dimensional assemblies in Chapter 8. Turning the sphere from the cube may be accomplished with the aid of Nomogram 10, as described for the ellipsoid projects. This project requires the sphere to be particularly accurate since, when boring the end, it needs to be rotated off its original turning axis in order to bring the segmented patterns to the position shown in Fig.327 (this is equivalent to standing the original cube on one of its corners). The fact that this particular design requires the pouring holes to be drilled straight into the original body of the piece (ie. there is no separate 'plug' insert at the pouring end) poses one further minor difficulty. The drilling and boring for the filling end must be carried out in a clamping-jig as described in Chapter 9, but without the benefit of a locating-pin at the chuck end. This requires care in initial mounting and even more when boring the filling-hole, to ensure that the sphere doesn't 'walk' angularly during the operation. The process should be started with a centre-drill and enlarged gradually, without attemping to remove a great deal of material in any one operation. When the hole is large enough to accommodate the smallest Forstner bit available, this should be started by very carefully boring the end of the hole with (say) the point of a skew chisel, just deep enough to give the bit an accurate start. This procedure must be carried out for each successive size of Forstner bit employed. The depth of the hole is also important, since it must provide a clean 'blind-end' to allow the pouring-holes to break through neatly. The piece may now be reversed and mounted on a pin-chuck in order to drill the pouring holes, as described in Project 5.

The *underside* of the base must be prepared first,

by boring and counterboring to suit a hollow cylindrical sleeve, as described in the 'ellipsoid' projects. The piece is then reversed on its pallet (a hot-melt adhesive type is highly desirable for this job), and hollowed to form a hemispherical recess to take the cruet body; note that the blank should be sufficiently large such that, at this point the size of the blank does *not* allow the recess to break through into the outer profile (which has yet to be formed anyway). The piece may then be mounted 'off-axis, and the three facets turned, thereby forming the scalloped recess for the body. In this case, given the making of only one base, it is very helpful indeed to have a 'guide-block' which encompasses more or less the entire remaining periphery of the mandrel (Fig.329); under these circumstances, turning will be found very easy. Protection of the 'points' of the scalloped recess can be materially assisted by fitting a dummy hemisphere (turned to the same Nomogram dimensions as the true body of the piece), as shown in Figs.329 and 330. This is of course turned down along with the base, and subsequently discarded.

Figure 329

Figure 330

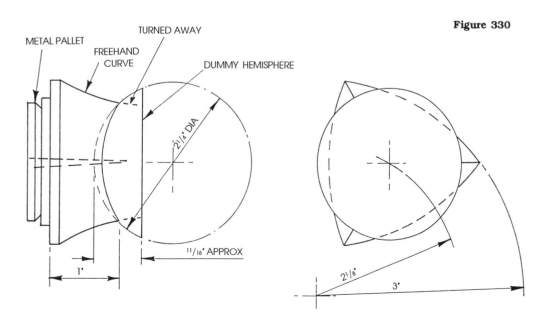

SALT CRUET (BASE ONLY)

This project is an alternative base for the salt cruet described in the 'three-axis' series of projects. It is carried out in much the same way as the pepper-cruet base, but has four facets (to match the essential body shape). Protection of the scalloped points is much easier in this case, since it is only necessary to make a dummy (solid) cylinder to fit the bored hole. This is again turned down with the base, and subsequently discarded (Figs. 331 and 332).

Figure 332

Figure 331

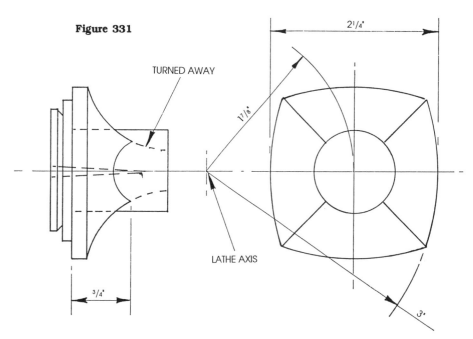

TURNED AWAY

2¹/₄"

1⁷/₈"

LATHE AXIS

³/₄"

3°

PROJECT 10. CUT AND JOIN TECHNIQUES
(Candlesticks, bowl)

The candlesticks illustrated are based upon a slight modification to an idea pioneered by Stephen Hogbin some years ago. The basic technique is that of turning a bowl, sawing it into two identical halves, and rejoining at the rim. It is illustrated in rather elementary form by the two larger pieces in Fig.333, but is *not* offered as an exercise or a project, since the idea essentially belongs to another turner. The modification consists of turning a small, approximately elliptical vessel, with the timber grain parallel to the lathe axis. Cutting and rejoining produces a vessel of elliptical planform and semi-elliptical side-elevation Fig.334(a). The resultant piece may be used as it stands, although

Figure 335

Figure 336

Figure 333

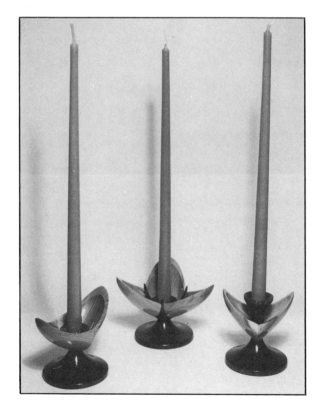

it is somewhat fragile, due to the necessarily limited gluing area, plus the fact that the joint is made in end-grain; it is also somewhat unstable unless attached to a base of some kind. The candlesticks utilise the same principle, but their appearance can be improved in a number of ways. It is possible, for instance, to drum-sand the vessel after joining the two half-shells, thereby modifying the elevation profile, this being perhaps the simplest approach. Figs.335(left) and 336 show a couple of the effects that can be obtained in this way. The three-leaved example represents a rather more difficult exercise, and will be found as part of Project 11.

Chapter 6 offers a number of drum-sanding techniques which may be employed to achieve more or less any desired radius of curvature. A slight improvement may be effected by pre-sanding the (original) rims of the half-shells to a predetermined mitre angle, joining the sanded faces, and then sanding a profile in the new rim. With this approach, it is possible to arrive at a fair depth of bowl at the centre, whilst retaining delicacy at the tips. A wide variation in profile is available by this means; two possibilities are illustrated in Fig.334 (b) and (c). A further method is that of sanding a mitre at the original rims, and then drum-sanding the 'secondary' rims separately, prior to final assembly; this produces a curved but discontinuous rim profile. The last-named technique requires care in assembly, in order to avoid an unwanted step at the joint; it also has the effect of reducing the bowl depth somewhat. Sanding of this nature may be implemented with the aid of the adjustable jig described and illustrated in Chapter 6. It is of course necessary to provide some form of attachment for the inside of the half-shell; this may be a section of an ellipsoid, turned to suit the inside of the half-shell, and provided with a hole for attachment to the metal arm of the jig, as shown in Figs.337 and 338. This arrangement also permits

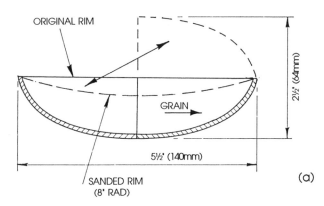

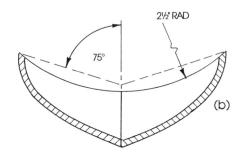

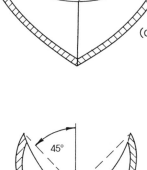

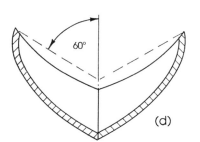

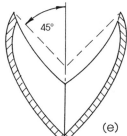

Figure 334

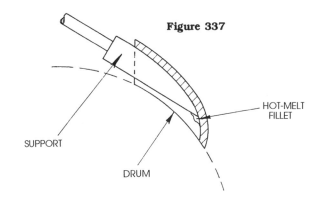

Figure 337

SUPPORT

DRUM

HOT-MELT FILLET

a wide range of profiles, two examples being given in Fig.334(d) and (e). All the designs shown may be based on a single elliptical shell-form. Dimensions are given in Fig.339, together with suggested base and candle-socket designs (the latter to suit a ½" diameter candle), but there is plenty of scope for individual expression. Note that the dimensions given in Fig.334(a) are associated with a small bowl design, to be described later.

In view of the fact that candlesticks rarely come as single items (one would normally make at least a pair), some means of ensuring that the form and

shape can be repeated is desirable; moreover, since the turned shells are to be split in half, the inner profile (and more importantly, the new rim) will also be visible; therefore, repeatability extends to the inner profile as well as the outer. Nomogram 10 may be used to generate any of these profiles, since all that is necessary is to decide upon the required major and minor axes for both the inside and outside ellipses, calculate the profiles and make the templates as discussed in Project 5. Indeed, the entire turning operation may be carried out by this means if desired. The reader is reminded, however, of the danger attendant upon applying any kind of inside-measuring device to revolving work.

Figure 338

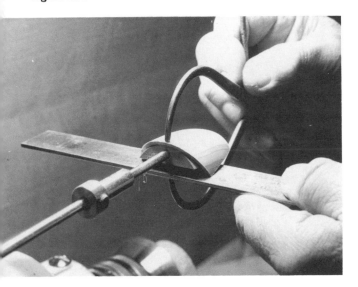

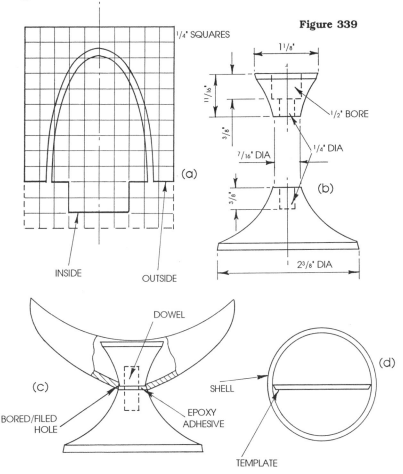

Figure 339

¼" SQUARES

INSIDE

OUTSIDE

(a)

1⅛"

1¹¹/₁₆"

3/8"

7/16" DIA

¼" DIA

½" BORE

3/8"

2³/₈" DIA

(b)

DOWEL

BORED/FILED HOLE

EPOXY ADHESIVE

SHELL

TEMPLATE

(c)

(d)

When sanding the inside of the workpiece bowl, the face should not be 'dubbed-over' at the rim, since this will tend to produce a poor finished profile (Fig.340(a)). One can produce this effect very easily without being aware of it at the time, if sanding is carried out by hand. It is suggested that a piece of abrasive sheet wrapped round a length of dowel produces a neater result, and is much safer. The outer profile may be turned at the same setting by providing tailstock support. The method does, however, have the disadvantage that the parting-off area must be finished by hand, and also that the outer template cannot be applied to the work with any real accuracy. Reversal of the work on the lathe mandrel will produce a much more accurate result; this procedure is simplicity itself given the type of hot-melt pallet assembly technique illustrated in (b) and described in Chapter 9, but can be somewhat tedious otherwise.

Since the bowl is turned as a 'one-piece' item it will require to be sawn in half, as accurately as possible. Two possible methods are shown in Fig.341, for use with a bandsaw. Method (a) involves attaching the shell rim with fillets of hot-melt glue to a scrap of plywood, which has one straight edge for use against the machine-fence (see also Fig.342). The extreme edge of the shell is arranged to be aligned with the straight edge of the plywood.

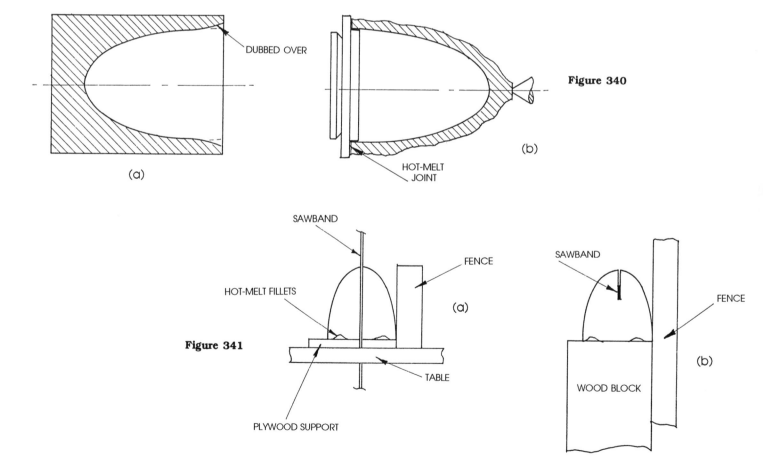

The fence is now set such that the centre of the sawband is at exactly half the diameter of the shell, and the assembly sawn through. Care in placement of the glue fillets is advised, since these must keep the shell stable on the base throughout the sawing process. Method (b) allows direct visual placement of the sawband relative to the shell, by attaching the latter to a block of wood (also with one straight edge), such that the domed end of the shell is fed into the sawband first. If, after turning, a small pencilled dot is made at the centre of the domed end with the lathe running, this may be readily aligned with the dead-centre position of the saw (possibly requiring a mirror if access to the rear of the machine is limited). This particular method has the disadvantage of lack of support of the free end of the shell during sawing; it works well nevertheless.

A further method which allows better utilisation of small offcuts, and eliminates the sawing problem, is that of joining two lengths of stock together with a sheet of paper between them, and turning as

an entity. The method requires great care in centring the work on the lathe in order to produce two identical halves. Moreover, since the joint strength is determined by the 'delamination-strength' of the paper, turning must be carried out carefully; in particular, the outside of the piece should only be 'roughed-down' initially, to the maximum diameter that the blank will allow, in order to deal with all intermittent cutting with the blank in its strongest condition, and then the inside turning (which generates forces tending to force the two halves apart) completed before any attempt is made to bring the outside to anything like its finished size. Separation of the two 'shells' may be made with a thin craft knife, and the paper/glue residue removed by drawing the shells gently across a flat sheet of abrasive.

It is obviously quite difficult to align the shells accurately by hand, to saw and sand the mitres. The shells may, however, be mounted on small prepared rectangles of thin ply with fillets of hot-melt glue, and the entire assembly finished by setting the machine-table to the required angle, with a fence on the table set at right angles (in plan view) to the saw or sanding-disc (Figs.343 and 344). When gluing the two half-shells together after sanding, electricians' plastic insulating tape provides an effective temporary holding medium. A shaped assembly-jig will also assist alignment of

Figure 342

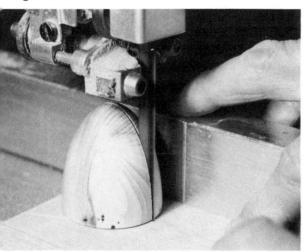

Figure 343

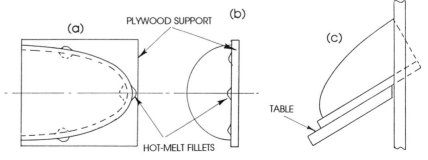

Figure 344

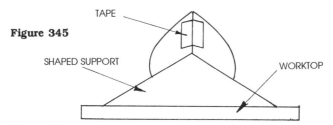

Figure 345

TAPE

SHAPED SUPPORT

WORKTOP

Figure 346

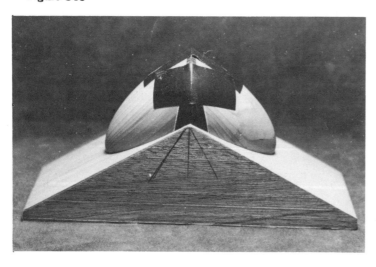

the two half-shells whilst taping. The method, illustrated in Figs.345 and 346, is very helpful if the rims are straight, but less so if they are sanded to a curve prior to joining. Assembly can be quite a difficult operation altogether, both in terms of unwanted movement between the two halves with consequent loss of registration, and also with regard to the removal of surplus adhesive on the inside faces. In this latter connection, it is sensible to completely finish the inside of the shells, inclusive of polishing, *before* assembly, since it is not easy to obtain a good unbroken finish, particularly at the joint-line, afterwards. If a wax finish is used, it should obviously be kept clear of the joint faces but should nevertheless be taken right up to the edge. Even if a wax finish is not used as a general procedure, a light rub with a discarded candle stub immediately adjacent to the joint faces will assist subsequent removal of excess adhesive. Finishing the outside of the shells after assembly is a simpler matter, and may be done in this way if preferred.

It is also necessary to drill a central hole to enable the candle-socket and base to be fitted. In view of the somewhat awkward shape presented by the workpiece at this point, the operation is best carried out on the assembly-jig where possible, and very carefully drilled out (from the outside of the piece) with a No. BS2 or BS3 centre-drill. A start for the drill may be made with a scriber, or even a very small sawcut, and the drill fed into the work very slowly and carefully. On no account should a normal twist drill be used, since this will simply tear at the work; neither should drilling be attempted from the inside of the vessel, since this can be quite dangerous to both workpiece and worker. Enlargement of the hole may be carried out by means of a round file, finishing off with a small piece of abrasive sheet wrapped around a dowel. Aside from its designated function, the hole provides a useful point of temporary attachment for a short length of dowel, to provide a handle when drum-sanding the rims.

A much more decorative effect on the shells may be obtained by using contrasting timbers at the centre, possibly with an interposed slip of veneer. The variation does of course demand a little extra fabrication, plus some care with assembly (Fig.347). The assembly jigs illustrated and described in Chapter 7 may be used (with minor modifications). The angles should be carefully matched on a dry assembly prior to gluing; if this is done, it is relatively easy to assemble the main sections and the slip of veneer in a single operation. This method of fabrication must of course be made with matching pairs (or sets) of blanks, which are afterwards joined with a sheet of paper between them, as described earlier. Although the initial surface preparation should be carried out with a view to ending-up with a flat face, some latitude is permissible with the veneer slip if the rims are to be subsequently sanded to a curve since any slight discontinuity will thereby be removed. In fact it may be seen from Fig.348 that some liberties may be taken with regard to assembly, given that the desired final profile is known beforehand. With regard to the designs offered, the sanding-angle 'B' is about 10° less than that of the final mitre angle 'A', but this may be varied if desired. It must be said that, although the entire project may appear fairly simple, it is in fact one of the more difficult projects offered, particularly with regard to obtaining a good match between pairs or sets of finished items. For this reason, it is suggested that one or two experimental pieces are made initially, using relatively inexpensive timbers.

To return to the small bowl (Fig.350): as it stands, this is a rather fragile component, but strength may be improved somewhat by providing a central

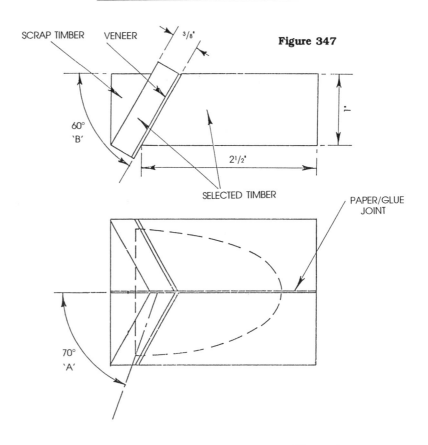

Figure 347

Figure 348

Figure 349

section in contrasting timber, which enables the two half-shells to be joined together in 'tongue-and-groove' fashion. Making the centre-section is an interesting exercise, since it must be grooved and shaped on both faces, with the shaping carried smoothly around such that it presents an unbroken curve. This may be made in a number of ways, but, in view of the likelihood that the section is likely to be made in relatively expensive timber, a rather economical means is illustrated in Fig.349. It will be seen that the workpiece comprises only half a disc (in this case, the darker timber), which is butted against another half-disc which forms part of the jig itself. The jig portion provides a guide for grooving and shaping the second half of the workpiece, because the jig and the first half of the

workpiece are shaped simultaneously to begin with. The workpiece is itself mounted to the jig by means of wood screws which permit reversal and realignment. The only real potential problem lies in parting-off, since this will allow the workpiece to fly out of the lathe if it is not controlled in some way. If the outer face is completely shaped to begin with, it may then be temporarily attached to the jig with a couple of small fillets of hot-melt glue, allowing some measure of freedom to (more or less) finish and part-off the inner face. Even so, the lathe must be run very slowly, and possibly even turned over by hand for the final breakthrough. Obviously the workpiece will require hand-finishing after removal. The tongued-and-gooved joint will render final gluing and assembly a simple matter, since the location is (or should be) firm, positive, and accurate. Once again, it is preferable to finish and lightly wax the component parts before assembly.

Assembly of the base pedestal is a little tricky, since there is not a great deal of scope for the provision of a strong joint whilst simultaneously avoiding some form of breakthrough to the inner face of the bowl. The pedestal top should be hand-shaped to fit the grooved centre-section of the bowl, thereby providing maximum gluing area, and provided with a small metal pin of about 1/16" or so diameter to assist location and give a little extra strength. There is a very strong case for the use of epoxy adhesive on this particular joint.

Figure 350

PROJECT 11. THREE ADVANCED DESIGNS
(Goblets, Pomander, Three-leaf Candlesticks)

The three designs to be described, although based upon previous work, are rather more difficult to execute repeatably. For this reason, it is strongly advised that they are not attempted until some experience with earlier projects has been acquired.

(a) GOBLETS (Fig.351)

Each goblet comprises five basic elements: the bowl, the stem, the base, and the two decorative collars, one at each end of the stem. For the sake of robustness of the finished piece, the two ends of the stem are dowelled into the bowl and the base with short lengths of metal rod. The two collars (Fig.353) are straightforward and will not be discussed.

The bowl follows previously described practice in that the blank is of laminated form with contrasting veneer slips between laminations (see Fig.229, Project 5. The blank is turned to a cylinder of the required length and diameter, followed by turning inside and out by means of the incremental step method described in Project 5, thus ensuring repeatability of form if more than one goblet is made. For convenience, the particular design offered is fully dimensioned in Fig.352 and Table 10. Where it is desired to change the design from that offered, it may be noted that the outer profile does not follow a true elliptical form, and cannot therefore be easily generated by mathematical methods. In such cases, a preliminary drawing of the re-

Figure 351

quired profile is made, which is then divided lengthwise into any convenient number of equal linear divisions. The diameter of the profile is then measured and noted at each step, from which point the turning procedure is as previously described. Note however, that this method cannot reasonably be expected to yield as accurate a result as the mathematical approach.

It will be noted that the base, which requires considerable care in making, is a four-segment construction; this matches the design formed by the bowl laminations. Initially, four triangular segments are prepared and veneered with a contrasting timber on each of the joint faces (Fig.354). A central web of crucifix form is then made in scrap hardwood, and the four segments glued temporarily into the recesses with one or two dabs of cyanoacrylate (superglue). The assembly is then drilled through in four positions (b). Drilling must be carried out with great care, using a Forstner or similar bit, to ensure clean sharp edges. The drill must also be centred accurately.

The web may now be bandsawn away, leaving just a little web timber on the segments. It is not advisable to attempt to split the web away from the segments, since this may tear the veneer surfaces. Short lengths of veneer are now glued into the indentations. The veneer grain must be as shown on the drawing. This procedure is easily carried out with the aid of a short turned cylinder, used as a cramp (Fig.355(a)). The remaining indentation is filled with a length of hardwood (ebony is very suitable, regardless of the other timbers used), turned to the required diameter, and bandsawn into segments (b). Each completed assembly is now disc sanded down to the veneer surface, and the

four pieces finally glued into a single assembly which may be turned as desired. It is wise to insert a disc of birch ply into the base of the assembly to obviate glue-line cracks due to timber movement. Fig.356 shows the possible unwanted effects of poor hole alignment and excessive sanding, but given due care in assembly and judicious choice of timbers, the effect can be quite stunning.

The design and construction of twisted stems or columns is a fairly substantial subject in its own right, and will not be covered in detail here, although the dimensions of the design illustrated are given in Fig.357. Readers who have yet to attempt a twisted column of any kind are advised that this is no place to begin; the relatively small size and the tight three-strand twist impose their own special difficulties. A turned stem to individual choice is perhaps to be preferred in such cases. For the benefit of readers who *are* prepared to make the attempt, it is suggested that a small workpiece is not ideally suited to the use of chisels and gouges, but hard close-grained timbers are amenable to the use of small scrapers; these are easily made from short lengths of discarded high-speed steel hacksaw blade, ground to the required shape. It will also be found convenient to mount the work in a small portable jig rather than in a lathe (Fig.358).

Figure 352

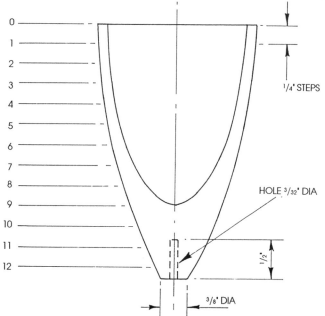

0 — 1 — 2 — 3 — 4 — 5 — 6 — 7 — 8 — 9 — 10 — 11 — 12

1/4" STEPS

HOLE 3/32" DIA

1/2"

3/8" DIA

TABLE 10

Dimensions in Inches

STATION	INNER DIA	OUTER DIA
0	1 25/32	2 1/32
1	1 3/4	2
2	1 23/32	1 31/32
3	1 5/8	1 7/8
4	1 9/16	1 13/16
5	1 13/32	1 3/4
6	1 1/4	1 5/8
7	1	1 1/2
8	21/32	1 11/32
9	–	1 5/32
10	–	31/32
11	–	23/32
12	–	1/2

HOLE ³/₃₂" DIA

Figure 353

¹³/₁₆"

³/₈"

¹/₄"

⁹/₃₂"

Figure 356

SEGMENT

CYLINDER

Figure 355

CRAMPING AXIS

SEGMENT

(a)

CRAMP BLOCK

VENEER SLIP

VENEER GRAIN

(b)

Figure 354

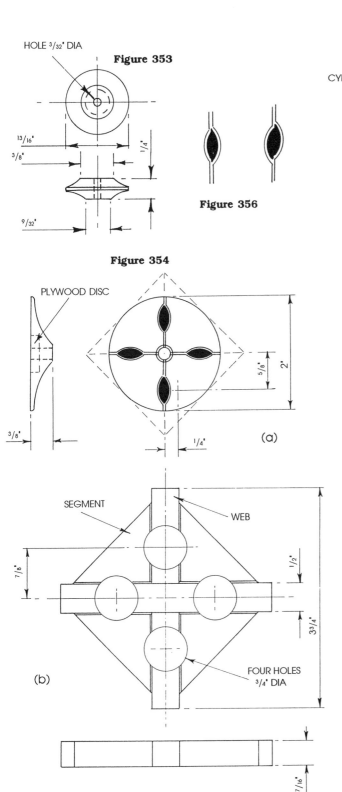

PLYWOOD DISC

2"

5/8"

³/₈"

¹/₄"

(a)

SEGMENT

WEB

7/8"

1/2"

3³/₄"

FOUR HOLES
³/₄" DIA

(b)

7/16"

Figure 357

¹/₈" DIA

3¹/₈"

HOLE ³/₃₂" DIA
BOTH ENDS

1¹/₄" PITCH

³/₈"

⁹/₃₂"

EFFECTIVE DIA

Figure 358

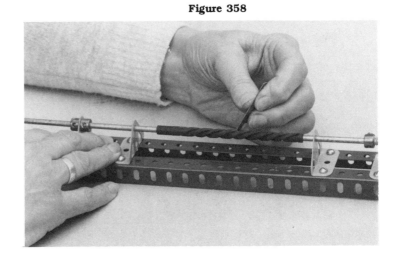

(b) **POMANDER** (Fig.359)

The tapered stave body of this piece is constructed in accordance with the dimensions given in Table 4, Project 2. The lid and base each comprise five segments which are curved in the piece illustrated, but which may be made straight if desired. The real difficulty lies with the five decorative apertures, and it is only these which are given detailed treatment.

The three turned spindles in each aperture are inserted in pre-drilled holes in the outer ring assembly, and their centre pegs are ultimately trapped in position by a split hub. The spindles and the hub represent a minor exercise in miniature turning, but some form of lathe indexing is required to ensure that the holes in the hub and the outer ring assembly are accurately drilled. Each half of any one hub must be turned and drilled as

Figure 359

a separate item and then parted off such that only half of each hole remains (Fig.360(c)). The holes in the five staves may be cut with a Forstner bit of suitable size, or bored in the lathe. In the latter case, each stave is mounted on a disc of birch ply which is itself then mounted in the lathe — this is in fact the method used for the piece illustrated. The hollow cylindrical rings (d) which are fitted into the holes in the staves, each comprise two annular rings of contrasting timbers, and must be made as individual items on a separate lathe mandrel. This procedure is necessary because they must be drilled with three holes in their rims *before* gluing into the staves. Final sizing of the rings must be carried out with care, with the staves being offered to them at regular intervals until the desired fit is obtained. It is also good practice to polish the inner surfaces of the rings at this stage, since any form of finishing will be found difficult after fitting. When gluing the rings into the staves, the alignment of the three small holes relative to the staves must be checked, to ensure that all five assemblies are alike.

In view of the fact that the inside of the vessel is to be turned, the holes must be plugged with well fitting discs of scrap hardwood, to obviate damage to the inner edges of the rings arising from intermittency of cut, and also possible damage to the operator during sanding and finishing. Each plug should be turned with a small flange on the outside, which is secured to the outer face of the stave with generous fillets of hot-melt glue. This procedure enables the plugs to be subsequently removed by slicing through the fillets with a craft knife, thereby reducing risk of damage to the stave outer faces.

The wide end of the assembled vessel is now mounted on the lathe by means of small blocks, as described in Chapter 8 (see also Fig.157), in order

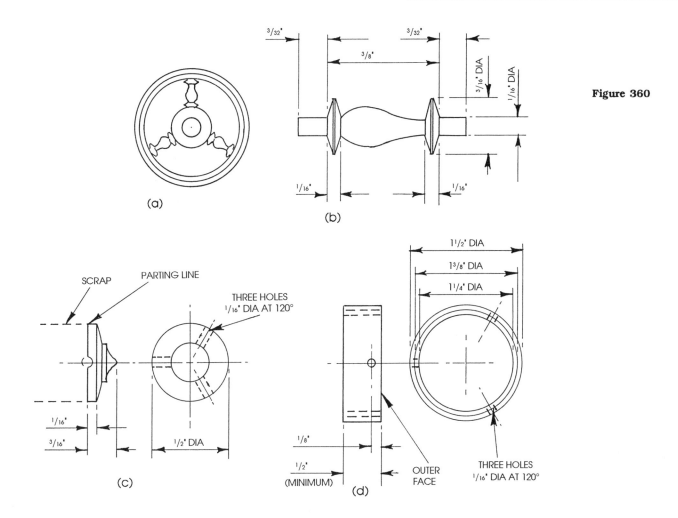

Figure 360

to turn the bottom end flat, and to incorporate a shouldered spigot fit into the segmented base. The base is prepared separately, and mounted on its own mandrel (preferably of the adhesive type), and turned to accept the bottom end of the vessel. The two parts are then glued together and turned inside and outside (where necessary) as an entity. Dependent upon the thickness of stave timber used, and the nature of the inner turned profile of the vessel, a small irregular hole may appear at the base on the inside; this may be drilled cleanly and

fitted with a decorative plug. All turned surfaces may now be given the desired finish.

The turned miniature spindles(b) and hubs(c) may now be fitted. If the fit of the spindle pegs into their holes is unduly loose, considerable difficulty will be experienced in manipulating all the parts and the necessary adhesive; a good close fit is therefore to be aimed for at the outset.

The lid (Fig.361) is a relatively simple turning exercise. A useful procedure is to drill the assembled blank (in the lathe) with a hole to receive the

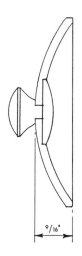

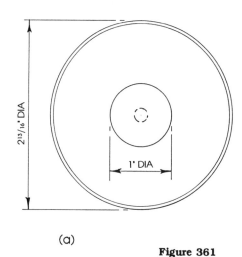

2¹³/₁₆" DIA

1" DIA

⁹/₁₆"

(a)

Figure 361

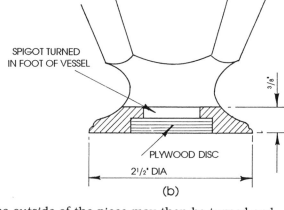

SPIGOT TURNED
IN FOOT OF VESSEL

PLYWOOD DISC

2¹/₂" DIA

³/₈"

(b)

turned knob, and then to turn and finish the inside surface. Note the decorative inner button, which also serves as a shrinkage protection disc. The piece may now be reversed in the lathe, over a suitable guide disc to ensure concentricity, and tailstock pressure brought to bear via a live centre.

The outside of the piece may then be turned and finished fairly easily. The contents of the pomander are best contained in a small bag of coloured silk or similar fabric. This, in addition to its primary purpose of containment, also provides an attractive setting for the miniature turnery.

(c) **THREE-LEAF CANDLESTICK** (Figs.335,336)

Construction of this piece is considerably more difficult than the two-leaf designs described in Project 10. Firstly, the requirement for three leaves demands the turning of *two* pairs of shells — and these must match closely. Secondly, the open ends of the shells must fit the three faces of the centre web, which is necessarily turned on an axis at right-angles to that of the shells (Fig.362 will assist clarification of the point). Readers with some experience of geometry will also doubtless note that the fact that the ends of the shells are sanded to a 70° angle with respect to their axis, changes the profile at this point from a semicircle to a semi-ellipse.

Fortunately the discrepancy is small, and may be dealt with by a little freehand sanding at the appropriate time. The major problem is in fact one of design; that of calculating the profile of the turned centre web such that the side profile on the three faces matches that of the shells.

Full dimensions of the centre web are given in Fig.362, but the dimensions of the shells may be taken from Fig.339. The method of fabrication, including the sanded curved profile on the top rims of the shells has been described in Project 10. It will be seen that the web is fabricated from a single triangular block with three blocks of scrap hard-

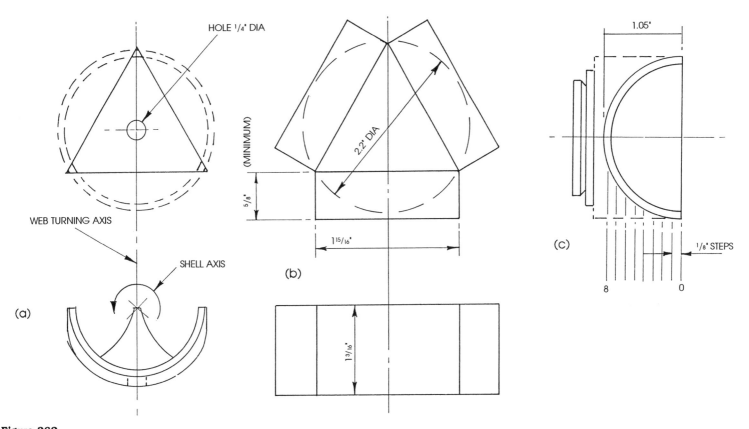

Figure 362

STATION	INNER DIA	OUTER DIA
0	1.9	2.1
1	1.9	2.1
2	1.84	2.05
3	1.75	1.97
4	1.6	1.85
5	1.45	1.73
6	1.2	1.5
7	0.8	1.2
8	–	0.77

TABLE 11
Dimensions in Inches

wood (preferably of a strongly contrasting timber as a visual aid) glued to the three faces of the triangle. The purpose of this assembly is to ensure that the web may be turned inside and out without risk of damage to the three rather delicate points that will arise as a result of the turning process. After turning, the scrap timber may be bandsawn away, leaving just a sliver of the scrap timber in place to allow final disc sanding. It will be found that with the dimensions given, the inner edges of the web profile will stand slightly proud of the corresponding edges of the shells. The excess may be sanded away by means of a small drum sander

Figure 363

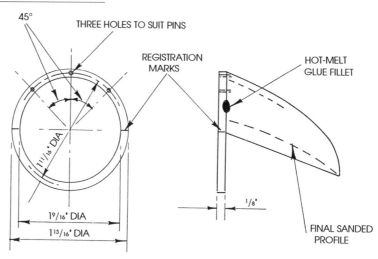

of a diameter equal to that of the inner diameter of the shells. It is important that the triangle is centred correctly with respect to the turning axis, otherwise the points of the web will not match. For this reason, it is a good plan to draw the triangle from a base circle which has been scribed with the work mounted in the lathe (see Fig.362).

A major problem arises on assembly, due to the difficulty of holding the shells firmly against the centre web whilst gluing them together. A further problem may be encountered due to the nature of the timber. Cocobolo, for example, as used in the piece illustrated, is notoriously difficult to glue. Given a little light metalworking, both problems are easily overcome by fitting three short pins (which may be panel pins clipped to a suitable length) into each of the shells, such that they locate precisely into three mating holes in each of the web faces. Panel pins of around .040" to .050" diameter are readily obtainable, but it is necessary also to acquire a twist drill of matching diameter. No firm advice may be given here, since the drill size chosen will be determined by the pins (although it will almost certainly turn out to be a metric size). Precise location of the holes in the shells and the web may be implemented by means of a metal ring

of outer diameter equal to that of the shells. Readers who are unable to acquire or make such an item are advised that it may be made from acrylic sheet at the expense of some difficulty in attachment to the turned items, plus possibly a little further difficulty in terms of subsequent wear and tear. The ring is drilled with three holes as shown in Fig.363. Given that the lathe in use has indexing facilities, a method of drilling a series of holes of this nature is given in Project 5, Fig.252. It is also necessary to mark the ring such that the shells and the web may be aligned accurately relative to the holes in the ring. The ring is temporarily attached to the turnery by means of fillets of hot-melt glue on the outer rim. The holes may then be spotted into the timber, using the ring as a drill guide. This operation is best carried out with the drill chuck mounted in the lathe, with only the required amount of drill protruding from the chuck; this obviates the risk of breakthrough due to excess drill penetration. Final gluing will be a fairly simple matter. If an adhesive requiring a lengthy setting period is used, the parts may be temporarily locked in position with hot-melt glue fillets, again on the outer surfaces of the work.

CONVERSION TABLE

	Decimal Equivalents of Fractions by $^1/_{32}$" Increments		Millimetre Equivalents	
	to 3 dec places	*to 2 dec places*	*to 3 dec places*	*to 2 dec places*
1	.031	.03	.794	.79
2	.063	.06	1.588	1.59
3	.094	.09	2.381	2.38
4	.125	.13	3.175	3.18
5	.156	.16	3.969	3.97
6	.188	.19	4.763	4.76
7	.219	.22	5.556	5.56
8	.250	.25	6.350	6.35
9	.281	.28	7.144	7.14
10	.313	.31	7.938	7.94
11	.344	.34	8.731	8.73
12	.375	.38	9.525	9.53
13	.406	.41	10.319	10.32
14	.438	.44	11.113	11.11
15	.469	.47	11.906	11.91
16	.500	.50	12.700	12.70
17	.531	.53	13.494	13.49
18	.563	.56	14.288	14.29
19	.594	.59	15.081	15.08
20	.625	.63	15.875	15.88
21	.656	.66	16.669	16.67
22	.688	.69	17.463	17.46
23	.719	.72	18.256	18.26
24	.750	.75	19.050	19.05
25	.781	.78	19.844	19.84
26	.813	.81	20.638	20.64
27	.844	.84	21.431	21.43
28	.875	.88	22.225	22.23
29	.906	.91	23.019	23.02
30	.938	.94	23.813	23.81
31	.969	.97	24.606	24.61
32	1.000	1.00	25.400	25.40

INDEX